TŪRANGA WAE WAE

TŪRANGA
WAE
WAE

Identity & Belonging in Aotearoa New Zealand

Edited by Trudie Cain, Ella Kahu and Richard Shaw

MASSEY UNIVERSITY PRESS

Contents

Kupu Māori / Glossary

WORD OR PHRASE	DESCRIPTION
ahi kā	Continued occupation; describes the home people of marae/hapū/iwi
awa	Ancestral river
Bastion Point/Takaparawhau	A marae site in Tāmaki Makaurau. It was marked for development, which led to a 506-day protest occupation that started in 1977
haka	Customary Māori recital, previously and commonly referred to as a 'war dance', which is a limited interpretation of this act
He Whakaputanga	He Whakaputanga o te Rangatiratanga o Nu Tireni — The Declaration of Independence
hei tiki	Customary pounamu (greenstone/jade) ornament, usually in the form of a necklace
hīkoi	To walk, but also adopted for the act of protest marches
Hine-ahu-one	The original human ancestor, the original female ancestor
Hine-nui-te-pō	Female ancestor and guardian of the underworld
hapū	Consists of a number of whānau sharing descent from a common ancestor; the primary political unit in traditional Māori society
hongi	Customary greeting enacted by two people pressing noses together and re-enacting the moment at which Hine-ahu-one drew her first breath — a moment of sharing time and space with another person
iwi	A large group of people sharing a common ancestry and associated with a distinct territory
kaitiakitanga	Guardianship, environmental sustainable management
kāwanatanga	Governance
Kīngitanga	The movement formed to provide a united iwi/Māori approach to mass land loss and colonisation
koru	Customary Māori art motif
kura kaupapa Māori	Te reo Māori immersion primary schooling
Mahuika	Female ancestor, deity and origin of fire

mana	Authority, control, influence, prestige, power, spiritual gift, spiritual authority and power
mana atua	Strength drawn from your ancestors and deities, and your responsibility to those connections
mana tangata	Your personal pursuits and achievements, your responsibility to be of service
mana whenua	Strength drawn from ancestral lands, your responsibility to protect those lands
maunga	Ancestral mountain
mihimihi	A speech of greeting, welcome or introduction at the beginning of a gathering, often following a more formal pōwhiri
moko	Māori designs tattooed on the face or body according to traditional protocols
Moutoa Gardens/ Pākaitore	A customary Māori site in Whanganui; site of protest occupation in 1995
Ngā Kete o Te Wānanga	Three baskets of knowledge, obtained by Tāne-mahuta (or Tāwhaki, depending on iwi narrative) for humankind to utilise
ngā matatini	Multidimensional (usually in reference to shapes), many faces
ngā matatini Māori	Māori diverse realities
Ngāpuhi	Iwi from Northland
Papatūānuku	Female origin, earth mother
pepeha	A form of words linking a person ancestrally with the communities and physical features of a particular landscape (mountains, rivers and oceans)
Raglan/Whāingaroa	A significant site of protest for land stolen for a First World War military base. The protest occupation started in 1978
rangatira	Chief, leader
rangatiratanga	Chieftainship, authority
Ranginui	Original male ancestor, sky father
rūnanga	A high council or legislative assembly called to discuss matters of significant concern to an iwi or community
Tāne-mahuta	Child of Ranginui and Papatūānuku, deity with authority over the forests and birds
taonga	Treasure
tāwhaki	Ancestor
Tāwhiri-mātea	Child of Ranginui and Papatūānuku, deity with authority over the winds, clouds, rain, snow and storms

te ao Māori	The Māori world, including the Māori language, rituals, processes, practices, sites of importance, and ties to whānau, hapū and iwi
Te Ika a Māui	The fish of Māui, the North Island of Aotearoa New Zealand
Te Kawariki	Northland-based activist group, responsible for developing the tino rangatiratanga flag
Te Kōhanga Reo	Te reo Māori early childhood education centre, language nest
Te Kore	The time of great potential, the nothing
Te Kotahitanga	Unity movements for liberation and resistance
Te Pō	The time of activation, the night
Te Reinga	The northernmost tip of Te Ika a Māui
te reo Māori	The Māori language
Te Tiriti o Waitangi	The Māori-language version, and mostly signed version, of the Treaty of Waitangi
tikanga Māori	Māori custom, protocol and practices
tino rangatiratanga	Absolute authority and independence, the right to self-determination
tipuna	Ancestor(s)
tupu	Urge for growth and expansion
tūrangawaewae	Place of belonging where you draw your strength from, your 'standing' place
wāhi tapu	Sacred site or place, often a place in which ritual restrictions on access or use apply
waiata	Song, chant, melody
wānanga	Place of higher learning
whāinga	Pursuit
whakapapa	Genealogy
whakataukī	A proverb or significant saying
whānau	Extended family or family group, a familiar term of address for a group of people
whenua	Land
wiri	The shaking of hands during waiata to demonstrate an affinity with nature

This glossary was compiled by Margaret Forster, Te Rina Warren and Veronica Tawhai. A small number of definitions were sourced from two online sites: the Māori Dictionary and the Ngata Dictionary.

Identity and citizenship in Aotearoa New Zealand

Ella Kahu

Introduction

This book has to do with identity, belonging and citizenship in Aotearoa New Zealand. At the individual level it explores some of the threads that comprise our personal identities and the relationships we have with others which help shape a sense of self, while at the broader societal level it critically examines some of those things said to define New Zealand's national identity.

It was once suggested that the English spend little time reflecting on what it means to be English 'because it is so simply and obviously a fact' (Barker, 1948, p. 195). The same can be said of us here in Aotearoa New Zealand. Except that it isn't that simple, of course: what it means to be a New Zealander or to be in this place (and these are not necessarily the same things) may be quite different for different people. Understanding this, the complexity of the social world and our place in it, requires reflection, a capacity to ask questions of things that are often taken for granted, and a willingness to be open to alternative ways of seeing things. These are what this book is intended to do: to probe, prompt and encourage you to reflect on aspects of your own sense of self, and of the ways in which we collectively make sense of who we are, that might otherwise continue to enjoy the status of received wisdom.

It would be difficult to overstate the importance of understanding the diversity of people, and of appreciating others' ways of being and doing at this point in place and time. So many of the large problems that are facing the world are grounded in issues of identity, such as the refugee crisis throughout Europe, the political tensions in the United States, and the increasing divide between the haves and the have-nots. A better understanding of oneself, and from that a better understanding of what it means to be a citizen of this place, are both essential to the tasks ahead.

This first section has two purposes. First, to introduce, define and illustrate the core ideas that form the foundation of this book. Much has been written and there are many debates around the concepts of identity and citizenship, so it is essential that we start with a clear explanation of the meanings we have chosen to work with. Its second purpose is to outline the structure of the book — to summarise the ideas that frame each of the four sections and the ties that bind them.

Identity and citizenship

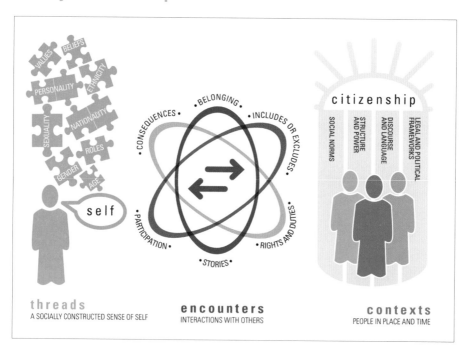

Identity

Who are you? How would you answer that question? You might talk about your personality and say 'I am shy', meaning, this is how I usually behave in certain situations. Or you might talk about a physical attribute and say 'I am 53'. Or you might talk about a role you have, 'I am a student', or even a belief such as 'I am an atheist'. These answers all reflect different aspects of your identity that together form your sense of self. As social science theorist Vivien Burr (2015) explains:

> A person's identity is achieved by a subtle interweaving of many different threads. There is a thread for age, for example they may be a child, a young adult or very old; that of class, depending on their occupation, income and level of education; ethnicity; gender; sexual orientation and so on. All of these, and many more, are woven together to produce the fabric of a person's identity. (pp. 123–124)

In the tūrangawaewae core concepts graphic, this idea of identity threads, or multiple identities, is illustrated by the figure of the self on the left. Some social scientists distinguish between personal and social identities. Personal identities are those characteristics that make us unique, such as our personality traits, preferences and values, while social identities are those identities derived from memberships in social groups and from social roles, such as being a lawyer or a member of the working class (Snow & Corrigall-Brown, 2015). However, the distinction between the personal and the social is not clear-cut, and the categories overlap. For instance, someone who is gay may view that as a personal identity, but, in the context of a conversation on homosexual law reform, being gay may function as a social identity — derived from and marking membership of a social group.

In many ways, all identities are social — identity is a way of marking out difference, delineating between 'us' and 'them' (Woodward, 2003). Identities are categories of people. It can even be argued that an identity exists only in comparison to others. For example, Liu, McCreanor, McIntosh and Teaiwa (2005) point out that, prior to European arrival, Māori were an iwi (tribal)-based people and the identity of 'Māori' did not yet exist: 'we have no sense of an ethnic self without a contrasting other' (p. 13).

Identity is important. Our identities shape how we experience the world, how we understand what we experience, and the opportunities and challenges we face through life. Not all identities are equally valued, and so identity also determines the allocation of social, political and economic power in society. We learn about our identities through our encounters and interactions with other people — through personal relationships, through institutions such as schools and workplaces, and through the vast array of media that depict and construct our social world. We express and present our identities to others in a multitude of ways — through our appearance, through what we say, and through the things that we own and display, the art we create or buy, the media we choose to consume. Identity is not just within us, it is all around us.

An important part of appreciating that identity is social — something that occurs between people rather than within people — is understanding that identities are socially constructed, fluid and dynamic. This means that how you experience being male, or Samoan, or 40, or a mother, or retired, is dependent on your social context and on the interactions and encounters that you have with others. To illustrate that idea with an example, consider age, an identity thread that on the surface is purely a matter of biology. A person between 13 and 19 years old is a teenager. But this identity label, this category, is socially constructed. Nothing specific happens the day you turn 13. And in some societies there is no word or idea that represents adolescence — you are a child and then you are an adult. But in most Western societies there is a period in between, and this period of adolescence is constructed as one of being impulsive and rebellious, as a period of identity-seeking and developing independence. And that social view of adolescence shapes how the individual experiences being a teenager.

Context is a critical concept here. Context includes the immediate context, such as one's family or workplace, but more importantly it also includes wider social contexts. So, for instance, my mother was a stay-at-home mother, and when I had my own children this is what I chose to do — my maternal identity was shaped in part by my encounters within my home and my family. But it was not just what I had learned from my mother. She had her children in the United Kingdom in the 1960s, whereas I had mine in Aotearoa New Zealand in the 1990s. Our social, political, cultural and historical contexts were different. Therefore, what it meant to be a mother and how we were supposed to do mothering was different, and this impacted on our individual experiences and identities as mothers — not just in terms of the choices we made, but also in terms of how we felt about those choices and ourselves. Language is a critical part of our context, and also helps shape our identity. The phrase 'stay-at-home mother' did not exist in my mother's time, because it was the norm. Now, 25 years after I had my children, that phrase can have a negative connotation, reflecting the shifting social views and norms about what being a mother means.

Another important contribution to the fluidity of our identity is that our identities are not separate and distinct. Coming back to Burr's (2015) metaphor of identity threads, those threads intersect and overlap, and in doing so each influences the other. So, being a mother and the way in which someone enacts their maternal identity will be shaped in part by their other identities, such as ethnicity, values and age. Some identity threads interact more easily than others (depending on the context). For example, in the current cultural context of Aotearoa New Zealand, teenage pregnancy is constructed as a social problem: 'teenager' and 'mother' is a socially undesirable combination of identities. As Wilson and Huntington (2006) point out, 'normative perceptions of motherhood have shifted over the past few decades to position teenage mothers as stigmatised and marginalised' (p. 59). There are other identities that do not easily align with 'mother' as well. In my own research on women's decision-making around family and paid work, first-time mothers talked about the challenge of weaving their existing identity as 'successful woman' in with this new identity of mother (Kahu & Morgan, 2007).

That is the self — a complex, fluid weaving of identities. But if the self is social, then, to understand fully we need to consider how we interact with each other within different communities. The word 'community' stems from the Latin bases of *communitas*, meaning 'the same', and *communis*, meaning 'shared by many'. So a community is a group of people with a common interest or a shared identity thread. Communities can be physical, a geographical area for instance; they can be digital, such as an online support group; and/or they can be social, based on relationships, such as a family. Communities can vary, too, in terms of size, from large, wide communities such as New Zealand, to small, specific communities such as the students in a particular class. Communities are powerful and important to our sense of self, as Mayo (2008) explains: 'communities are the source of social attachments, create interdependencies, mediate between the individual and the larger society, and sustain the well being of members' (p. 147). So being a member of a community can give people a sense of belonging, an idea we will return to in a moment.

Citizenship

One useful way of understanding membership within a community is as citizenship. Most commonly, 'citizenship' refers to membership of a nation state, a particular geographical and political context, and to the various rights and responsibilities that flow from this. In this instance, legal citizenship is represented by holding a national passport. But in this text we conceive of citizenship more broadly, referring to membership of any community — your local sports club, your workplace, your family even. Citizenship is important because it has consequences. It determines material benefits, it fosters a sense of belonging (or a sense of alienation), and it legitimises participation and voice.

Citizenship is about more than just membership of the community; it is about the rights and obligations that accompany that membership. The nature of citizenship in any particular community, like identity, is socially constructed, contextual and fluid. Who gets to be a member of a community, as well as the level of rights and obligations that members have, often depends on the identity threads a person has: 'Identity is a fundamental organising principle in the enactment of power, the mobilisation for and the allocation of resources, and a critical marker of inclusion and exclusion' (Liu et al., 2005, p. 15). It also depends on the context — who is a citizen and what that means are different in different communities, and change through time.

As mentioned, the term 'citizenship' is often used specifically in reference to membership of a nation state; our nationality is an important thread to most people's identities. While we are interested in how the individual functions in a range of communities, this book is about identity and citizenship within Aotearoa New Zealand. It is useful, therefore, to use Aotearoa New Zealand as an example community to illustrate the links with identity. Note, however, that everyone who lives here is a member of this community, but not all have a New Zealand passport, and therefore are not citizens in the narrow, legal definition of the word (they may be permanent residents, temporary visitors or even illegal residents). However, in the broader understanding of citizenship as membership of a community, they are citizens, albeit with different rights.

The nature of citizenship is influenced by a range of forces, such as political and legal frameworks, social norms, structures of power, and discourse and language, as shown in the illustration of tūrangawaewae's core concepts. The most tangible of these influences are the political and legal frameworks — the laws of the land. These laws establish, among other things, who counts as a citizen, and which of those citizens has what rights. There are four broad types of citizenship rights: legal rights, such as personal security and access to justice; political rights, such as the rights to vote, to protest and to access information; social rights, such as healthcare, education and welfare; and participatory rights, such as access to jobs and protection from discrimination (Janoski & Gran, 2002).

Not all citizens have access to the same rights, and in part that is determined by their identity. For example, until recently, the right to marry was limited to heterosexual couples — homosexual New Zealanders were denied that right on the basis of their identity. Critically, this type of legal exclusion sent a clear message that a homosexual identity thread was not as valued as a heterosexual identity thread.

Laws exert explicit influences on citizenship, but there are other less tangible influences, such as social norms and language. For instance, there is a strong discourse (a way of talking about and understanding the world) in New Zealand and most of the Western world these days (i.e. in the current socio-historical context) that paid work is essential — for personal wellbeing and also as a contribution to society. Within this narrative, those who are not in paid work (including beneficiaries, retirees and stay-at-home parents) are seen as a burden — they are not doing their bit for the community. Phrases like 'dole bludger' make this clear. So, while in terms of legal frameworks a person on a benefit may have the same rights as everyone else, the social norms and the way we talk about the world position these identities as lesser citizens. As with the previous example, a significant thread in those people's identity is deemed less valuable, less desirable.

There are two other ideas that link closely to citizenship and identity that need more exploration so we can understand why this all matters: participation and belonging. Participation refers to the actions we undertake as members of a community, as active citizens. For example, if the community is the local school your children attend, then your participation includes activities such as helping out at the school fair, attending parent–teacher interviews and voting in the school's board of trustees elections. Participation is the things we do that contribute to the smooth running of our communities, but it is also how we have a say on how our communities function. So an important part of participation is voice — and not just being able to have a say, but also having our voice listened to. As British political scientist Richard Bellamy (2008) puts it: 'Those who enjoy a certain status are entitled to participate on an equal basis with their fellow citizens in making the collective decisions that regulate social life' (p. 1).

In the same way that not all citizens have equal rights, not all citizens are able to have an equal say, and not everyone's voice is equally heard. Part of the exclusion and marginalisation of identities that occurs in a community is the silencing of people's voices. Again using the nation state as our example community, Māori have a long history of being silenced in Aotearoa New Zealand — of not being able to participate equally. The obvious example of this is that Māori were long denied equal voting rights, as Richard Shaw discusses in Chapter 3. But the silencing, and therefore the exclusion, of Māori was also evident in other formal and informal social actions, such as the confiscation of Māori land by government and the banning of Māori language in schools. When people are marginalised and their voices are not heard through formal channels, such as voting, they may turn to less formal ways of speaking, such as protest and art, as we discuss in Part 2 of this book. It is unsurprising, then, that we have a long history in Aotearoa New Zealand of Māori protest (Harris, 2004).

Closely linked to participation is the idea of belonging. Belonging is the sense of being an important part of a community — of feeling like a valued member. As illustrated above, different groups of people have been marginalised and excluded in different ways in Aotearoa New Zealand: through being denied equal rights, through social norms and language, through active silencing. In all of these cases, their identity is socially constructed as of less value, as less important. This can have a powerful impact on people's sense of self, and potentially impacts negatively on their sense of belonging in the community of Aotearoa New Zealand. Conversely, participation and belonging have a cyclical relationship. The more someone actively participates (and is allowed and encouraged to participate) in a community, the stronger their sense of belonging. And the stronger a person's sense of belonging within a community, the more they are likely to participate in the running and decision-making of that community.

I started with the idea that people come together along shared identity lines to form communities to which people belong. The final piece of puzzle needed to complete the foundations of this book is the idea of 'collective identity'. Polletta and Jasper (2001) describe collective identity as 'an individual's cognitive, moral and emotional connection with a broader community category, practice or institution' (p. 285). The reciprocal link between citizenship and identity is evident in this definition, and Snow and Corrigall-Brown (2015) make it clearer when they describe collective identity as our 'shared sense of "one-ness" or "we-ness" anchored in real or imagined shared attributes' (p. 175). So our identities bring us together into a community and, at the same time, our membership in that community helps shape our individual identities. Aotearoa New Zealand as a community therefore has a collective identity. When we talk about New Zealanders being friendly or when we draw on metaphors of 'No. 8 fencing wire', we are drawing on perceived attributes of our collective identity. It does not mean that all New Zealanders are friendly or good at DIY, but nonetheless these ideas form a part of our sense of self. And a collective identity is as fluid and as socially constructed as a personal identity, and so what it means to be a New Zealander is changing — an idea that resonates throughout this book.

These interrelated ideas — identity, citizenship, participation and belonging — form the foundation of this volume. Each section addresses these ideas from a slightly different perspective, and, by looking at various identities, events and communities, together the chapters form an understanding of what it means to be of this place, Aotearoa New Zealand, at this time.

Structure of the book

The book is arranged in four parts, each of which opens with a short discussion in which the central questions and issues pursued in the subsequent chapters — what we call a 'conceptual template' — are set out.

The chapters

Part 1, 'Faces of Aotearoa New Zealand', sets the scene by exploring both the rapidly changing demographic composition of our population, and several other ways in which the individual and the collective faces of New Zealand are altering. It examines some of the diverse identities that make up Aotearoa New Zealand. The central theme is that the use of the singular category 'citizen' can mask what is, increasingly, a rich, messy and tremendously diverse national population. In Chapter 1, Trudie Cain explores the shifting face(s) of Aotearoa New Zealand through the lens of demography. Inevitably, she cannot cover each and every important dimension of these changes in full detail; what Trudie does provide, though, is a portrait of a country in which ethnicity, age, income and geographical location — and the intersections of these — all feature. In Chapter 2, Te Rina Warren, Margaret Forster and Veronica Tawhai offer a Māori perspective on notions of identity, belonging and citizenship. Drawing on sacred stories, and Māori experiences of colonisation, one of the important things they do is gently show us that the range of intellectual tools that we can use to make sense of things such as identity, belonging and citizenship is probably greater than many of us are aware.

Part 2, 'Voices of Aotearoa New Zealand', explores some of the ways in which we give voice, individually or as part of a group, to our views, fears, hopes and aspirations. This section is explicitly about participation — how people express their points of view and seek to have them acknowledged as legitimate contributions to public debate; it has to do with how people's identities are expressed and heard. Richard Shaw's chapter explores the ways in which people seek to express their voice through formal parliamentary politics, but he also suggests that choosing not to engage with politics is a legitimate expression of voice (albeit one with potentially disturbing consequences). In Chapter 4, I look at participation outside of Parliament, exploring what motivates people to protest. I then use two case studies to illustrate the impacts of voice on identity. In Chapter 5, Trudie Cain considers the role of the arts in both representing and constructing identity.

The penultimate section, Part 3, 'Places in Aotearoa New Zealand', looks at the ways in which our identity is connected to places of significance to us, and examines how both tacit and explicit conventions, norms and rules structure relationships between people in these places. Beyond the level of the individual, our encounters with others in these contexts also have implications for notions of citizenship. Some places comprise environments in which the communities we belong to (or to which we aspire to belong) come together; others can provide a refuge and disengagement from such collective interactions. Juliana Mansvelt, Trudie Cain and Ann Dupuis begin this section with a chapter in which they explore different understandings of home as a place of significance. In Chapter 7, Richard Shaw examines the tacit and explicit 'rules of the game' that structure relationships within universities, while, in Chapter 8, Sy Taffel looks at the relationship between people's sense of self and their engagement with the digital world.

The chapters comprising Part 4, 'Stories of Aotearoa New Zealand', critically engage with three of the major narratives told in this country as a way of asserting national identity. The narratives we examine — which are about inequality, the environment and Anzac — are examples of the ways in which national narratives convey powerful messages about what it means to be in and of this country. In so doing, they can shape both our individual and collective (or national) senses of who we are. Clearly, each has elements of truth; equally, each tells only a partial story, and masks both the lived experiences of some members of our society and competing accounts of the way things are.

David Littlewood begins this process in Chapter 9 by examining the origins, evolution and accuracy of the idea that New Zealand is an egalitarian society, that we are all equal. In doing so, he highlights the complex links between equality of opportunity and equality of outcome. In the following chapter, Juliana Mansvelt examines another story we like to tell — that New Zealand is clean, green and 100% pure. After tracing the history of the story, including its links to Brand New Zealand, Juliana puts our environment under the microscope to reveal a very different image of New Zealand. In Chapter 11, Carl Bradley and Rhys Ball turn our attention to the Anzac story that talks of New Zealand's national identity being founded on the shores of Gallipoli. They contrast Gallipoli with the Vietnam War in order to shine a light on a different view of war, and then highlight some of the groups in our society whose experiences of war are missing from the Anzac story. In the conclusion, the editors, Richard, Trudie and I, offer some concluding thoughts on the issues and debates raised throughout the book. Stepping back from the detail of earlier chapters, we reflect on the magnitude of what is presently happening in Aotearoa New Zealand, on the long-term challenges and opportunities these trends present, and on how we might as a national community react to the sorts of changes discussed in this book.

The choice of topics

Finally, a word or two on our choice of topics. Deciding what we were going to focus on was no easy matter. For every choice we made, others were forgone. Given the amount of time many of us spend in sports clubs, charitable organisations or churches, for example, Part 3 could happily have included chapters on each of these places. And in Part 4 we might well have chosen other narratives — that this is a great place to raise kids, perhaps, or that farming is the backbone of the nation, or that New Zealand is now a bicultural nation — each of which contains elements of truth, while also obscuring inconvenient facts. In the end, we stand by our choices — but in future editions of the book we may well take the opportunity to explore these alternatives.

Several reasons lie behind our decision to dedicate a chapter to Māori ethnicity. First, the chapter serves as a specific study of how and why ethnicity is important to all of us; the authors introduce us to terms and concepts in the context of tangata whenua, but many of these have analogues in other ethnic contexts. That said, the voice of Māori — which, as Mason Durie (2003) has shown us, is not one but a chorus of voices — is still, even in these purportedly post-Treaty settlement times, often silenced. Māori imagery and symbolism are important elements in our collective identity, and central to the way we represent — and overtly market — ourselves as a nation to others. Indeed, we have used a Māori term in the title of this publication, and for many it would be inconceivable that an All Black test could start without a haka. Yet Māori views on and understandings of citizenship are not as widely understood as they should be. This choice of ours, therefore, is explicitly intended to showcase Māori, but this is not to deny other ethnicities, including Pākehā: indeed, the entire book comprises an extended invitation not only to learn about others' ways of doing and being, but also to reflect on the ethnic and other bases of your own sense of self.

We are mindful that our decision may trigger calls for balanced coverage; for an equivalent amount of attention to be paid to a point of view or position that is the obverse of that which has suddenly been rendered visible. Therefore, some might argue that a chapter on Māori should be complemented with one on Pākehā (or, depending on your linguistic preferences, European New Zealanders). As editors, that is not a view we share. Rather, our position is that — with the exception of Chapter 2 — the bulk of this book is framed by a Pākehā/European New Zealander lens. It may not be obvious at first sight, because — to reiterate the point made by Barker (1948) at the beginning of this introduction — for many of us this is what is natural and therefore taken for granted, but both the content of each other chapter, and the cultural frameworks within which those chapters' authors work, are predominantly non-Māori. Seen in this way, a single chapter on things Māori in a book numbering 11 chapters seems if anything insufficient rather than overly generous.

Conclusion

Making sense of the complex intersections between these ideas of identity, belonging, citizenship and participation is fundamental to understanding people — and to understanding ourselves. Moreover, in the bigger picture, understanding identity and citizenship is fundamental to many of the large social problems that the world is facing. How countries are responding to the current refugee crisis is shaped by understandings of identity and citizenship, for example. Closer to home, debates about the influence of migration on 'the New Zealand way of life' or about the proper place of the Treaty of Waitangi in our system of government — these, too, are fundamentally shaped by contrasting understandings of identity. Whichever way you look at it, identity matters.

Making sense of these complex issues requires different intellectual tools, a range of which we will offer you throughout the book. Some are from social scientists, who typically assert the need for greater reflexive identity, 'a greater awareness of how our concepts of ourselves affect our daily lives; from high level political decisions (to go to Iraq) . . . to personal decisions (stance on seabed) . . . to mundane choices (who to invite for dinner, what school for our kids, what music)' (Liu et al., 2005, p. 13). Others are from the disciplines of the humanities, which tend to 'study the meaning-making practices of human culture, past and present, focusing on interpretation and critical evaluation, primarily in terms of the individual response' (Small, 2013, p. 57).

It is our hope that you will draw on these contributions and read this book reflectively. That as you come across different ideas, learn about different identities and hear about different events, you will stop and think about you and your place in Aotearoa New Zealand. And that through this process you will have gained a better understanding of what it means for each of us to be a citizen of this place and time.

How to use this book

At several points in each chapter, you will find a QR code and URL that will take you to a video or a piece of text that offers you further information. It looks like this:

Visit the Tūrangawaewae website for more online resources: http://turangawaewae.massey.ac.nz

As well as these links there will be a further QR code and URL at the very end of each chapter. Scan the code or insert the URL into your browser and you will find an interview with someone who knows a good deal about the topic, as well as a series of suggestions about other online resources. Taking time to browse through these links will help you make sense of the material covered in the chapter. Here is a complete list of all the chapter videos:

Introduction

Chapter 1

Chapter 2

Chapter 3

Chapter 4

Chapter 5

Chapter 6

Chapter 7

You will also see that every chapter concludes with an extensive list of references. Of course that is an academic convention and we wouldn't expect you to go to all of them. But amongst these titles there are some that we do urge you to read as they will deepen your knowledge and thinking. Each chapter, therefore, also ends with a 'recommended reading' list.

Recommended reading

Beausoleil, E. (2017). Twenty-first-century citizenship: Critical, global, active. In A. Brown & J. Griffiths (Eds.), *The citizen: Past and present* (pp. 25–35). Auckland, New Zealand: Massey University Press.

Liu, J. H., McCreanor, T., McIntosh, T., & Teaiwa, T. (2005). Introduction: Constructing New Zealand identities. In J. H. Liu, T. McCreanor, T. McIntosh, & T. Teaiwa (Eds.), *New Zealand identities: Departures and destinations* (pp. 11–20). Wellington, New Zealand: Victoria University Press.

References

Barker, E. (1948). *National character and the factors in its formantion* (4th ed.). London, England: Methuen & Co.

Bellamy, R. (2008). *Citizenship: A very short introduction.* Oxford, England: Oxford University Press.

Burr, V. (2015). *Social constructionism* (3rd ed.). London, England: Routledge.

Durie, M. (2003). *Ngā kāhui pou: Launching Māori futures.* Wellington, New Zealand: Huia Press.

Harris, A. (2004). *Hikoi: Forty years of Māori protest.* Wellington, New Zealand: Huia Press.

Janoski, T., & Gran, B. (2002). Political citizenship: Foundations of rights. In E. F. Isin & B. S. Turner (Eds.), *Handbook of citizenship studies* (pp. 13–53). London, England: Sage.

Kahu, E. R., & Morgan, M. (2007). Weaving cohesive identities: New Zealand women talk as mothers and workers. *Kōtuitui: New Zealand Journal of Social Sciences Online, 2*(2), 55–73.

Liu, J. H., McCreanor, T., McIntosh, T., & Teaiwa, T. (2005). Introduction: Constructing New Zealand identities. In J. H. Liu, T. McCreanor, T. McIntosh, & T. Teaiwa (Eds.), *New Zealand identities: Departures and destinations* (pp. 11–20). Wellington, New Zealand: Victoria University Press.

Mayo, M. L. (2008). Community. In V. N. Parrillo (Ed.), *Encyclopedia of social problems* (pp. 147–149). Thousand Oaks, CA: Sage.

Polletta, F., & Jasper, J. M. (2001). Collective identity and social movements. *Annual Review of Sociology, 27*, 283–305. doi:10.1146/annurev.soc.27.1.283

Small, H. (2013). *The value of the humanities.* Oxford, England: Oxford University Press.

Snow, D. A., & Corrigall-Brown, C. (2015). Collective identity. In J. D. Wright (Ed.), *International encyclopedia of the social and behavioral sciences* (2nd ed., Vol. 4, pp. 174–180). New York, NY: Elsevier.

Wilson, H., & Huntington, A. (2006). Deviant (m)others: The construction of teenage motherhood in contemporary discourse. *Journal of Social Policy, 35*(1), 59–76. doi:10.1017/S0047279405009335

Woodward, K. (2003). *Understanding identity.* London, England: Arnold.

PART ONE: FACES OF AOTEAROA NEW ZEALAND

Faces:
Introduction

Richard Shaw

Welcome to the first of the four parts — faces, voices, places and stories — comprising this book. Each part begins with one of these brief discussions, the purpose of which is to introduce the conceptual template that gives shape to each of the individual chapters within it. Think of this short piece, then, as a sort of map designed to guide both the structure of each subsequent chapter and your engagement with it.

About Part 1

Let me borrow (and in so doing possibly butcher) a metaphor from art to explain the specifics of Part 1 and its two constituent chapters. The diversity that now characterises this country — ethnic, linguistic, religious, familial and so on — is so pronounced that we need many colours to paint its portrait. In this context, the fundamental purpose of Part 1 is to provide a sense of the breadth, depth and richness of the people of Aotearoa New Zealand, by examining some of the different demographic characteristics of those who live here. Although we will look primarily at the changing ethnic composition of the population, consistent with the points Ella made in the introduction, we will also acknowledge other identities, such as age, gender and place of residence. Put these and other identity threads together — as occurs in Chapters 1 and 2 — and you will begin to develop a sharper sense of the ways in which the individual faces within, and the collective face of, Aotearoa New Zealand are changing.

The conceptual template for the two chapters in Part 1 has four elements:

1. We examine the shifting patterns of identity in Aotearoa New Zealand in

the twenty-first century, and take a close look at the ways in which the demographic profile of the population is evolving.

2. We also explore some of the ways in which our identity threads intersect with wider social, political and other forces to continuously shape and reshape our personal sense of self, and our understandings of national identity.

3. We assess some of the ways in which identity is expressed (through, for instance, rituals, symbols and art).

4. Finally, we consider some of the present and future consequences and challenges of the changing face of Aotearoa New Zealand. We analyse what the demographic and other trends explored in Part 1 mean to different groups, and look at some of the reactions to those developments.

Overview of chapters

In Chapter 1, 'Demographic diversities — the changing face of Aotearoa New Zealand', Trudie Cain explores the contested, shifting and changing face of citizenship in Aotearoa New Zealand. Trudie's is something of a scene-setting chapter. Focusing on broad demographic developments, but also incorporating insights into the relationship between ethnicity, age and factors such as income and geography, she works through some of the consequences these seismic shifts are having for what counts as identity and citizenship at the individual and societal levels. What Trudie offers is a portrait of a country that is quite different from that which existed only a few short decades ago.

In Chapter 2, Te Rina Warren, Margaret Forster and Veronica Tawhai introduce historical and contemporary conceptions of identity, belonging and citizenship that are particular to Māori. If Trudie's was a scene-setting chapter, then 'Tangata whenua — Māori, identity and belonging' is a detailed exploration of the ways in which these conceptions are shaped by the contextually specific experiences of a particular ethnic group (albeit one containing, as they point out, diverse realities). Among other things, what the authors provide are insights into notions of identity, belonging and citizenship that are indigenous to Aotearoa New Zealand. In doing so, they remind us of the dissonant chord that can be struck when Māori understandings of such notions are placed alongside those that emerge from different cultural contexts. Neither is more or less correct: the point to be made is that what makes sense (and is perhaps taken for granted) by some is far from obvious for others.

Conclusion

Part 1 provides a context for the rest of the book. As such, its first and most important job is to sketch, at a necessarily broad level, the rich and varied nature of the individual and collective identities that comprise Aotearoa New Zealand. A second and somewhat tacit aim is to invite you to begin (or perhaps to continue) the process of challenging or reappraising your own assumptions about what it means to be in and of this country.

A third objective is to encourage you to think about what the term 'citizen' means in the context of the country that begins to emerge from Chapters 1 and 2. 'Citizen' is a unitary category (in formal terms, at least — you either are one or you are not), but the word masks a wide range of different identities: what it means to be a New Zealander will differ, and often quite significantly, from one person to another. There is no one template for being a citizen of — or indeed a visitor to, or a migrant or refugee in — this place. The face of Aotearoa New Zealand is far more colourful and diverse than it was even a couple of decades ago. These developments, and the profound consequences they are having for the ways in which we make sense of who we are as people and as a nation, are the focus of the two chapters you are about to read. And, indeed, this colourful picture provides the backdrop to the rest of this book.

CHAPTER ONE:

Demographic diversities

The changing face of Aotearoa New Zealand

Trudie Cain

Introduction

The main title of this chapter is 'Demographic diversities'. The word 'demography' is derived from Ancient Greece: the prefix *demo* refers to 'the people', while *graphy* suggests 'describing, measuring or writing about'. Hence, 'demography' can be defined as 'the statistical study of human populations'. Does this mean you are about to read a chapter full of statistics? Well, yes and no. There are certainly some statistics included, but they are introduced to paint a picture of how this country's population has changed (and continues to change) over time. This is an important point that requires underlining. Population change has social, cultural, economic and political implications, each of which impacts on the lives of those who live here in New Zealand.

In the book's introduction, Ella discussed the multiple threads of self that weave together to create an individual and collective sense of identity. This chapter extends this work by considering how two very specific and significant identity threads — ethnicity and age — influence our individual and collective sense of self, including how these aspects of identity shape the encounters we have with others.

Importantly, ethnicity and age can provide both opportunities and challenges for fully participating in society and securing a sense of belonging and inclusion. The chapter also explores how changing patterns of ethnicity and age have altered the demographic face and complexion of Aotearoa New Zealand. What I hope will become clear is the extent to which rapidly changing populations create new contexts in which diverse identities might emerge.

Ethnicity and identity

Ethnicity is a particularly significant identity thread for many New Zealanders. But what is even meant by ethnicity? The term 'ethnicity' is largely taken for granted, but in the Aotearoa New Zealand context it is strongly contested. Statistics New Zealand (2005) defines 'ethnicity' as 'the ethnic group or groups that people identify with or feel they belong to. Ethnicity is a measure of cultural affiliation, as opposed to race, ancestry, nationality or citizenship. Ethnicity is self-perceived and people can affiliate with more than one ethnic group' (p. 1).

This definition highlights a number of important points. First, although ancestry (biological and social roots) continues to perform an important role in ethnic identification, it provides only part of the story. More important are the subjective understandings and perceptions that individuals might have of a given ethnicity, what it means to them, and the extent to which they feel they belong or not. Ethnic identity is fluid and dynamic, and can change over the course of one's life and, perhaps relatedly, many New Zealanders (especially younger New Zealanders) identify with more than one ethnic group.

Indeed, official classifications of ethnicity in the five-yearly New Zealand census are regularly updated to reflect the fluidity and multiplicity of ethnic identity, moving away in recent years from an emphasis on biological criteria and descent. Profoundly personal, ethnic identification is a powerful marker of shared cultural values, knowledge and beliefs, and customs and practices that are shaped in a given historical and socio-cultural context. In a local context, ethnic identification can be complex, especially in relation to ethnic categories such as Māori, Pākehā and New Zealander.

 If you are interested in the approach Statistics New Zealand takes to defining and classifying ethnicity, visit: http://www.stats.govt.nz/methods/classifications-and-standards/classification-related-stats-standards/ethnicity/definition.aspx

Our ethnic affiliation and identification weaves its way into many, if not all, aspects of our lives. With regard to our everyday lives, ethnicity can shape the clothes we wear, the way we wear our hair, and the food we choose to prepare and eat. The body itself can also be an important marker of ethnic identity. For example, culturally specific tattoos such as moko (traditional Māori tattoo), tatau (traditional male Samoan tattoo) and malu (traditional female Samoan tattoo) provide ways of ascribing culture and ethnicity onto the body. Such tattoos are often deeply personal, and serve as a symbol of respect for cultural heritage and whakapapa (genealogy). Ethnicity is also likely to shape our religious beliefs and linguistic practices; ultimately, ethnicity shapes how we understand and make sense of the world.

Importantly, ethnicity also intersects with other aspects of our identity, such as age and gender, each of which shapes how ethnicity is experienced. Socio-cultural norms and conventions shape how people with different combinations of identity threads interact with each other in particular temporal and spatial contexts. To illustrate the point, consider the title of the excellent New Zealand baking book *Ladies, A plate* (2008). The author, Alexa Johnston, consciously invokes a time and place (post-war New Zealand) in which an invitation to a social gathering would as likely as not be accompanied by a request that women should bring a plate. The plate, it was assumed, would contain food (of the sort profiled in Johnston's book). The important point is that the assumption was tacit: women (and men) from the dominant culture would be able to decode the request, but anecdotes abound about women from other ethnic and cultural contexts who would wonder quite why they were being asked to bring a plate to a social gathering.

Some of you might find it fairly easy to identify your ethnicity in the first instance, and also to think about the ways you perform your ethnic identity in different settings. Others of you might find it a little trickier. As Ella noted in the introduction, it can be especially difficult when we identify with the dominant ethnic group — as Pākehā/New Zealand European. Arguably, when we identify with the majority ethnic group we have less reason to reflect on our own ethnic identity, because our way of seeing and being in the world becomes the norm by which others might be measured. To paraphrase the point Ella made early in her chapter, we may struggle to reflect on our own ethnic identity 'because it is so simply and obviously a fact' (Barker, 1948, p. 195). But whether you are part of the majority or not, there is nothing 'given' about ethnic identity.

I encourage you to take some time to reflect on your own ethnic identity while you continue reading this chapter. To what extent does your ethnicity as New Zealand European, Māori, Hong Kong-Chinese, Pākehā, and so on, impact on how you see the world, how you behave in the world, and how you negotiate the world in everyday life?

From individual ethnicity to collective diversity

I want to turn away now from an understanding of an individual ethnic identity and move towards a discussion of the demographic change that is occurring in Aotearoa New Zealand. For a long time now, this country has been described as 'ethnically diverse'. But we are increasingly being described as 'superdiverse' (Chen, 2015). The term 'superdiversity' was coined in 2007 by anthropologist Steven Vertovec to describe the 'level and kind of complexity' (p. 1024) of diversity that now exists in many migrant host nations, such as New Zealand. Vertovec argues that, as the world has become 'smaller', with people moving more easily between one place and another, increasingly complex social formations have developed that produce a dynamic interplay of country of origin, ethnic identification, migration pathways, languages spoken, religious affiliation and socio-cultural practices and values. So superdiversity is not simply about 'more ethnic groups' represented in a given country, although that is certainly part of it: it is about the 'diversification of diversity' (p. 1025).

Viewed in this way, it is not difficult to think of New Zealand as superdiverse. As a settler society, New Zealand has a long history of attracting migrants from the United Kingdom, to the point where, historically at least, the country was often described as 'the Britain of the South Seas' (Beilharz & Cox, 2006, p. 560). In Chapters 9 and 10 we look at some of the stories of New Zealand that were told to attract those migrants. However, in 1986/87, the country's immigration policy context changed, and the privileging of immigrants from the United Kingdom was abandoned in favour of a new immigration policy that explicitly targeted those with the skills, capital and other means of contributing to the economy (Spoonley & Bedford, 2012) that New Zealand required. Since then, the number of New Zealanders born overseas has increased dramatically in a very short space of time, climbing from just 19.5 per cent of the total population in 2001 to 25 per cent in 2013 (Statistics New Zealand, 2013).

Ethnic group	Number	Per cent of total population	Per cent change since 2006
European	2,969,391	74%	+14%
Māori	598,605	15%	+6%
Asian	471,711	12%	+33%
Pasifika	295,944	7%	+11%
Middle Eastern/Latin American/African	46,953	1%	+35%

Source: Statistics New Zealand, 2013

This change in policy context also substantially impacted on the ethnic makeup of New Zealand. There are now more ethnic groups represented in this country (213 ethnicities were counted in 2013) than there are countries in the world (Statistics New Zealand, 2013). The table above shows the number and percentage of people who identified with the 'top five' ethnic groups at the time of the 2013 census. The 33 per cent increase in the number of people identifying as Asian since 2006 is telling. Some of the largest increases within this broad ethnic category have been from China (increased by 16.2 per cent), India (48.4 per cent), and the Philippines (138.2 per cent) (Statistics New Zealand, 2013).

These new migration flows have certainly changed the face of Aotearoa New Zealand. A report produced by the Royal Society of New Zealand (2013) states that 'New Zealand is, increasingly, a country with multiple "national" identities and values' (p. 8). These identities and values can be seen in a range of ways. For example, over 160 different languages are now spoken across the country, and nearly 30 per cent of people are able to speak more than one language (after English, te reo Māori, Samoan and Hindi are the most common) (Statistics New Zealand, 2013; Royal Society of New Zealand, 2013).

Changing (and increased) migration flows have also shaped the religious beliefs of New Zealanders. Post-colonisation, the majority of New Zealanders identified as Christian, and Christianity certainly remains the largest single religion in the country. However, of those who stated a religion in the 2013 census, just 49 per cent identified as Christian (down from 55 per cent in 2006), and more people than ever before do not identify with a religion at all. There are also changes *within* the Christian faith, with Catholicism overtaking Anglicanism to become the largest Christian denomination (Statistics New Zealand, 2013). One of the reasons for this change is the flow of migrants from the Philippines to work in the dairy, health and construction sectors, along with other migrants arriving from countries such as Samoa and Tonga, both of which have a strong Catholic faith. Alongside these changes, adherents to non-Christian religions doubled between 1996 and 2006, such that there are now sizeable Hindu, Buddhist, Muslim and Sikh communities, each comprising various ethnic and language groups with very different migrant experiences.

 Visit Te Ara for more on New Zealand's religious diversity: http://www.teara.govt.nz/en/diverse-religions/page-1

Religious and ethnic diversity is not distributed evenly across New Zealand. Historical migrant settlement patterns have created marked religious differences between various regions. For example, the historical settlement of Scottish immigrants in Otago and Southland is reflected still in the dominance of Presbyterianism in the bottom half of the South Island, while English Anglican settlers tended to settle in the top half of the South Island and in the North Island. With regard to ethnic diversity, Auckland continues to serve as a 'gateway city' for newly arrived immigrants, two-thirds of whom arrive and stay in Auckland. This makes Auckland the most ethnically diverse city in New Zealand, with nearly 40 per cent of the city's residents born overseas (Statistics New Zealand, 2013); moreover, two-thirds of New Zealand's Asian and Pasifika residents live in Auckland (Auckland Council, 2014). Those figures stand in stark contrast to the situation in, for instance, Gisborne, Southland and the West Coast, where, respectively, only 9.7, 10.1 and 11 per cent of the resident populations were born overseas (Statistics New Zealand, 2013).

Rapid population change not only alters the face of New Zealand society, but it also alters its complexion. As the country, and especially Auckland, becomes 'diverse in new ways' (Hawke et al., 2015, p. 7), new emerging identities take shape. Cultural festivals are a material consequence of population change in New Zealand, and they provide opportunities for the construction, negotiation and expression of ethnic identity. Writing about the annual Pasifika Festival, held in Auckland, for example, Mackley-Crump (2015) argues that the event, which attracts more than 225,000 visitors each year, provides an opportunity for Pasifika peoples to deploy 'polycultural capital'; that is, to draw on an 'accumulation of distinctive cultural resources, intertextual skills, the power to negotiate between them and the ability to deploy these cross-cultural resources strategically in different contexts' (p. 8). What this means in practice is that people are able to straddle the boundaries of the Pacific and Aotearoa at this festival.

The Chinese Lantern Festival is another example of what is now an annual event that brings together diverse groups from across the country. Celebrating and showcasing the Chinese New Year, and the country's rich ethnic diversity, the festival has grown since its inception in 2000 to become one of the biggest and most popular cultural events in Auckland, with over 200,000 visitors annually. Clearly, such events are not confined to Auckland. In 2015, for instance, over 150,000 people attended Diwali lights festivals across the country (Asia New Zealand Foundation, 2016).

Festivals provide just one example of a context within which intercultural encounters might take place. Another example is the rise of ethnic precincts — new sites of work and consumption that are designed to meet the employment, social and consumer needs of new immigrant communities at the same time as providing both social and culinary experiences for non-migrants. Ethnic precincts are defined as the 'co-location of businesses that are owned by members of the same ethnic/immigrant group' (Cain, Meares, Spoonley, & Peace, 2011, p. 7). For migrants, especially those who are recently arrived, ethnic precincts help foster a sense of belonging and connectedness by offering the familiar sights, sounds and tastes of home. The sights of home include roast ducks hanging in restaurant windows and the presence of Chinese script on the streetscape — what Cain et al. (2011) describe as the street's 'linguistic landscape' (p. 33). The sounds of home reference being able to hear and communicate in their own language. Finally, the tastes of home are concerned with the very specific provincial flavours of their hometown; much of the Chinese food on offer in ethnic precincts is not generic, but reflects styles and flavours of cooking that are redolent of very specific places in China (Meares et al., 2015). Both food and language are important cultural identity markers, and being able to embody them in this space fosters and reinforces a sense of familiarity, belonging and connectedness both in New Zealand and in migrants' home countries.

Importantly, these sites of consumption also perform an important role for non-migrants. For example, the primarily Chinese ethnic precinct located in the Balmoral shops (Dominion Road, Auckland) is also frequented by many non-Chinese New Zealanders (both overseas- and local-born); nearly two-thirds of the people who visited the precinct identified with a non-Chinese ethnicity (Meares et al., 2015). An Auckland Council study asked visitors to the precinct about their reasons for visiting. The responses often centred on the diversity of 'ethnic' foods available to them, and the 'authenticity' of the flavour profiles (Meares et al., 2015). Visitors also reported their appreciation for the vibrancy of the place and its unique

Embracing diversity

Auckland's annual Lantern Festival, with its astounding lit-lantern artworks, celebrates and marks the Chinese New Year and traditional and contemporary Chinese culture. It has drawn thousands of visitors every year since it was first staged in 2000. By 2016 attendances had grown so much that it was moved from Albert Park in the central city to the Auckland Domain. The 2013 census recorded 171,411 Chinese living in Auckland, up from 105,057 at the 2001 census.

characteristics, especially when compared with the ubiquitous food halls that can be found in most shopping malls. Overall, shoppers were eager to embrace Auckland's new ethnic diversity, and many felt it provided opportunities for better understanding others' ethnicity and culture, as the following quote from a male Pākehā shopper attests:

> I don't think it facilitates a real sort of intense mixing, it does [however] provide a place where people from other ethnicities [can] be together in the same space . . . which is kind of cool, I don't think you could minimise the sort of value of that so yeah I think it is quite good actually when I think about it. (Meares et al., 2015, p. 81)

Ethnoburbs are also a feature of new ethnic diversities. 'Ethnoburbs' are defined as suburban residential areas with notable clusters of particular ethnic minority populations (Friesen, 2015; Li, 2009), and there are a number of developments of this kind across Auckland in particular. In the West Auckland Census Area Unit of LynnMall, for example, Chinese Aucklanders represent 31 per cent of the total population (Meares, Ho, Peace, & Spoonley, 2010a, p. 18). There are also significant concentrations of Korean Aucklanders in a number of middle-class areas of Auckland's North Shore, including Pinehill and Northcross (comprising 17 per cent and 13 per cent of the total populations of these Census Area Units, respectively) (Meares, Ho, Peace & Spoonley, 2010b, p. 22).

While some might argue that ethnoburbs are divisive, research suggests that these co-ethnic residential concentrations have social, cultural and economic benefits for the people who live there (Skop & Li, 2010), creating a sense of connectedness, belonging and a shared social context in which migrants can feel at home (Cain, Meares, & Read, 2015). Where we live is important for fostering a sense of identity, community and belonging. We create a sense of place through the physical environment we inhabit, but also through the relationships we have there — relationships that are socially and culturally specific and reflect one's 'place-in-the-world' (McCreanor et al., 2006, p. 198). (You'll read more about the relationship between place and identity in Part 3.)

A sense of identity and belonging is also mediated by the extent to which a person feels 'included and accepted within the institutional fabric of neighbourhood and community' (ibid.). There is a large body of literature that speaks to the difficulty of 'making home' in a strange land (Phillip & Ho, 2010; Li, Hodgetts, & Ho, 2010), and for those who are newly arrived in a country it can be difficult to attain this sense of belonging. This goes *some* way to explaining the rise of ethnoburbs (although there are other important structural and historical explanations, too). The interactions and encounters that people might have in these diverse regions across the country are undoubtedly shaped by the socio-political context in which they are situated.

Age and identity

Age is also an important and significant thread of identity that shapes the kinds of experiences we might have on a daily basis, as well as how we might make sense of those experiences. Our age structures the kinds of encounters we have with the outside world: whether we celebrate our birthday with 21 shots or a quiet meal with friends and family; whether we watch Netflix or TV1; or whether we take a river cruise or backpack around India. Of course I am not suggesting that our age *determines* what we can and cannot do — there is nothing stopping a 75-year-old from backpacking around India. But what I am saying is that the 'life course' approach to understanding human experience across the lifespan suggests that a series of socially defined events and roles shape the way an individual's life plays out over time. Although these events are not predetermined, they are shaped by biological, psycho-social, cultural and structural contexts, and include starting school; (perhaps) going to university; (maybe) finding a life partner; and (potentially) starting a new career. Again, everyone's life is different, and the socio-cultural environment in which we live will influence whether various events become part of our individual life story and when.

Just like ethnicity, age intersects with other threads of identity to shape how life is experienced at any given time. Income level and living situation, for example, are likely to determine the kind of lifestyle that someone has. Those of us who live at home for free with our parents while studying full-time, for instance, might have social lives that afford us great freedom and autonomy. In contrast, others of us who must necessarily work significant hours to contribute to the household income at the same time as studying full-time are likely to feel socially and financially constrained.

Following the pattern of the previous section, I want to turn now to the demographic profile of Aotearoa New Zealand and consider the extent to which age, like ethnicity, is changing the face of this country. In short, populations are ageing worldwide, and New Zealand is no exception. The population aged 65 and over is expected to almost double from 635,200 in 2013 to 1,100,000 in 2030. As life expectancy continues to climb, the number of people who are among the 'oldest old' (i.e. aged 85 or over) will also continue to climb, increasing from around 74,000 to over 144,000 during the same time period (Dale, 2015). Another way of expressing this is to point out that the country's population aged 65 or more will increase from 13 per cent to 21 per cent by 2031 (Jackson, 2011).

This global and local phenomenon is the direct result of large numbers of soldiers returning home at the end of the Second World War and very quickly marrying and starting a family. And families were large at this time; in the mid-1950s, Pākehā women could expect to have an average of nearly four live births, while Māori women could expect an average of almost seven. To put this in perspective, the current birth rate is at its lowest ever of nearly two births per woman (Jackson, 2016). This dramatic reduction in fertility rates is due at least in part to the introduction of the contraceptive pill in 1961, and to women's greater presence in the paid workforce (Tolerton, 2016). But regardless of the reason for the change, post-war demographic trends contributed to a 'baby boom' that reverberates still.

Understanding the economic, social and cultural impact of those people who were born during this period (approximately between 1946 and 1964) is important for thinking about identity and belonging in Aotearoa New Zealand. Baby boomers (as they have become known) have largely experienced economic growth and prosperity across their lifetime. In Aotearoa New Zealand, baby boomers have arguably benefited from free tertiary education, a generous 'cradle to the grave' welfare system, and affordable state housing, then private ownership and rising property prices. As the oldest of the baby boomers start to retire, they do so as members of a comparatively successful and affluent generation.

I use the word 'comparatively' to strike a cautionary note. For many baby boomers, access to non-income-tested government pensions and the possession of considerable equity in the form of their family home means that retirement does indeed represent the 'golden years'. However, this is by no means the case for all of them. Disquieting recent research suggests that a sizeable minority of the boomer generation do not own their own homes, and are only just getting by (if that) on government-provided superannuation (Johnson, 2015a). For these elderly, the future is likely to be uncomfortable and uncertain.

The rapid ageing of New Zealand's overall population has serious consequences for the country, including but extending well beyond the costs of providing age-appropriate healthcare, housing and other services. Demographer Natalie Jackson points out that the 'bulge' in New Zealand's older adult population puts pressure on an already 'demographically tight labour market' (Jackson, 2016, p. 53).

Statistics New Zealand's Interactive Population Pyramid for New Zealand illustrates the country's changing age–sex distribution over time: http://www.stats.govt.nz/tools_and_services/interactive-pop-pyramid.aspx

This means that, assuming present policies remain as they are, there are not enough of us who are of working age to fully support the growing number of retirees. A related concern is around the provision of the necessary health and social services to support an ageing population. While immigration plays an important role in filling local labour market needs, it is not sufficient to keep up with demand. This is a national problem that is not going to disappear in a hurry. (See Spoonley, 2016, for an extended discussion of these regional concerns.) As Jackson (2016) points out, it is an issue for local and central government, organisations and the business sector that requires a better understanding of the 'local drivers of demographic change' (pp. 76–77).

So far, I have been writing as though population age structure is evenly distributed, but this is not the case. For one thing, age intersects with ethnicity in different ways. Māori and Pasifika, for example, are significantly younger than those who identify with European and Asian ethnic groups: the average age of Māori and Pasifika in this country is 23.9 years and 22.1 years, respectively. By comparison, the average age of European and Asian New Zealanders is 41.0 years and 30.6 years, respectively (Statistics New Zealand, 2013).

 Data from the 2013 census shows our changing cultural diversity: http://www.stats.govt.nz/Census/2013-census/profile-and-summary-reports/quickstats-about-national-highlights/cultural-diversity.aspx

Similarly, age and geography play out in different ways. While Auckland, Wellington and Christchurch, for example, are comparatively young, other regions, such as Thames-Coromandel, are structurally 'very old'. In part, regional distinctions are created by a 'disproportionate influx of retirees' to some regions (Jackson, 2011, p. 20), and is exacerbated by the inward migration of working-age migrants to the country's largest cities as discussed earlier. Structural ageing (the increase in the *proportion* of a region's population that is old) will have a profound impact on those regions that are ageing rapidly or facing substantial population decline (Spoonley, 2016). Challenges associated with labour market

Baby boom sprawl

Local mothers meet on a street corner in
a new housing area of Waiuku, south of
Auckland, in the 1970s. Bare new housing
subdivisions like this were common across
New Zealand during the 1970s baby boom.
Builders were busy as new shops, schools,
churches and community facilities sprang up
to meet the needs of young families.

supply will be felt especially keenly at regional levels, but there are also significant infrastructure development challenges: how, for instance, can local governments create infrastructure to support an ageing population with a declining total population?

Regional differences matter because they shape the 'types of opportunities people have and the quality of life they might expect' (Johnson, 2015b, p. 5); where we live impacts on our lives in material ways. A 2015 report by the Salvation Army, *Mixed fortunes: The geography of advantage and disadvantage in New Zealand*, showed that location has a profound impact on economic opportunities (Johnson, 2015a). While areas such as Northland, Gisborne and Waikato — which, coincidentally, have significant Māori populations — have faced economic stagnation, large cities such as Auckland have benefited from a positive agglomeration effect (which is the self-reinforcing process via which large, prosperous cities attract more business and become larger and more prosperous as a result). These regional diversities not only contribute to inequitable outcomes (more on this in Chapter 9), they also contribute to the identity threads of residents.

Ultimately, different age cohorts have different life experiences that are a function of the political context into which they were born. Many millennials (those born in the 1980s and 1990s) argue that 'rolling back the state' in 1984 and removing free tertiary education in 1989 has disadvantaged them and created an unfair financial advantage for older New Zealanders. The story that is often told is of the retiree who has had it all through their life course and continues to have it all in their retirement, while millennials face the impossible task of locating an affordable home in which to live. Such rhetoric is powerful and has traction; but this distinction not only misrepresents the material circumstances of some older people, it also creates a false dichotomy that stigmatises older adults and constructs them as a financial burden on other members of society. As we explore in Part 4 of the book, national narratives such as that of the 'selfish boomer generation' may contain elements of truth, but they also obscure others, which results in the exclusion of the experiences of those to whom the narrative does not apply.

 You don't have to look very far to find articles that speak to the 'selfishness' of baby boomers and the martyrdom of millennials: https://www.theguardian.com/commentisfree/2015/sep/04/why-are-the-baby-boomers-desperate-to-make-us-millennials-hate-ourselves

The new New Zealand

Māori and Pasifika children in their school playground. They are the face of an increasingly diverse city, and will have been joined in recent years by children from China, India, Africa and the Middle East. The New Zealand education system has had to be flexible over the decades to accommodate the language needs of such a diverse population, many of whom arrive at school not having English as their first language.

Conclusion

All too often when diversity is discussed in the public arena, it is framed as a conversation about ethnicity. But the core purpose of this chapter has been to show that ethnic diversity is just one strand of diversity that impacts on the lives of New Zealanders. Age, sexuality, household income level (to name just a few variables): each shapes expressions of identity and belonging in this country. In this chapter, I have opted to focus on ethnicity, but have complemented this with attention to age and, to a lesser degree, geography. I have done so because when we weave these threads together we can start to see the particularly rich context from which identity can emerge.

The increasing ethnic diversity of New Zealand has created a new context for thinking about identity and belonging in this country. The new superdiverse context creates social and economic opportunities for individuals and the country, but there are also challenges. With regard to the former, ethnic diversity generates opportunities for entrepreneurship and new kinds of social encounters. As to the latter, newly arrived migrants must negotiate their identity in a new land, and, relatedly, although I haven't really discussed this here, local residents must negotiate a new social context that might be very different from the one in which they grew up. There are also challenges for policy-makers who must respond to a rapidly changing social milieu in ways that are inclusive, allow for linguistic and cultural difference, and promote participation and social cohesion.

The rapidly changing age structure of Aotearoa New Zealand has also altered the face of this country, and generated new kinds of encounters that are both explicitly and implicitly embedded in relations of power. As the so-called 'silver tsunami' puts pressure on the labour market, as well as on the country's health and pension policies, government and business must respond to these changing (region-specific) dynamics. As suggested by Spoonley (2016), a possible way forward is to harness the 'silver economy' and leverage the opportunities of a knowledgeable and experienced community of older adults. Doing so could generate new kinds of social and economic encounters that could benefit individuals, communities and regions as well as the country more broadly.

This chapter argues that new demographic diversities are changing the face and complexion of Aotearoa New Zealand. This necessarily places emphasis on a rapidly changing population, and this is undoubtedly important. But it is also important to remember that a population comprises many individuals. And these individuals each have a complex sense of identity that is informed by the socio-cultural, economic and political context into which they were born and raised, and currently live.

Chapter 1 — Demographic diversities: The changing face of Aotearoa New Zealand: http://turangawaewae.massey.ac.nz/chapter1.html

Recommended reading

Friesen, W. (2015). *Asian Auckland: The multiple meanings of diversity*. Wellington, New Zealand: Asia New Zealand Foundation.

Hawke, G., Bedford, R., Kukutai, T., McKinnon, M., Olssen, E., & Spoonley, P. (2015). *Our futures — Te pae tāwhiti: The 2013 census and New Zealand's changing population*. Wellington, New Zealand: The Royal Society of New Zealand.

Jackson, N. (2011). *The demographic forces shaping New Zealand's future: What population ageing [really] means* (NIDEA Working Paper). Hamilton, New Zealand: University of Waikato/National Institute of Demographic and Economic Analysis (NIDEA).

Spoonley, P. (Ed.). (2016). *Rebooting the regions: Why low or zero growth needn't mean the end of prosperity*. Auckland, New Zealand: Massey University Press.

References

Asia New Zealand Foundation. (2016). *Arts and culture*. Retrieved from http://www.asianz.org.nz/content/diwali-festival-lights

Auckland Council. (2014). *Auckland profile: Initial results from the 2013 census*. Auckland, New Zealand: Auckland Council.

Barker, E. (1948). *National character and the factors in its formantion* (4th ed.). London, England: Methven & Co.

Beilharz, P., & Cox, L. (2006). Nations and nationalism in Australia and New Zealand. In G. Delanty & K. Kumar (Eds.), *The Sage handbook of nations and nationalism* (pp. 555–565). London, England: Sage.

Cain, T., Meares, C., & Read, C. (2015). Home and beyond in Aotearoa: The affective dimensions of migration for South African migrants. *Gender, Place and Culture*, 22(8), 1141–1157.

Cain, T., Meares, C., Spoonley, P., & Peace, R. (2011). *Halfway house: The Dominion Road ethnic precinct*. Auckland, New Zealand: Massey University/University of Waikato.

Chen, M. (2015). *Superdiversity stocktake: Implications for business, government and New Zealand*. Auckland, New Zealand: Superdiversity Centre.

Dale, M. C. (2015). *Turning silver to gold: Policies for an ageing population* (Working

Paper 2014-2). Auckland, New Zealand: Retirement Policy and Research Centre/ University of Auckland.

Friesen, W. (2015). *Asian Auckland: The multiple meanings of diversity.* Wellington, New Zealand: Asia New Zealand Foundation.

Hawke, G., Bedford, R., Kukutai, T., McKinnon, M., Olssen, E., & Spoonley, P. (2015). *Our futures — Te pae tāwhiti: The 2013 census and New Zealand's changing population.* Wellington, New Zealand: The Royal Society of New Zealand.

Jackson, N. (2011). *The demographic forces shaping New Zealand's future: What population ageing [really] means* (NIDEA Working Paper). Hamilton, New Zealand: University of Waikato/National Institute of Demographic and Economic Analysis (NIDEA).

Jackson, N. (2016). Irresistible forces: Facing up to demographic change. In P. Spoonley (Ed.), *Rebooting the regions: Why low or zero growth needn't mean the end of prosperity* (pp. 49–77). Auckland, New Zealand: Massey University Press.

Johnson, A. (2015a). *Homeless baby boomers: Housing poorer baby boomers in their retirement.* Auckland, New Zealand: The Salvation Army Social Policy and Parliamentary Unit.

Johnson, A. (2015b). *Mixed fortunes: The geography of advantage and disadvantage in New Zealand.* Auckland, New Zealand: The Salvation Army Social Policy and Parliamentary Unit.

Johnston, A. (2008). *Ladies, a plate: Traditional home baking.* Auckland, New Zealand: Penguin.

Li, W. (2009). *Ethnoburb: The new ethnic community in urban America* [ebook]. Honolulu, HI: University of Hawaii Press.

Li, W., Hodgetts, D., & Ho, E. (2010). Gardens, transitions and identity reconstruction among older Chinese immigrants to New Zealand. *Journal of Health Psychology, 15*(5), 786–796.

Mackley-Crump, J. (2015). *The Pacific festivals of Aotearoa New Zealand: Negotiating place and identity in a new homeland* [ebook]. Honolulu, HI: University of Hawaii Press.

McCreanor, T., Penney, L., Jensen, V., Witten, K., Kearns, R., & Moewaka Barnes, H. (2006). 'This is like my comfort zone': Sense of place and belonging within Oruāmo/ Beachhaven, New Zealand. *New Zealand Geographer, 62,* 196–207.

Meares, C., Cain, T., Hitchins, H., Allpress, J., Fairgray, S., Terruhn, J., & Gilbertson, A. (2015). *Ethnic precincts in Auckland: Understanding the role and function of the Balmoral shops* (TR2015/015). Auckland, New Zealand: Auckland Council.

Meares, C., Ho, E., Peace, R., & Spoonley, P. (2010a). *Bamboo networks: Chinese employers and employees in Auckland.* Auckland, New Zealand: Massey University/University of Waikato.

Meares, C., Ho, E., Peace, R., & Spoonley, P. (2010b). *Kimchi networks: Korean employers and employees in Auckland*. Auckland, New Zealand: Massey University/University of Waikato.

Phillip, A., & Ho, E. (2010). Migration, home and belonging: South African migrant women in Hamilton, New Zealand. *New Zealand Population Review, 36*, 81–101.

Royal Society of New Zealand. (2013, March 5). *Languages in Aotearoa New Zealand.* Retrieved from http://www.royalsociety.org.nz/2013/03/05/new-zealand-superdiversity-presents-unprecedented-language-challenges-and-opportunities/

Skop, E., & Li, W. (2010). From the ghetto to the invisiburb. In J. W. Frazier & F. M. Margai (Eds.), *Multicultural geographies: The changing racial/ethnic patterns of the United States* (pp. 113–124). New York, NY: Global Academic Publishing.

Spoonley, P. (Ed.). (2016). *Rebooting the regions: Why low or zero growth needn't mean the end of prosperity*. Auckland, New Zealand: Massey University Press.

Spoonley, P., & Bedford, R. (2012). *Welcome to our world? Immigration and the reshaping of New Zealand*. Auckland, New Zealand: Dunmore Publishing.

Statistics New Zealand. (2005). *Statistical standard for ethnicity 2005*. Wellington: New Zealand: Statistics New Zealand.

Statistics New Zealand. (2013). *Census 2013*. Wellington, New Zealand: Statistics New Zealand. Retrieved from http://www.stats.govt.nz/Census/2013-census.aspx

Tolerton, J. (2016). Contraception and sterilisation: 19th-century contraception. In *Te Ara: The Encyclopedia of New Zealand*. Retrieved from http://www.TeAra.govt.nz/en/graph/26967/new-zealands-fertility-rate

Vertovec, S. (2007). Superdiversity and its implications. *Ethnic and Racial Studies, 30*(6), 1024–1054.

Tangata whenua

Māori, identity and belonging

Te Rina Warren,
Margaret Forster and
Veronica Tawhai

Introduction

I te timatanga ko Te Kore, ko Te Pō. Ka piri a Ranginui rāua ko Papatūānuku, ka puta a rāua tamariki, ki te Whai ao, ki te Ao Marama. In the beginning there was pure potential, Te Kore, shrouded in epochs of blackness, Te Pō. Eons elapsed into a period of activation where Ranginui and Papatūānuku emerged, and within Te Pō they discovered each other. From their union came children who sought a new world, a World of Light. One of the children, Tāne-mahuta, amidst the vigorous debate of his siblings, inverted the failed attempts of the others and with great effort detached Ranginui from Papatūānuku. Te Ao Marama, a world of light and space, poured through the darkness, releasing the children from within the tight embrace of their parents. After establishing themselves across several domains, it was Tāne-mahuta who searched for the earthly female element, and, on fashioning Hine-ahu-one, from their union came forth humankind.

Couched in this narrative and others are key markers from which Māori notions of identity and belonging are drawn. On a symbolic level, this particular Creation narrative is represented in our national 'tino rangatiratanga' flag, where black represents Ranginui as sky father, red represents Papatūānuku as earth mother, and the space in between represents the World of Light where we, humankind, now dwell: Te Ao Marama.

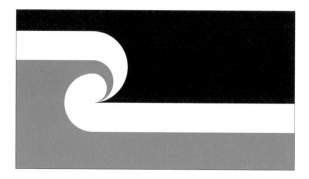

We locate ourselves within this narrative and acknowledge our closeness to Papatūānuku and Hine-ahu-one through the use of the terms 'tangata whenua', people of the land, and 'tūrangawaewae', one's sacred or special place of belonging.

On a more personal level, from the narrative above comes our explanation for the innate urge for growth and expansion we take to be a critical attribute of the human condition: what Te Pakaka Tawhai (1978) referred to as 'tupu' (p. 16). The separation of Ranginui and Papatūānuku involved deep and emotive debate among the siblings, with valid concern for both parents. Today we are reminded of the consequence of this decision during extreme weather when siblings like Tāwhiri-mātea remind others of their opposition to the separation, and note that overall care and wellbeing must be at the forefront of all our decisions. Growth and expansion, debate and informed decision-making, obligations and responsibilities, agitation for change and living with the consequences of those actions (positive and negative) are present in our Creation narratives and provide essential guidelines for the future.

This chapter explores Māori understandings of identity, belonging and citizenship, and notions including tupu, mana, rangatiratanga and whenua as expressed through media such as our traditional narratives. The significance of these notions is reflected in their inclusion in key documents central to citizenship in Aotearoa, such as He Whakaputanga o te Rangatiratanga o Nu Tireni 1835 (see below) and Te Tiriti o Waitangi 1840. The diversity of Māori today — a key theme in the chapter — in part reflects forces such as colonisation that have sought to dismantle Māori identity, and which have shaped Māori historical and current experiences of citizenship. These diverse Māori realities are also reflected in, and have emerged from, the many ways Māori have resisted, struggled, negotiated

The Empire flexes its muscles

In the early nineteenth century, Māori were becoming anxious about increasing European activity in Aotearoa. Not only were the numbers of British increasing, but the French were also snooping around. In 1831, a number of Ngāpuhi chiefs sent a petition to King William IV asking for his protection. In 1835, the British Resident, James Busby, presented a document to Northern chiefs called 'A Declaration of the Independence of New Zealand'. The declaration effectively gave sovereign power in New Zealand to this group of chiefs, who in return would protect British subjects residing in Aotearoa; King William IV would become the 'Protector and Matua of their State'. The document was signed by 34 Northern chiefs, and later by 18 other chiefs, and formally acknowledged by the Crown in 1836. Māori who signed the Declaration thought that it gave them independence and their own state. The British saw it as an intermediary form of governance until such time as full annexation was needed, which eventuated with the signing of the Treaty of Waitangi in 1840.

and continued to develop our identity in contemporary settings. Perhaps the primary purposes of this chapter, then, are to briefly explore these historical and contemporary developments and to demonstrate how they continue to shape Māori conceptions of the notions that are central to this book: identity, belonging and citizenship.

Narratives: our sacred stories

As Ngahuia Murphy (2016) argues, '[o]ur sacred stories carry the instruction of our tīpuna about proper conduct to maintain the balance' (p. 190). Within these sacred stories, including the Creation narrative, are a number of expressions about citizenship. One is the notion of mana. Reverend Maori Marsden (1992) defines 'mana' as 'spiritual authority and power ... a spiritual gift delegated by the gods' (pp. 118–119). In general terms, mana is often described as spiritual power, authority, influence and prestige. The belief as to the presence of this innate quality within each member of society is derived from an understanding of our place within the world and greater universe: that is, as descendants of Hine-ahu-one and Tāne, who emerged from Te Pō to Te Ao Marama, we are all embodied with an innate spiritual potential and power to grow and expand. Tāne-mahuta went on to ascend to the heavens to retrieve Ngā Kete o te Wānanga, the Baskets of Knowledge, and then gifted these to humankind to provide us with the knowledge for development in all areas of life. Other narratives recall the ancestor Tāwhaki as having achieved this task; irrespective, these narratives reinforce the idea of growth and the pursuit of knowledge in order to reach one's goal and fulfil one's potential.

The ancestor Māui, responsible for retrieving Te Ika a Māui (the Fish of Māui, commonly known as the North Island), for slowing the sun and for obtaining fire from Mahuika, among other things, is another example of a sacred narrative. In his final feat, Māui attempts to reverse mortality through Hine-nui-te-pō, which results in his death. In the legacy of Māui are lessons about challenging boundaries, discovering new horizons, and creating advantageous situations, limited only by mortality. Tāwhaki, and countless other regional heroes such as Tamatea (Ngāti Kahungunu), Paikea (Ngāti Porou), Hinemoa (Te Arawa), Wairaka (Mataatua) and Rangi Topeora (Raukawa), also leave handsome legacies of achievement for us, their descendants. These are living narratives of great expeditions across time and space, remarkable relationships with the natural world, determination, strategy, intuition and intellect. These ancestors and many others are celebrated with waiata, whakataukī and haka that descendants continue to sing, recite and perform, passionate expressions where we recount their feats and the examples they leave us for today.

Māori understanding of the nature of humankind and our impulse to explore and strive towards fulfilling our potential can therefore be mapped from (i) our seeking of light and space from Te Kore to Te Pō to Te Ao Marama, (ii) Tāne-mahuta seeking Hine-ahu-one to bring forth further life, (iii) Tāne's (or Tāwhaki's) endeavour for Ngā Kete o Te Wānanga, (iv) Māui's slowing of the sun and other achievements, (v) Māui's search for immortality, and (vi) the many feats of our more recent ancestors.

These relate to the notion of mana in the following ways. 'Mana atua' is the spiritual power and prestige we all derive from our whakapapa or genealogy, which connects us to these ancestors and their great achievements (Mead, 2003; Reedy, 2000). Mana atua is our understanding that this potential for growth, expansion and achievement lies within all of us.

'Mana whenua' is the power we draw from our whenua or lands that our ancestors inhabited (Kawharu, 2000; Reedy, 2000). Acknowledging maunga or ancestral mountains, awa or ancestral waterways, and wāhi tapu or sacred places make up a part of tūrangawaewae, each person's sacred, special place where they feel they belong (Kawharu, 2000; Reedy, 2000). Mana whenua is where our desires, obligations and responsibilities to cherish our tūrangawaewae for future generations come from (Kawharu, 2000). Closely linked to this notion and others expressing our connections to land are concepts such as kaitiakitanga (responsibilities for guardianship) and ahi kā (continued occupation).

'Mana tangata' is, then, the authority and prestige we receive from our own whāinga, or pursuits; the greatness we develop from what we do and achieve in our lifetime. The responsibilities we have to the collective means that mana tangata is most enhanced when our personal pursuits are for the benefit of others (Mead, 2003). This is reflected in our narratives, and in recent times in the accounts of early Māori business practices (Warren, 2009).

Mana atua, mana whenua and mana tangata subsequently shape our responsibilities and rights as citizens. These notions of mana as a basis for citizenship also appear in our founding written constitutional documents, the 1835 He Whakaputanga o te Rangatiratanga and 1840 Te Tiriti o Waitangi.

He Whakaputanga and Te Tiriti o Waitangi

After decades of interacting globally with other peoples overseas for trade, business and other purposes, He Whakaputanga o te Rangatiratanga o Nu Tireni (The

Declaration of Independence) was signed by rangatira between 1835 and 1839. The Declaration proclaimed Aotearoa New Zealand an 'independent state' under the sovereignty of rangatira, who would continue to meet in congress once a year to 'frame laws', 'dispense justice', 'preserve peace and good order' and 'regulate trade'. It also invited an alliance with Britain, based on the relationship of mutual growth and benefit developed between us since the early 1800s. Some of the terms within the Declaration specific to notions of citizenship include:

- rangatiratanga — independence
- w[h]enua rangatira — independent state
- mana i te w[h]enua — sovereignty
- rūnanga — congress.

Most of these terms and others were repeated in Te Tiriti o Waitangi (the Treaty of Waitangi, Māori texts), each of the four articles of which express important provisions for citizenship in Aotearoa New Zealand today. In Article One, Māori granted the British Queen 'kāwanatanga', the authority to extend British-style governance over British citizens living in Aotearoa. In Article Two, the British Queen guaranteed to Māori the 'tino rangatiratanga' recognised by Britain in the 1835 He Whakaputanga, our ongoing independence. In Article Three, the Queen offered to Māori 'ngā tikanga katoa rite tahi ki ana mea', all the rights and customs of British citizenship should Māori wish to use them. As a fourth and final article, an Oral Article was given, stating 'e tiakina ngatahitia e ia', that all the faiths of the peoples of Aotearoa New Zealand, including that of Māori, would be protected by the Governor.

Differences in the text — for example, in the English-language version of the Treaty Māori did not retain independence, but instead gave sovereignty to the Queen — are where the notion of 'Treaty principles' have arisen. The principles are a blend of the te reo Māori and English versions, and are suggestions as to how the Treaty might be applied today. Many have been applied to citizenship in Aotearoa, including the introduction of British-style citizenship in Aotearoa, the continuance of Māori notions of citizenship to hapū and iwi, the partnership between Māori and the government, equality between Māori and other citizens (including the rights of Māori to fully participate in te ao Māori as well as in Pākehā society alongside others), the active protection of the identity, voices, places and treasures of Māori as the indigenous peoples of Aotearoa, and the wellbeing of all citizens who come here so we may flourish together.

Colonisation and assimilation

As opposed to the Tiriti texts, and long before Treaty principles came into being, the assumption by British authorities was that the Treaty had established British sovereignty over Aotearoa, and that Māori, as inferior native peoples, had willingly relinquished their authority to Britain. Māori lands, resources and lives were to be colonised and assimilated: that is, they were to come under the control of British colonisers who had assumed the right to govern in Aotearoa, and, consistent with the approach towards some other indigenous peoples of the day, would be absorbed into British systems (as opposed to, say, being eradicated, as had occurred on other continents, notably Australia).

Māori enthusiasm for capitalising on the opportunities that emerged from a formal relationship with the British (e.g. access to British-based markets, commerce and new technologies) was mistaken for a willingness to be colonised and assimilated (Warren, 2009). Although the Waitangi Tribunal (2014) has confirmed that Māori did not cede sovereignty to Britain, at the time it was assumed that a new colony had been founded and would be based on what was believed by British authorities to be superior British traditions (e.g. individual property rights), institutions (e.g. Westminster-style governance) and values (e.g. Christianity and colonialism). It was expected that Māori would adopt these modern, more progressive ways of being and, with 'proper guidance', abandon Māori values and ways of life to progress towards 'civilization' (Sorrenson, 1975, p. 97).

As the number of British settlers immigrating to Aotearoa overwhelmed the Māori population and decisions began to be made by settler authorities for Māori, Māori were forcibly disconnected from our lands, culture, language and identity. To colonise Māori minds, policies like the Education Ordinance 1847 established English as the only language of instruction in what would become compulsory British-based schools for Māori. To assimilate Māori lands and make them more accessible for British settlements, the Native Lands Act 1862 established compulsory individualisation of Māori land title through a Native Land Court. To assimilate Māori politically, and quash Māori political autonomy, the Maori Representation Act 1867 gave Māori the option of four seats amongst the (then) 72-seat settler Parliament, as opposed to providing political representation for hapū or iwi.

As outlined in Te Tiriti o Waitangi, Māori (or more specifically, hapū) clearly desired to retain tino rangatiratanga, and thus vigorously resisted via armed warfare, peaceful resistance, autonomous movements, political lobbying and participation in the settler Parliament. The Kīngitanga, Te Kotahitanga mo Te Tiriti

REF: AAQT 6539 W3537 54 A/54871, ARCHIVES NEW ZEALAND

New Zealand's passive resisters

The Māori settlement of Parihaka was established in Taranaki by Te Whiti-o-Rongomai and Tohu Kākahi in the late 1860s. After government survey teams moved into the lands north of the Waingongoro River in south Taranaki, the people of Parihaka began a programme of passive resistance in 1879, erecting fences across road lines and ploughing Pākehā farmers' paddocks. So many were arrested and held without trial that an embarrassed government decided on military action. Armed constabulary advanced on Parihaka pā in late 1881, part of a combined force of more than 1,500. On 5 November the forces surrounded the township and arrested Te Whiti-o-Rongomai and Tohu Kākahi. Over the next few weeks many of the residents were evicted and their houses destroyed. The two chiefs were given an enforced tour of the South Island, designed to demonstrate the advantages and power of Pākehā society. They were returned to Parihaka in 1883. After many years of decline, the village of Parihaka was rejuvenated in the late twentieth century. Since 2006 it has been the venue for the annual Parihaka Peace Festival, which draws visitors from all over New Zealand. ABRIDGED FROM TE ARA — THE ENCYCLOPEDIA OF NEW ZEALAND

(Unity for the Treaty), Parihaka, Maungapōhatu and other expressions of resistance in our history are testament to these efforts (Walker, 1990).

To find out more about Rua Kēnana and Maungapōhatu, visit: https://nzhistory.govt.nz/arrest-of-rua-kenana

Yet, Māori resistance to colonisation and assimilation was met with further policies, including the Suppression of Rebellion Act 1863 and the Maori Prisoners' Trials Act 1879, which introduced Māori to the settler criminal justice system, albeit without the same rights as settlers within that system — for example, Māori land could be confiscated for any opposition to colonial invasion of homeland, and Māori could be imprisoned without trial. Confiscations of land, indefinite imprisonment and/or death were punishments for resisting British coloniser rule. For the following decades (1860–1900), as significant numbers of Māori found ourselves landless, homeless, without access to shelter or food, and with a dwindling population (due to the ongoing onslaught of diseases and the poor nutrition of new mothers), the expression and exercise of identity, belonging and citizenship for Māori began to radically change.

Changes to Māori society

Building on the resistance initiatives of the 1850–1900s, a new wave of Māori leadership, including James Carroll, Te Puea Herangi, Āpirana Ngata, Te Rangi Hīroa (Peter Buck) and Māui Pomare, resisted the negative impacts of colonisation in their own ways, and sought to adapt to Western lifestyles while retaining a strong cultural identity (Walker, 1990). With our people in crisis — in survival mode — politicians like Ngata encouraged Māori to take advantage of what was now thought of as Pākehā citizenship, and specifically the demanding of equal citizenship. Ngata (1943) called the sacrifices made by Māori in the two world wars 'the price of citizenship', and a new era of Māori–Crown relationship began, during which the government was called to honour the sacrifices Māori had made in the war efforts overseas.

For more on the life of Sir Peter Buck, visit: www.teara.govt.nz/en/biographies/3b54/buck-peter-henry

As a result, following the two world wars Māori were assisted to move into cities and to take up places in state homes, in order that they might find employment in urban centres. Māori responded to these new lived realities: however, they also continued to struggle against assimilation policies and face discrimination from 'mainstream' New Zealanders who were not used to contending with these Māori neighbours, schoolchildren, patients, employees or community members now living alongside them in the cities, and for whom that mainstream society had not, culturally or socially, been designed. Recovering from the mass loss of land, and the ongoing policy of assimilation and now integration in schools, health systems, the workplace and the community, Māori access to culture, to te reo Māori, and to sources of identity, health and wellbeing diminished greatly.

A key development in Māori identity occurred with the establishment of new urban marae and group-based collectives in the cities, set up to address key Māori issues and provide for the Māori collective living away from traditional hapū and iwi lands, particularly those who were marginalised. Examples include the Maori Women's Welfare League (1951), Nga Tamatoa (1970), Te Reo Maori Society (1970), Te Whanau o Waipereira Trust (1984), and the National Maori Congress (1990). Each group emerged to address specific issues of the time: health concerns, Treaty rights, te reo Māori, urban living and assimilation, and ownership of Māori development.

Growing awareness of collectively experienced historic injustices also led to a re-emergence of Māori resistance in the form of protest movements against unjust decisions made by government about Māori and Māori land and resources. You will read more about the importance of protest as a means of expressing voice in Chapter 4. This involved a number of land occupations (e.g. Bastion Point, Raglan Golf Course and Moutoa Gardens/Pākaitore), and the famous Māori land march led by Dame Whina Cooper in 1975. Eighty-year-old Dame Whina left Te Hapua by foot and walked to Wellington with the mantra 'not one more acre' in opposition to the ongoing theft, confiscation and alienation of Māori lands. Nearly 30 years later, in 2004, this trend in Māori expression continued with the hīkoi supporting then Labour Member of Parliament Tariana Turia's opposition to the proposed Foreshore and Seabed Act. Since then there have been several other such instances, and these actions are critical in raising the country's awareness around the oppression of the Treaty, Māori identity, and the failure of governments to honour equal Māori citizenship.

The severe impacts of the historic contests are also being revisited today through the Waitangi Tribunal, which investigates and then makes recommendations to government about how Treaty of Waitangi breaches should be remedied. Although many fervently argue that the compensations are woefully inadequate (see Mutu,

Long march to recognition

In early 1975, the idea was raised of a 'Māori Land March' from Te Hapua in the far north to Parliament to focus on landlessness and cultural loss. A meeting of tribal representatives was convened at Mangere marae by the founding Maori Women's Welfare League president Whina Cooper. In her address to the hui, Cooper implied that she was operating under the mantle of great Māori leaders such as James Carroll, Āpirana Ngata and Peter Buck, all of whom she had known. She asserted customary Māori protocol through a 'Memorial of Right', thereby linking the march to a long tradition of earlier petitions to the Crown, especially those by Kings Tawhiao and Te Rata in 1886 and 1914.

The Land March combined the forces of Ngā Tamatoa-type radicalism with the wishes and protocols of traditionalist elders, attracting the support of Māori from urban areas and rural marae throughout the country. When it first set off from Te Hapua on 14 September, there were few on the road, but before long numbers swelled. Marchers sought respect for communal ownership of tribal lands, believing that Labour's reforms had fallen short. They demanded, that 'not one more acre of Maori land' be alienated. As a leaflet entitled 'Why We Protest' explained: 'Land is the very soul of a tribal people . . . [We want] a just society allowing Maoris to preserve our own social and cultural identity in the last remnants of our tribal estate . . . The alternative is the creation of a landless brown proletariat with no dignity, no mana and no stake in society.'

Five thousand marchers converged on Parliament on 13 October, bearing a petition with 60,000 signatories. Government ministers felt chagrined that the government's extensive consultation procedures and 'progressive' Māori policies and legislation had been rebuked, but, in a sense, the march was not so much about specific land policies or, necessarily, even about land at all. It was a reassertion of autonomist Māori demands and aspirations at a time when the political and social climate was becoming more receptive to them. As one historian later noted, the march represented Māori, at an auspicious moment, 'symbolically reclaiming the tino Rangatiratanga promised by the Treaty of Waitangi'. ABRIDGED FROM NZETC

2015), others argue that this amounts to Māori privilege and special treatment (Brash, 2004). These debates are central to understanding Māori citizenship as shaped by colonisation and assimilation policy and contemporary notions of Māori identity.

Diverse Māori realities

The layers of dispossession for Māori — land alienation, disease, the land wars (responsibility for which was once rhetorically laid at the feet of Māori through the simple expedient of calling them the 'Māori Wars'), assimilation policies, the world wars, urbanisation and loss of language — reshape Māori cultural identity and sense of belonging. These variations also create wide disparities in understandings of what it means to be Māori today. These days, Māori are often positioned as a 'homogeneous, disadvantaged ethnic group' (Kukutai, 2011, p. 49); a group that looks the same and has the same values and life experiences. In reality, the term 'Māori' 'can refer to a wide range of people of varying ethnic compositions and cultural identity' (Greaves, Houkamau, & Sibley, 2015, p. 541). The characteristics of the contemporary Māori population include the following:

- one in seven people living in New Zealand are of Māori ethnicity
- one in seven Māori are living in Australia
- one-third of Māori are aged under 15 years
- nearly a quarter of all Māori live in the Auckland region
- one-fifth of Māori can hold a conversation in te reo Māori
- labourers and professionals are the most common occupational groups for Māori
- some 18.5 per cent of Māori are not aware of, or do not identify with, their iwi affiliations. (Statistics New Zealand, 2013)

All of this has a significant impact on Māori identity and notions of citizenship. Sir Mason Durie (1995) refers to this diversity across a range of identity factors as 'nga matatini Maori', 'the many faces of Maori': in other words, 'diverse Maori realities' (p. 1). Diverse Māori realities mean there are a range of answers to the question 'Who is Māori?', and to the query that sometimes follows it: 'How Māori are you?' For some people, it might mean self-identifying as Māori, yet having very little access to other Māori people and sources of culture. At the other end of the spectrum, it may mean being completely immersed in Māori language and culture. For some, it could mean living 'successfully' in two worlds; for others, it means feeling uncomfortable in both. Māori identity and belonging can mean quite different things for males and females, the young and the old, Māori living in their iwi territory or outside, or Māori living in Aotearoa or abroad. But regardless of lived experience or on which part of the spectrum people find themselves, the capacity to whakapapa or demonstrate genealogical links to Māori ancestors means that they are all Māori.

Typologies can be used to provide an understanding of the nuances associated with the questions 'Who is Māori?' and 'What does it mean to be Māori?' Durie (1994) explores a typology for Māori, distinguishing between:

- those who know whakapapa, te reo Māori and Māori custom: the 'culturally Māori'
- those who live easily in the Māori world and the Pākehā world: 'bicultural Māori', and
- those who do not relate to either world: the 'marginalised Māori'.

Similarly, Williams (2000) describes the following Māori typology:

- a 'core' that is centred in the Māori world and language
- the 'primarily urban' who are bicultural
- the 'unconnected' or those who are marginalised from the Māori world, and
- Māori who are 'indistinguishable' from Pākehā.

Wehipeihana (1995) offers a quadrant approach to Māori identity that moves vertically between positive and negative dispositions, and horizontally between close and distant interactions. The quadrants are described as:

- the 'cultural inheritor', who displays clear cultural competency in te reo Māori and protocols (positive disposition and close cultural interaction)
- the 'cultural dissenter', who feels pressured by cultural expectations (negative disposition and close interaction)
- the 'cultural seekers', who are rediscovering Māori identity (positive disposition and distant interaction), and
- the 'cultural rejectors', who reject being Māori and embrace assimilation into Western conventions, norms and rules (negative disposition and distant interaction).

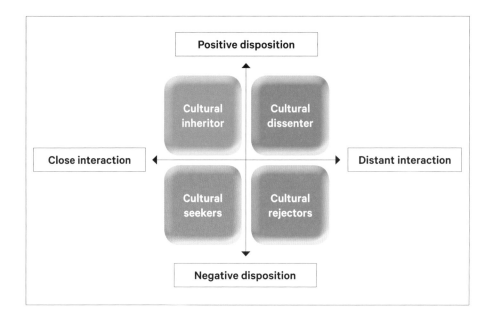

In short, being Māori is fluid and dynamic and can have multiple meanings. Houkamau and Sibley (2015) describe this situation in terms of 'experiential domains', which include: group membership evaluation, socio-political consciousness, cultural efficacy and active identity expression, spirituality, interdependent self-concept and authenticity beliefs. In other words, there are many factors to consider when exploring contemporary notions of Māori identity.

Māori identities are complicated by media coverage of poor Māori outcomes, which stands in stark contrast with the national pride expressed in Māori symbols, such as the haka, the koru, the hei tiki and the hongi. In one sense, this demonstrates a dilemma for Māori identity — a sort of love–hate tug-of-war. This is further complicated by the fact that Māori culture sets Aotearoa apart from other nations: it makes us distinct. That said, links to Māori ancestors and the desire to identify as Māori qualifies a person to claim identity as Māori. As an individual's capacity to access culture and to express mana atua, mana whenua and mana tangata develops across their lifespan, so the likelihood increases that the individual will have a secure cultural identity and be located in the more positive dimensions associated with the typologies listed above.

Conclusion

Although Māori realities are diverse, all realities are derived from particular social, economic, historical and political contexts that are explicitly interconnected with relationships to whakapapa, whenua and whāinga. For some, those are long-lost relationships; for others, they are hard-fought renewed; and for some, they were never lost, impacting on senses, experiences and aspirations for identity, belonging and citizenship. Our socio-political history transverses He Whakaputanga and Te Tiriti o Waitangi, the land wars and legislative impositions, but is experienced in different ways, leading to different outcomes for individuals. Notions of Māori citizenship are based on mana atua and kinship rights and responsibilities, mana whenua and environmental rights and obligations, and mana tangata with duties for service.

However, an individual's understanding and expression of these notions will be influenced by their connection/dispossession and experiences of being Māori. In this sense, initiatives that encourage the revitalisation of Māori knowledges and practices — such as Kōhanga Reo and Kaupapa Māori in education, and other initiatives in health, justice and other areas — are important citizenship initiatives. In many ways, resistance, struggle and liberation have become part of many citizens' sense of their Māori identity because of the necessity to assert and protect a positive Māori identity (should they have one). In this sense, too, the Treaty of Waitangi remains a vital document from which dialogue between Māori and other New Zealanders might continue to occur, so that, as a part of their understanding of the notions of citizenship indigenous to these lands, mana atua, mana whenua and mana tangata might continue to be honoured as central to the landscape of identity, belonging and citizenship that is unique to Aotearoa.

Chapter 2 — Tangata whenua: Māori, identity and belonging:
http://turangawaewae.massey.ac.nz/chapter2.html

Recommended reading

Commissioned by Kuia and Kaumātua of Ngāpuhi Nui Tonu. (2012). *Ngāpuhi speaks: He wakaputanga o te rangatiratanga o Nu Tireni and Te Tiriti o Waitangi. Independent Report, Ngāpuhi Nui Tonu Claim*. Whangarei, New Zealand: Te Kawariki & Network Waitangi Whangarei. It includes: He Whakaputanga o te Rangatiratanga o Nu Tireni: The Declaration of Independence 1835; Te Tiriti o Waitangi: The Treaty of Waitangi 1840.

Durie, M. H. (2009). *Ngā kāhui pou: Launching Māori futures.* Wellington, New Zealand: Huia Publishers.

O'Malley, V. (2016). *The great war for New Zealand: Waikato 1800–2000.* Wellington, New Zealand: Bridget Williams Books.

Walker, R. (1990). *Ka whawhai tonu matou: Struggle without end.* Auckland, New Zealand: Penguin.

References

Brash, D. (2004, January 27). *Orewa 2004 — nationhood* [address to the Orewa Rotary Club, Auckland]. Retrieved from http://www.donbrash.com/national-party/orewa-2004-nationhood/

Durie, M. (1994). *Whaiora: Māori health development.* Auckland, New Zealand: Oxford University Press.

Durie, M. (1995). *Ngā Matatini Māori: Diverse Māori realities.* Unpublished paper presented at Wananga Purongo Korerorero, Tūrangawaewae Marae, Ngāruawāhia, New Zealand.

Greaves, L. M., Houkamau, C., & Sibley, C. G. (2015). Māori identity signatures: A latent profile analysis of the types of Māori identity. *Cultural Diversity and Ethnic Minority Psychology, 21*(4), 541–549. doi: http://dx.doi.org/10.1037/cdp0000033

Houkamau, C. A., & Sibley, C. G. (2015). The revised Multidimensional Model of Māori Identity and Cultural Engagement (MMM-ICE2). *Social Indicators Research, 122,* 279–296.

Kawharu, M. (2000). Kaitiakitanga: A Māori anthropological perspective of the Māori socio-environmental ethic of resource management. *Journal of the Polynesian Society, 109,* 349–370.

Kukutai, T. (2011). Māori demography in Aotearoa New Zealand: Fifty years on. *New Zealand Population Review, 37,* 45–64.

Marsden, M. (1992). God, man, and universe: A Māori view. In Michael King (Ed.), *Te Ao Hurihuri: Aspects of Māoritanga* (pp. 117–137). Auckland, New Zealand: Reed Books.

Mead, H. M. (2003). *Tikanga Māori: Living by Māori values.* Wellington, New Zealand: Huia Publishers.

Murphy, N. (2016). Te awa atua. In J. Hutchings & J. Lee-Morgan (Eds.), *Decolonisation in Aotearoa: Education, research and practice* (pp. 182–193). Wellington, New Zealand: New Zealand Council for Educational Research.

Mutu, M. (2015). Unravelling colonial weaving. In P. Little & W. Nissen (Eds.), *Stroppy old women: 52 kiwi women, who've been around long enough to know, tell you what's wrong with the world* (pp. 165–178). Auckland, New Zealand: Paul Little Books.

Ngata, A. T. (1943). *The price of citizenship: Ngarimu, V.C.* Wellington, New Zealand: Whitcombe & Tombs.

Reedy, T. (2000). Te reo Māori: The past 20 years and looking forward. *Oceanic Linguistics, 39*(1), 157–169.

Sorrenson, M. P. K. (1975). How to civilize savages. *New Zealand Journal of History, 9*(2), 97–110.

Statistics New Zealand. (2008). *New Zealand long term data series.* Wellington, New Zealand: Statistics New Zealand. Retrieved from http://web.archive.org/web/20080305185447/http://www.stats.govt.nz/tables/ltds/ltds-population.htm

Tawhai, T. P. (1978). *Ngā tipuna whare o te rohe o Uepohatu.* (Unpublished MA thesis). Massey University, Palmerston North, New Zealand.

Te Kawariki & Network Waitangi Whangarei. (2012). *Ngāpuhi speaks: He wakaputanga and Te Tiriti o Waitangi. Independent Report, Ngāpuhi Nui Tonu Claim.* Kaitaia, New Zealand: Te Kawariki & Network Waitangi Whangarei.

Tomlins-Jahnke, H., & Warren, K. T. (2011). Full, exclusive and undisturbed possession: Māori education and the Treaty. In V. M. H. Tawhai & K. Gray-Sharp (Eds.), *Always speaking: The Treaty of Waitangi and public policy* (pp. 21–33). Wellington, New Zealand: Huia Publishers.

Waitangi Tribunal. (2014). *He Whakaputanga me Te Tiriti — The Declaration and the Treaty: The report on stage 1 of the Te Paparahi o Te Raki Inquiry.* Wellington, New Zealand: Waitangi Tribunal.

Walker, R. (1990). *Ka whawhai tonu matou: Struggle without end.* Auckland, New Zealand: Penguin.

Warren, K. T. R. (2009). *Once upon a tikanga: A literature review of early Māori business practice.* Palmerston North, New Zealand: Te Au Rangahau, Māori Business Research Centre, Massey University.

Wehipeihana, N. (1995). *Factors facilitating Māori participation and entry into professional occupations.* Wellington, New Zealand: Te Puni Kōkiri, The Ministry for Māori Development.

Williams, J. (2000, October). *The nature of the Māori community.* Paper presented at the PSSM Conference, New Zealand State Services Commission, Wellington, New Zealand.

PART TWO: VOICES OF AOTEAROA NEW ZEALAND

Voices:
Introduction

Trudie Cain and Ella Kahu

The previous section of this book considered the many diverse faces of Aotearoa New Zealand. Its purpose was to consider the extent to which individual and collective faces of New Zealand have altered, and to reflect on the implications of rapid demographic change. This next part, 'Voices of Aotearoa New Zealand', considers how voice might be expressed in this country by different people and in different contexts. A related aim is also to consider what the impact of expressions of voice might have for individuals, communities and the nation.

About Part 2

Here, then, we explore voice in Aotearoa New Zealand. But what does voice even mean? In *Tūrangawaewae*, we define voice as being able to express one's view or tell one's story, and have that view taken as a valid contribution to public debate. Clearly, this statement has two very distinct parts. The first is about having a voice, and there are many different ways this can occur, depending on the context. Casting one's vote in local or national elections, marching up Lambton Quay with a banner in hand, or creating films that tell our individual and collective stories are all avenues for the expression of voice. But to have a voice is one thing, to be heard is quite another. It might make someone feel good that they have vented on a troubling issue, but if no one was listening and nothing changed, what does it matter? Which brings us to the second part of the definition: having one's voice acknowledged as a legitimate contribution to public debate. This is an important point that is worth underlining.

We can think about voice as operating at two levels: individual and collective. A single person's voice can be expressed or silenced; and, equally, collective voices — those of the élite or of the marginalised, for instance — may be heard or ignored. Clearly, not all voices are in agreement, and in a world of wide-ranging people with wide-ranging views it would be nonsense to expect that they would be. The problem emerges, however, when some voices are privileged, or, alternatively, when some voices are muted entirely. The extent to which a voice might be amplified or silenced is influenced by a range of factors, perhaps the most important of which is identity. Individual or collective threads of identity shape how people choose to engage with public issues, their opinions on such issues, and also the extent to which their opinions and stories are heard. This links closely with the relations of power that are embedded in our encounters with others. Some groups of people in this country have to struggle for the right to participate in public affairs; in other words, they must struggle to have their voices heard and be legitimated. Gender, sexuality, ethnicity and geographical location are all threads of identity that might amplify or mute one's capacity to speak out and be heard. Often it is the majority voice that is privileged, and it is their views and stories which are taken for granted as the norm in society.

Another important influence on how and when the different faces of Aotearoa New Zealand get to speak is the norms or formal rules of a particular place (an idea we return to in Part 3). For instance, Parliament has very specific protocols about who can speak, and when, in the debating chamber. The Speaker of the House of Representatives chooses who will be invited to speak during debates, and ensures that the Standing Orders, the written rules of conduct that govern the business of the House, are observed.

To learn more on the history and role of the Speaker, visit: https://www.parliament.nz/en/visit-and-learn/how-parliament-works/office-of-the-speaker/role-history-of-the-speaker/role-election-of-the-speaker/

The influence of identity threads on the right to speak can also be heard in the university setting. While lecturers take the floor as a matter of right, students are typically silent until invited to speak. And when they do speak, their words do not carry as much weight as those of their lecturer. In both these examples, power structures are again evident.

Debates around issues of inclusion and participation are central to an appreciation of identity, belonging and citizenship in Aotearoa New Zealand. As Ella discussed in the introduction, there is a reciprocal link between participation and belonging. Being able to participate equally in a particular community and have one's voice heard and acknowledged increases people's sense of belonging to that community. Equally, people who already have a strong sense of belonging are more likely to use their voice and take an active role in the community. Voice, then, is important.

The conceptual template underpinning this part of the book and connecting it to the book as a whole has the following three components:

1. Giving voice to what you think and feel. We look at different ways in which people express or 'voice' their views in the public domain. We also examine what motivates people to engage in these various strategies, and probe the connections between a person or group's sense of identity and belonging and them seeking to have their voice heard.

2. From silence to voice. We explore the struggles different groups have had in gaining a legitimate voice as members of the community of citizens of Aotearoa New Zealand. We ask whether there is room in this country for dissenting voices, and look at what can happen to people who adopt unpopular or contentious positions.

3. Voice, identity and citizenship. We probe the consequences of giving voice for broader issues of citizenship. Voice contributes to the construction of identity and reveals certain assumptions about citizenship. Therefore, the central question here is: how does participation and engagement in the public domain (or being refused those things) shape understandings of identity and belonging at the individual, group and national levels?

Overview of chapters

The following chapters explore three different ways in which 'voice' is expressed: first, through political participation and representation; second, through political protest; and third, through various forms of art. Each topic provides a different means of illuminating the challenges associated with securing the right to engage in public life, and the subsequent consequences of this for identity.

In Chapter 3 Richard Shaw discusses New Zealand's political system and how citizens of this country can exercise their voice through voting in general elections. He also shines a light on an apparent turn away from political engagement, and raises concerns about poor voter turnout for New Zealand. The implications for citizenship are great, given that the most vulnerable members of society are those least likely to exercise their right to vote.

In Chapter 4, 'Shout it out — participation and protest in public life', Ella Kahu writes about political protest as a way of exercising one's voice and bringing about social, political or economic change in this country. Ella reflects on what motivates people to exercise their voice in this way, including the unity and sense of belonging that collective action brings for those with shared threads of identity. She draws on two historical case studies — the gay rights movement and the 1981 Springbok Tour — to illustrate the ways in which political protest can mobilise communities, create social change, and challenge and contest understandings of national identity.

The final chapter in this section, 'Express yourself — voice through the arts', takes a different focus, and considers the capacity of the art world to speak for those who might be marginalised, excluded or otherwise silenced. Here, Trudie Cain draws on three specific case studies to consider the extent to which the arts can: represent the identity of groups who are on the margins; construct identity threads for those who might be negotiating new forms of identity that straddle the boundaries of place and time; and contribute to place-making and community development.

Conclusion

This text encourages you to think critically about issues of identity and belonging within Aotearoa New Zealand. The focus on voices in this section expands on our examination of the identities that make up our country in Part 1, and explores the different ways in which those identities are expressed. The ability to exercise one's voice, to have one's story heard, and to have a say in how the community functions is fundamental to citizenship. New Zealand's history is saturated with examples of groups of people who have been excluded and marginalised, but who have fought to have their voice heard — through our political systems within government, through protest outside of government, and through the diverse media of the arts. This section of *Tūrangawaewae* tells some of those stories to illustrate these important social processes, and in doing so widens our understanding of the links between identity and citizenship and the central importance of voice. And, most importantly, it can help us to hear those identities and voices that continue to be silenced.

CHAPTER THREE:

Voices in the House
Political representation and participation

Richard Shaw

Introduction

In 2015, a protest against the Trans Pacific Partnership Agreement, a trade agreement entered into by 12 Pacific rim nations, ended with an energetic, raucous gathering on the forecourt of the New Zealand Parliament. One way or another (as will become even clearer in the following chapter by Ella), Parliament is often the focus of protests: people come to the nation's most powerful law-making authority to voice — loudly, enthusiastically and often angrily — their views, opinions and concerns. Others, however, come because it is where they are employed as Members of Parliament (MPs). There is a direct link between those who protest on Parliament's steps and those who walk up them to go to work: in addition to doing so by protesting, the former can also express their political sentiments by participating in the election of the latter. And while it may appear that protesting occurs outside the political system while voting takes place within it, that false dichotomy should be avoided: in a parliamentary democracy, both are forms of political activity.

Voting is one of the main ways in which citizens give voice to their political hopes, fears and aspirations. In this chapter, then, we focus on the exercise of voice via engagement with and participation in politics at central-government level, especially — but not exclusively — through the act of voting. We begin with some definitions of key terms, and take a quick tour around New Zealand's voting system. Then we explore why people are motivated to vote, and look at the connection between this specific form of voice and people's sense of identity and belonging. We touch on the struggles some groups have had in gaining this citizenship right, and we end by examining some of the possible identity consequences — for both individuals and the wider national community — of both participation and *non*-participation in politics.

A few words on democracy and politics

If you are not familiar with the language of politics, it can be a little daunting. But if you let that put you off, you risk not acquiring the knowledge you need to understand and participate in politics, and may, as a result, quietly drift away and leave the business of democracy to others. Let's begin, therefore, by defining three terms that are central to this chapter: citizenship, democracy and politics.

Citizenship

You have already met the word 'citizenship' in this book: in Ella's introduction, for instance, it is defined as membership of a social community. This broad, encompassing conception of social citizenship is a relatively recent development. Traditionally, the term is and has been associated with membership of a political community — usually, but not necessarily, a nation state — and tends to come with certain legal rights and duties. Two points about citizenship are especially relevant in the context of this chapter. First, citizens' rights and duties are defined by political institutions. Parliament is particularly important, but so are the courts and the executive branch of government (Cabinet ministers and government departments). The benefits and obligations you might enjoy today are neither inevitable nor immutable: rather, they are a product of encounters and interactions between people — often with widely diverging views about what should be done — in the political process.

 Parliament's website gives you access to pretty much everything going on in our legislature (including the passage of legislation): https://www.parliament.nz/en/

Second, at different points in history, qualification for citizenship has rested on aspects of a person's identity. At various times the right to vote (suffrage) has depended on someone's place of birth, ethnicity, socio-economic class, gender, wealth, ability to read (sometimes in the language of a colonising nation), income, age, and so on. In New Zealand, suffrage was originally subject to wealth, property and gender qualifications. In short, the right to participate as a full member of a political community is often determined on the basis of what we refer to in this publication as a person's 'identity threads'.

Democracy

The terms 'citizenship' and 'democracy' are closely related but are not synonyms. The former concerns notions of membership of some form of community, and the attendant rights and obligations; the latter describes different models for structuring and apportioning political power.

Most definitions of 'democracy' describe political systems characterised by: universal suffrage (i.e. the right to vote); governments chosen by free, regular and competitive elections; and political rights to freedom of speech and association (Stoker, 2006). Abraham Lincoln's defence of 'government of the people, by the people, for the people' in the 1863 Gettysberg Address captures the essence of this way of understanding democracy. It is an approach to politics based on the principle that people consent to being governed by others on the understanding that they get to participate in choosing those who do the governing.

Most of us would intuitively recognise this definition, but might not know that the formal term for this way of organising politics is 'representative democracy'. A representative democracy is one in which citizens delegate their political authority to elected representatives (MPs, in New Zealand) through a formal electoral process and for a defined period of time (three years in New Zealand's case). This delegation does not preclude directly participating in the business of making laws and policies: through the select committee process, for instance, New Zealand citizens are able to comment on virtually all legislation developed in Parliament. It does mean, however, that the day-to-day work of crafting and passing laws is done by MPs on behalf of all citizens. Elected parliaments connect those who govern with those who are governed: to use the language of this chapter, when MPs stand up in the House (or a committee room) to speak, they are often giving voice to the views of those they represent.

Representative democracy is sometimes contrasted with 'participatory democracy', which describes systems in which citizens directly engage in the business of designing, passing and implementing policy. The classical example of this kind of model is ancient Athens, where citizens — a category which excluded women, slaves and *metics* (resident aliens) — directly participated in the business of governing. At the national level, at least, the size of most political communities these days is such that direct participatory democracy à la Athens is simply not possible, although the spirit of direct participation remains very much alive and kicking, particularly in debates about the pros and cons of making decisions through referendums.

Politics

Time now to turn to a working definition of 'politics'. Again, democracy and politics are not synonyms: it is not difficult to think of countries in which politics is profoundly anti-democratic. I think 'politics' is best defined as the processes through which people both give voice to their views *and* listen to those of others. Politics is much more than political institutions (e.g. Parliament) or actors (MPs and ministers). Clearly, these are important, but an over-riding concern with them prevents us adopting a broader appreciation of politics as the ways in which we express and try to address the things we disagree on (Stoker, 2006). Even using this generous definition, some people don't go near politics (more on that shortly), but lots do: by writing letters to newspapers, having arguments with friends, family or flatmates about the issue du jour, signing online petitions, phoning or listening to talkback radio, marching in a protest, boycotting certain products or joining a political party (not so popular these days). All of these are ways in which people express their political voice and (sometimes) listen to those of others.

That said, voting in parliamentary elections is one of the most significant forms of political engagement. Yes: voter turnout — in New Zealand and internationally — is declining. Yes: if it's all you do, then casting your vote (two of them, technically — more on which below) once every three years is a pretty limited means of engaging with politics. And, yes, there is a strong case for arguing that *not* voting is also a way of exercising the right to voice (we'll come to that shortly, too).

Nonetheless, voting matters because it is how we collectively decide who gets to make the rules that govern our lives. Indeed, voting *really* matters. Here are three things that happen as a direct consequence of New Zealand's triennial general elections. First, a Parliament is chosen. Second, a government is formed from that Parliament (by the party or parties controlling a majority of parliamentary seats). Third, that government starts doing things that have material consequences for people's lives — including yours. Governments and parliaments decide what is legal and what isn't, and what public money is spent on, and what it is taken away from. Governments' policies may validate, valorise and include, but they can also stigmatise, stereotype and exclude. One way or another, this stuff counts — and voting is where it all begins.

Some background on elections and electoral systems

Because voting is one key way in which people give voice to their political views, it is important to understand how the voting system in New Zealand operates and what its main functions are (see Hayward, 2016; Shaw & Eichbaum, 2011). Elections are staged according to various laws and procedures that collectively comprise an electoral system, the core function of which is to allow voters to influence the shape of the Parliament. When (or if, as voting is not compulsory here) you cast your votes in a general election, you are choosing the people you want to serve as MPs for the next parliamentary term. The job of the electoral system is to take your choice and that of every other voter, and allocate the correct number of parliamentary seats to the various political parties contesting the election.

 Visit the Electoral Commission for information and research on the voting system, the outcomes of general elections, political parties and so on: http://www.elections.org.nz/

Different electoral systems perform this task in contrasting ways. Under our Mixed Member Proportional (MMP) system, each elector has two votes. Voters generally give the party vote to their preferred political party, and the electorate vote to the candidate they want to represent their electorate (a specific voting district). It is the party vote that determines the composition of Parliament, because the number of parliamentary seats a party is allocated reflects its support amongst voters. The maths is pretty simple: a party that wins 47 per cent of the party vote, for example, as National did in 2014, will be awarded an equivalent proportion of all seats in Parliament. In 2014, National's share of the vote entitled it to 60 seats: its candidates won 41 electorate seats and so the party received 19 list seats to take it to its entitlement. The sting in the tail is that parties have to cross an electoral threshold before they are entitled to list seats: they must win at least 5 per cent of all valid party votes or one constituency seat (either general or Māori).

There is one other important feature of New Zealand's political system that is useful to understand. In this country we do *not* directly elect the prime minister. (Nor do we have any say in the selection of our head of state. Rather, at the apex of our political system sits a hereditary monarch who resides 20,000 kilometres away. I will leave you to ponder whether or not this is consistent with our claim to be a fully sovereign and independent state.) In many other democracies, voters have a more or less direct voice in the process of choosing their head of government (whether called a president or a prime minister). Not here. Here, we directly elect the Parliament at national elections, but the formation of a government — the prime minister and the 20 or more members of her or his Cabinet — happens after the election. The outcome of that process depends on the distribution of parliamentary seats, and specifically on which party (or parties) can negotiate an arrangement with other parties allowing it (or them) to control a majority of parliamentary seats. The voters' contribution to this is an indirect one: our votes for the Parliament directly influence the number of seats each party has, and therefore how strong a voice, if any, each has in the government formation process, but we do not directly choose our governments. People living in countries like France and the United States, where citizens participate directly in the election of the head of state and the head of government (who are sometimes the same person), are inclined to find our way of doing things slightly odd.

Politics as voice: identity threads, encounters and contexts

You will recall that one of the aims of this part of the book is to explore what motivates people to give voice to their thoughts, feelings and views in different ways. In the context of this chapter, that requires exploring the range of reasons behind people's decisions to vote (or not to do so). For some, the motivation stems from a deeply held view that voting is a fundamental act of citizenship; an assertion of belonging to a sovereign, self-governing political community. For others, voting is a civic virtue (if not a requirement): this view is reflected in the argument that you *should* vote because others fought (and sometimes died) in order that you might maintain that right. Most people, however, vote because they want to have a say — however small that contribution may seem — in the political processes that directly influence our daily lives. The cost of a tertiary education and the size of our student debt, the price of houses, the number and quality of jobs available — these and myriad other things are influenced, if not wholly determined, by decisions made by parliamentarians and ministers. Many people have firm views on at least some of these things, and voting is one way in which we can express this and help shape decision-making.

In this respect, voting is as much an emotional and expressive act as it is a strictly rational one. When people exercise their voice through voting, they are

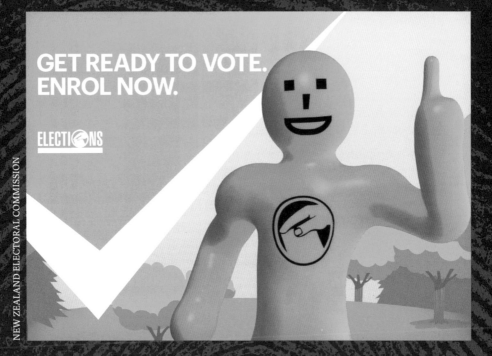

GET READY TO VOTE.
ENROL NOW.

ELECTIONS

Exercising citizenship

You can't just rock on up to a voting place on election day in New Zealand; you first have to be enrolled for your vote to count. This means enrolling with the Electoral Commission before election day. To enrol, you have to be 18 years or older and be a New Zealand citizen or permanent resident. You also have to have lived in New Zealand for one year or more at some point in your life. People from Australia, the Cook Islands, Niue and Tokelau who do not have permanent resident visas may vote as long as they have lived in New Zealand for more than 12 months and are enrolled to vote. People on student, work and tourist visas cannot vote if they have to leave New Zealand by a set date.

taking a position on things they often feel strongly about. There is a relationship between a person's views, values, beliefs and so forth — their identity threads — and the positions they take on matters of public concern. For example, someone with social justice values may feel particularly strongly about income inequality in New Zealand; another person will have firm opinions on how we should treat the environment (you will read more about these issues in Chapters 9 and 10, respectively). These positions might motivate them to vote, and to do so for a party whose policies are consistent with their values.

In addition, our political identities are to some extent shaped by the relationships — or identity encounters — we have with others. For instance, while there are no iron-clad rules, the sociological explanation of voting behaviour stresses the significant roles played by those with whom we have important social relationships — particularly family members, partners and peers — in shaping our political views and, therefore, how we vote. Another account, the party identification model, suggests that people develop an attachment to particular parties — based on a person's history, experiences, their families' voting preferences, past policies and so forth — which shapes their voting behaviour. According to this view, unless given compelling reasons to do otherwise, people tend to stick with 'their' party — it becomes a part of their political sense of self.

There are other connections between voting, and political engagement more generally, and people's personal sense of identity and belonging. Whether you use it or not, having the right to vote signifies that you are a member of a political community; not having that right marks you as an outsider. Furthermore, you are far more likely to feel connected to that political community, even if its decisions aren't always the ones you'd like, if you know you can contribute by selecting those responsible for making the decisions that influence everyone. The reverse also applies: people who cannot vote or who are disengaged from a political community are less likely to feel part of it (even though the rules will continue to apply to them).

Voting is one way of expressing membership of a political community: 'I vote, therefore I belong'. But it also works the other way: that community — which is part of the context in which people's sense of identity is shaped — will do things that have consequences for individuals' sense of who they are. The language and substance of politics send messages about who matters and who does not. For instance, tax cuts for higher-income earners send one type of message ('We will reward you because you are earning well'), while punitive sanctions against those on benefits send a very different message ('If you just tried harder, you could find work'). Look hard enough and you will see that governments' policies almost always reflect preferences for certain values, and serve the interests of some groups over others.

But policies do more than that: they also shape people's material circumstances, and in doing so have impacts on their sense of self. American political scientists Anne Schneider and Helen Ingram (1993) explain how this happens. Government policies are imbued with socially constructed images of the populations they are targeted at (high-income earners, the unemployed, sick people, business owners, students, investors, refugees, property owners, migrants or whomever). Those images may be positive or negative. Either way, the implicit messages — worthy/not worthy; lazy/hard-working; deserving/undeserving, etc. — that are communicated by such images are absorbed by members of the target populations.

Whether positive or negative, these representations can have consequences for people's feelings of self-worth and their willingness to participate in (or withdraw from) the life of their communities. New Zealand writer Andrew Dean (2015) provides a local example of this very thing, explaining how the economic policy reforms of the 1980s and 1990s were associated with both a growing sense of alienation and rising suicide rates amongst young people in this country.

The consequences of these politically constructed representations can also reverberate out into the wider public domain. The public acceptance of the negative portrayal of a certain group may produce stereotypes based on a poorly informed understanding of that group's circumstances. Worse still, the process can become self-reinforcing. Negative stereotypes can influence voters' choices at the ballot booth, which in turn may lead to more punitive government policies that have further corrosive consequences for members of marginalised groups.

From silence to voice

Another core theme of this section of the book is that membership of any sort of political community is rarely inevitable. Often what we take for granted today is something that previous generations have been denied. That is certainly the case with voting: there is nothing natural about having the right to vote, or to engage in politics more generally, as a brief political history of Māori and women shows. Aspects of both stories are well known, but there is more to them than many of us realise.

The Māori seats were established in 1867 by Donald McLean's Maori Representation Act. The legislation — indeed, the whole history of Māori parliamentary representation, which remains one of the great untold (or misunderstood) political stories of our nation — was fascinating for a number of reasons. For one thing, for the purposes of the Act a 'Maori' was defined as 'a male aboriginal native inhabitant of New Zealand of the age of 21 years and upwards, and shall include half-castes'. You can see how at least three identity threads — ethnicity, gender and age — are in play here. For another, had the number of seats been established on a population basis (as was the case for what were then known as the 'European seats'), there would have been 14 or 16 seats rather than the four that were established. Third, at the time, Māori weren't the only ones with dedicated parliamentary representation. Ring-fenced seats were de rigueur in the mid-1800s. Two had already been set aside for Otago goldminers by the time McLean's legislation was enacted, and there was a Pensioners Settlement electorate in Auckland. In fact, 1867 was a good year for separate representation: not only were Māori bequeathed four seats, but Westland goldminers were also tossed an electorate of their own.

 For more detail on the history of the Māori seats see Te Ara: http://www.teara.govt.nz/en/nga-mangai-maori-representation/page-1

There remains a surprisingly entrenched view that the Māori seats represent a privilege. I am not sure why, given that (a) the voting process on the Māori and general rolls is identical, (b) no voter can vote on more than one electoral roll, and (c) the Māori electorates are generally much larger, and therefore harder to service, than general electorates. Also, we are certainly not alone in providing for the dedicated parliamentary representation of indigenous people. It also exists in Lebanon, Fiji, Zimbabwe, Singapore, India and the United States' dependencies of Guam and Puerto Rico. Admittedly, one or two of these are countries some of us might not like being compared with, but the point is that separate representation isn't uncommon.

Indeed, the history of the Māori voice in Parliament is replete with instances in which being treated differently has not been to the advantage of tangata whenua. The secret ballot was established for male European voters in 1870, but Māori voted by show of hand until 1910, and then by declaration (in front of a returning officer and a Māori witness) until 1937. Between 1919 and 1951, voting in the Māori seats was held the day before voting in European seats ('European' seats became known as 'general' seats in 1975). Māori could not stand as candidates in European electorates until 1967, and between 1893 and 1975 a person deemed to be more than half Māori could not vote in a European seat. Indeed, for long periods of time, without the Māori seats there would have been few, if any, Māori MPs.

As to women, while we are forever invoking the 1893 legislation granting all

LADY VOTERS GOING UP TO POLLING-BOOTH, ELECTION DAY, AUCKLAND.   Beattie and Sanderson, Photo.

The battle for equality

New Zealand women won the right to vote in 1893, with the
passing of the Electoral Act, but the battle for equality was
not quite over: they could not stand for Parliament until 1919.
The push to get the vote was known as the women's suffrage
movement and Kate Sheppard was its leader: 'We are tired
of having a "sphere" doled out to us, and of being told that
anything outside that sphere is "unwomanly",' she once
said. The movement grew out of concern at alcohol-related
violence; women thought that if they could vote they would
have more say in promoting laws to ban liquor and encourage
higher moral standards, as well as enjoy more participation
in society, rather than only in their homes.

women the vote as part of our progressive, egalitarian nation-building story (which we explore further in Part 4 of the book), there are less tasteful elements of that history that rarely feature in the official narrative. For instance, while women won the right to vote in 1893, the law prevented them from *standing* for parliamentary election until 1919, and it was 40 years after the landmark suffrage legislation before the first woman — Elizabeth McCombs — took her seat in Parliament.

 The history of women and the vote in Aotearoa New Zealand is told here: http://www.nzhistory.govt.nz/politics/womens-suffrage

More than a century later, women still number just 30 per cent of all MPs, and comprise around the same proportion of government ministers. That under-representation raises questions about women's voice in the House. It is an especial concern for those who support women's representation on the grounds that Parliament should resemble — in demographic terms — the wider population. (That view is itself based on the assumption that women have specific interests that can only be represented by those with the same interests, which is open to the challenge that this downplays other aspects of women's identity, such as class, ethnicity or age.) To some extent, too, it is also at odds with one of our national articles of faith, which is that everyone is, or should be, treated equally (which David discusses in Chapter 9).

From voice to silence?

There is one final story we should talk about here, which is the declining turnout of voters at elections. Once upon a time voter turnout routinely hovered around the 80 to 90 per cent range, but in the 2014 election nearly 23 per cent of registered voters did not vote, and a further 252,581 people who were eligible to vote did not enrol at all (Shaw, 2016). Those drifting towards the democratic margins include young people (in 2014, only 75 per cent of eligible voters aged 18 to 24 enrolled, and 37 per cent of them did not vote), Māori (46 per cent of Māori aged 18 to 24 who enrolled to vote did not do so), the unemployed and those on low incomes, and members of some migrant communities (Henderson, 2013).

Before delving into this issue, there are two points worth making. First, be careful not to assume that non-voters are politically disengaged. They may well be, but voting is just one way of participating in politics, and it is entirely possible that your daughter/son/partner/flatmate who does not vote is happily engaging in other types of political activity. This is the twenty-first century, after all, and one obvious form this might take is online political activity — sometimes called 'information activism' — which is connective rather than collective in nature (Marsh, Vines, & Halupka, 2016). There is a smug tendency among more traditional types to dismiss such activity as 'mere clicktivism', but there is evidence that online activity also spills over into more concrete, embodied political arenas (Bennett & Segerberg, 2012, p.19).

 Listen to this TED talk by Evgeny Morozov if you think the internet is innately democratising: https://www.ted.com/talks/ evgeny_morozov_is_the_internet_what_orwell_feared

Second, while the act of voting is a statement ('I have a stake in this community and I wish to participate in it'), non-voting is not necessarily a statement of *not* belonging. By choosing not to vote, a person may well be saying 'I don't feel I belong to this community'. Equally, they might be saying 'I belong, and feel so strongly about the direction in which things are going that I will choose not to vote', or 'I don't see my particular identity reflected in the people standing for election'. This, too, is an active choice and a legitimate expression of a view. In short, resist the temptation to blame non-voting on lazy, irresponsible or apathetic individuals. Of course those can be factors, but, as Marsh, Vines and Halupka (2016) put it, the issue might not be 'political apathy, but alienation from politics as it is practised' (p. 1).

Why some people don't vote (spoiler alert: it's not to do with apathy)

Rather than blame people, then, we should ask two very serious questions: 'Why is non-voting on the rise?' and 'Is this a problem?' The first thing to be said is that falling voter turnout is one expression of a deeper trend towards political disengagement from formal politics. The reasons for this are deep and complex, but one is that some people no longer believe in the capacity of politics and politicians to address their problems and issues. If you are facing a future of insecure employment, low wages and increasingly unaffordable housing — and some people in this country face all of those challenges and more — and see no way out of this vortex, you may well question the point of engaging with politics, via voting or other means.

The New Zealand Herald's Insight page — http://insights. nzherald.co.nz/category/politics — contains some excellent infographics demonstrating voting trends and other phenomena

This loss of faith is sometimes expressed in what has become known as 'anti-politics' (Hay & Stoker, 2009). Even if you have never heard it before, you will be familiar with what the term represents — anti-politics is that bleak view of politics that sees mendacity, duplicity and sleaze everywhere, and which holds that politicians are, without exception, lazy, self-serving, dishonest liars. There is some truth in elements of the anti-politics perspective; equally, it provides a partial explanation of affairs (often enthusiastically promoted by a media less interested in objectivity or balance than in sensationalism and reader-market share) which rests on negative assumptions rather than rigorous evidence.

Of most concern, perhaps, is where the anti-politics analysis leads us. If the diagnosis is that politics amounts to nothing more than the rampant pursuit of self-interest, then the solution, surely, is less politics. Unfortunately, 'less politics' really means that most of us get less and less (and eventually no) say in what gets decided. Instead, decision-making is removed from the public domain and becomes the preserve of other people: in effect, it gets 'subcontracted . . . to non-elected agencies and institutions' (Hay & Stoker, 2009, p. 228). This happens in one of two ways, the first of which is through the delegation of decision-making authority to appointed officials in institutions such as the Reserve Bank and sundry Crown entities. Those agencies can possess very significant powers: changes in interest rates decided by the governor of the Reserve Bank, for instance, have major consequences for home owners, property investors and those who rent. But the public cannot hold the (appointed) Reserve Bank governor to account in the same way it can the (elected) Minister of Finance.

Second, we have come to rely heavily on the free market to organise social and economic life. But as the public sphere has shrunk, so the private domain has expanded. There are three potential issues with this. First, marketisation has direct impacts on individuals, especially for those who are struggling (and who therefore, for instance, go cold during winter). Second, it also has a bearing on what politics can achieve, because the government's influence in markets (for electricity, housing, food, etc.) is, by definition, limited. This means that politics is constrained in its capacity to support people who suffer through a lack of means. Finally, the more we rely on markets to resolve what were once public debates about who gets access to what, the less we are able to collectively resolve these issues through the political process. In competitive markets, unlike in politics, we are not all equal: it is in the nature of competition that some voices will miss out.

And this is a problem, why?

As to the second question posed above — is falling voter turnout an issue? — in the section in the book about voice we should reflect on some of the possible long-term consequences of political disengagement (see Shaw, 2016). However compelling the reasons may be, there are risks associated with what amounts to a voluntary silencing of voice. Most obviously, non-voters' voices stand less chance of being heard when decisions are taken, and over time it may be that those decisions start to disproportionately reflect the views of those who *do* engage. Whether you vote or not, governments will go on governing, and will make choices — usually sooner rather than later — that will directly influence you. In other words, even if your voice has not been part of the relevant conversation, you will have little choice other than to live with the consequences of the decisions that will inevitably be taken.

There is another, possibly less obvious risk of long-term political disengagement, which is that at some point anti-politics becomes so systemic it starts to threaten the very structure of our democracy. There are a couple of ways this could play out. One scenario sees a populist demagogue riding a wave of public anger to electoral victory, following which he or she drives illiberal laws through the New Zealand Parliament as the nation embraces a politics of intolerance and suspicion (see Shaw, 2017). The second path can be glimpsed in data from a poll undertaken by the Lowy Institute for International Policy (2013), which revealed that just 48 per cent of 18- to 29-year-old Australians thought that 'democracy is preferable to any other kind of government'. Put differently, a majority of those polled thought some other form of political system would be preferable to Australia's parliamentary democracy.

I am not aware of equivalent New Zealand data, but we need to be careful about what we wish for. If we disparage, dismiss and denigrate our form of democracy to the point that it collapses, what will we replace it with? An absolute monarchy? A dictatorship? Some other form of authoritarian regime? Whatever its faults (and heaven knows they need remedying), our type of democracy does permit people to voice their views and engage should they choose to. In some other political systems the only voices to be heard are those of what American sociologist C. Wright Mills (1956) once called the 'power élite'. But if we leave the field of political play to the powerful, they may ignore the rest of us completely and simply write the rules in their favour.

Conclusion

There is a clear link between voting, and political engagement more broadly, and the wider narrative in this book regarding citizenship. Participation in public life is a central aspect of citizenship. As Hay and Stoker (2009), two eminent British political scientists, put it, 'in politics the only way to get something is to use voice — to express your concerns in concert with others' (p. 234). In other words, politics is something that we do with the others with whom we share this place. The bases on which participation in such processes is allowed (or prohibited), the groups who get to participate (and those who do not), the ways we can (or cannot) participate through voting — each is central to an appreciation of identity, belonging and citizenship in Aotearoa New Zealand.

Little of this is simple or straightforward. One of the central themes of this book is that the faces, places, voices and stories that characterise Aotearoa New Zealand are rich and varied. It is hardly a surprise, then, that this diversity often means people take opposing views on issues. In politics, people speak with different voices because they hold diverging views on things that are fundamental to their sense of self. In a diverse society like ours, there cannot always (or even often) be unanimity on what matters to us: unless some false uniformity is imposed from on high, there will always be different voices regarding our values and the things we believe in. That is both healthy and entirely to be expected.

Politics is the process through which all of this occurs. Done well, it can help us 'find ways for those who disagree to rub along together . . . [and to] potentially patch up the disagreements that characterise our societies without recourse to illegitimate coercion or violence' (Stoker, 2006, p. 2). But, for this to happen, two things have to occur. First, *all* of our voices need to be heard in the political conversation; second, we must do better at *listening* to what others have to say. The current drift towards political disengagement — of which the reduction in voter turnout is just one symptom — means that some voices are falling silent and there is a whole lot less listening going on. As a political community, our challenge is to find ways for those voices to rejoin the conversation about how we wish to live together, and to nourish our ability to listen to them. It won't have escaped even the most casual observer of the 2016 presidential election in the United States that the price of failure to rise to this test might be very high indeed.

Chapter 3 — Voices in the House: Political representation and participation: http://turangawaewae.massey.ac.nz/chapter3.html

Recommended reading

Hayward, J. (Ed.). (2016). *New Zealand government and politics* (6th ed.). Melbourne, Australia: Oxford University Press.

Shaw, R. (2016). The harvest we will reap. In N. Legat (Ed.), *The journal of urgent writing*. Auckland, New Zealand: Massey University Press.

Stoker, G. (2006). *Why politics matters*. New York, NY: Palgrave Macmillan.

References

Bennett, W., & Segerberg, A. (2012). The logic of connective action: Digital media and the personalization of contentious politics. *Information, Communication & Society, 15*(5), 739–768.

Dean, A. (2015). *Ruth, Roger and me: Debts and legacies*. Wellington, New Zealand: BWB Texts.

Hay, I., & Stoker, G. (2009). Revitalising politics: Have we lost the plot?. *Representation, 45*(3), 226–236.

Hayward, J. (Ed.). (2016). *New Zealand government and politics* (6th ed.). Melbourne, Australia: Oxford University Press.

Henderson, A. (2013). *Immigrants and electoral enrolment. Do the numbers add up?* (Statistics New Zealand Working Paper 13-01). Wellington, New Zealand: Statistics New Zealand.

Lowy Institute. (2013). *The Lowy Institute poll*. Retrieved from https://www.lowyinstitute.org/publications/lowy-institute-poll-2013

Marsh, I., Vines, E., & Halupka, M. (2016). Two cheers for Richards and Smith: Beyond anti-politics? *The Political Quarterly.* doi: 10.1111/1467-923X.12247

Mills, C. Wright. (1956). *The power élite*. New York, NY: Oxford University Press.

Schneider, A., & Ingram, H. (1993). Social construction of target populations: Implications for politics and policy. *American Political Science Review, 87*(2), 334–347.

Shaw, R. (2016). The harvest we will reap. In N. Legat (Ed.), *The journal of urgent writing* (pp. 124–39). Auckland, New Zealand: Massey University Press.

Shaw, R. (2017). We're all in this together? Democracy and politics in Aotearoa New Zealand. In A. Bell, V. Elizabeth, T. McIntosh, & M. Wynyard (Eds.), *A land of milk and honey? Making sense of Aotearoa New Zealand* (pp. 43–56). Auckland, New Zealand: Auckland University Press.

Shaw, R., & Eichbaum, C. (2011). *Public policy in New Zealand: Institutions, processes and outcomes* (3rd ed.). Auckland, New Zealand: Pearson Education.

Stoker, G. (2006). *Why politics matters*. New York, NY: Palgrave Macmillan.

CHAPTER FOUR:

Shout it out
Participation and protest in public life

Ella Kahu

Introduction

In ancient Athens, political participation, activity intended to influence government, was a duty of all citizens. (As an interesting aside, as we learned in Richard's chapter, 'citizens' excluded women, slaves and *metics* [aliens] — which left a mere 30 per cent of the population.) The value that was placed on participation, and on the role of active citizen, is evident in our language: the English word 'idiot' derives from the Greek *idiōtēs* meaning 'private and self-centred' — in direct contrast to *politēs*, meaning 'citizen' or 'public' (Parker, 2005). While participation in public life is no longer seen as an obligation (even voting is not compulsory in New Zealand), the right to have a say on how things happen, to participate, remains a critical right in modern democracies (Kaase, 2011). In the previous chapter, Richard explored a particular form of political participation: voice through voting. In this chapter we step outside of the formal structures of Parliament and look at protest: groups of citizens with a common goal, aiming to bring about social, political or economic change by making their voice heard through methods such as letter/email writing, marches, petitions, boycotts and occupations (Grey, 2015). Protest is vital to a democratic, dynamic society — it is one of the key ways that politicians get to hear citizens' views on important issues. It is often through citizen activism that change occurs.

The first key aim for this part of the book is to explore how people express their voice and what motivates them to do so. So why do people protest? The phenomena of social movements and protests have been the focus of disciplines in social science and the humanities, such as social psychology, sociology, political science, history and anthropology, with each taking a different view of this complex topic (Roggeband & Klandermans, 2010). For instance, a social psychologist may look at the individual identities of activists, whereas a sociologist may look at the cultural context that shapes a protest movement. Both of these approaches are relevant to the theoretical framework that informs this text.

At an individual level, protest is strongly linked to identity; for example, the rights granted to citizens are often determined by the threads of their identities, and it is often shared dimensions of identity, such as gender or class, that bring a group together in protest. For instance, Anthony Marx (1995) argues that exclusion from citizenship based on ethnicity solidifies ethnic identity and results in collective action against the state — exactly the phenomenon Te Rina, Margaret and Veronica discussed in Chapter 2. Protest also links closely to individual belonging, both as a motivation and as an outcome. The sense of belonging stemming from a shared identity can increase the likelihood of an individual protesting, and participation in collective action is often described with terms such as 'solidarity' and 'unity', with such feelings strongly associated with continued involvement in the cause (Drury et al., 2005). Of course, protest is not always founded on pre-existing collective identities. It may be an event, political decision or action that brings a group together; for example, the Springbok Tour protests, as discussed shortly. In this instance, bonding over a shared belief also results in a sense of belonging, a camaraderie of protest (Friedlander, 2013).

But to fully understand why people protest and what they protest about, we also need to consider the context: 'collective struggles are rooted in a social and political context' (van Stekelenburg & Klandermans, 2013, p. 899). For instance, Anita Lacey at the University of Auckland (2015) highlights how the nature of protest has changed. Prior to the 1960s, protests tended to be driven by the working class, primarily aimed at the redistribution of power and resources. Following that era, the focus shifted to wider social issues, such as rights, identity and ecology. The homosexual law reform movement, discussed shortly, is one such example. It is also an example of how, in contemporary movements, people also protest in solidarity — using their voice to strengthen the voice of minority groups. Many of those calling for the legalisation of same-sex marriage in 2013 were heterosexual.

Aotearoa New Zealand's history is replete with examples of citizens using their voice to protest — not always with success — from the peaceful Māori occupation of Parihaka in the 1880s (and the many other instances of Māori protest explored in Chapter 2) to the Trans Pacific Partnership (TPP) protests in 2015. The other two aims for this part of the book are to explore the struggles that different groups face in expressing their voice, and to understand the consequences of voice in terms of issues of identity and citizenship. Here we use two historical case studies to illustrate voice and consequences. Both are powerful, but they are very different stories of the forging of identity at individual, group and national levels: the gay rights movement from the 1970s until the present, and the Springbok rugby tour protests in 1981.

The gay protest movement

Homosexuality has been a longstanding focus of protest in New Zealand. Sexuality is an important identity thread for people, particularly for those who are not heterosexual, and who have therefore been excluded from many aspects of life in New Zealand (and indeed the world). Here we take a quick overview of some of the challenges and consequences of the gay protest movement. While recent protests centred on issues of sexuality have tended to focus explicitly on rights (protests leading up to the passing of the same-sex marriage bill in 2013 for instance), the goals of the movement have been much deeper and wider than just legislative change. As American sociologists Polletta and Jasper (2001) remind us, a key goal of many social movements is the development of a stronger collective identity — a sense of group pride. For the lesbian, gay, bisexual and transgender (LGBT) community, the fight has been, and continues to be, for acceptance of their identity as both valid and valued.

As with all protest movements, the socio-political context is critical to understanding events. Following the Second World War, New Zealand prided itself on being strongly equalitarian (Hansen, 1968), an ideology that is associated with conformity — pride in not just equality of income, but also equality of customs and outlook: a 'high degree of uniformity' (Dunstall, 1992, p. 452). In Chapter 9, David explores the egalitarian element of that ideology in some depth. The conformity of the New Zealand culture was evident in rigid gender roles, with the New Zealand masculine identity of rugged rural man sharply defined. Deviation from this strongly held norm was deeply problematic. In a book based on a doctoral thesis exploring public debate in New Zealand on homosexuality from 1960 to 1986, Laurie Guy (2002) points out that holding on to that sense of conformity requires a blindness to others: 'it was a case of ignoring Maoris [sic], ignoring women,

REF: EP/1985/4285/25. ALEXANDER TURNBULL LIBRARY, WELLINGTON

Resisting reform, unsuccessfully

Politician Peter Tait and businessman Keith Hay, of the
Coalition of Concerned Citizens, carry a petition against
homosexual law reform into Parliament in 1985. Despite the
strenuous efforts of a loose coalition of conservative and
Christian groups, in July 1986 the Homosexual Law Reform
Act was signed by the Governor-General, decriminalising
consensual sexual relations between men aged 16 and over.
No longer would they be liable to prosecution and a term
of imprisonment. Since then a raft of gradual reforms,
including legalising same-sex marriage, has been enacted,
addressing the legal status and improving the access to
equal rights of LGBT New Zealanders.

ignoring homosexuals — male Pakeha heterosexuality ruled' (p. 25). In addition to rigid gender roles, the sexual values of the time stemmed from strong Christian beliefs that sex was acceptable only within marriage. Legally, male-on-male sex was a criminal act, and morally it was held to be a sin. This was a time when the two-parent family was the only acceptable structure, and so it is unsurprising that, in this context, homosexuals were seen as sick or sinful, and homosexuality was at best ignored and at worst abhorred.

 See this *New Zealand Herald* article for an excellent timeline of gay rights in New Zealand: http://www.nzherald.co.nz/nz/news/ article.cfm?c_id=1&objectid=1087813

But contexts change, and as contexts change so do identities. The late 1960s and the 1970s was a period of significant social change in New Zealand, with the emergence of numerous social movements, including second-wave feminism, abortion rights, anti-war protests and Māori land issues. Alongside these changes, we saw a shift in sexual morality and a decrease in the Church's influence over society. Together, these changes provided a context in which the gay liberation movement, and more specifically homosexual law reform, could become part of the New Zealand conversation (Guy, 2002). It is not possible to pinpoint the exact start of the movement, although Guy argues that a tragic case in 1964, where a homosexual man was attacked and killed by six youths in Christchurch, acted as a catalyst for change. The offenders were subsequently acquitted, following a trial that focused, in part, on the victim's sexual preferences. This event stands both as a reflection of the societal attitudes in New Zealand of the time, and as a mark of the start of the protest movement.

One of the challenges facing the early homosexual protest movement was that it did not centre on a single shared identity. For instance, Guy's historical examination of the gay movement in New Zealand, from the 1960s until the homosexual law reform in 1986, highlights that lesbian women faced very different issues to gay men in this period. Homosexual women faced a battle not just against heterosexism, but also against the male patriarchy. But male homosexual behaviour was seen as more abhorrent than female homosexual behaviour, which was not legally proscribed and therefore not a criminal offence. In addition, much of the early debate and protest centred on viewing homosexuality and heterosexuality as binary identities. Despite there being an increasing acknowledgement, particularly in academia, of the fluidity and variability of sexuality in terms of both orientation and behaviour, viewing homosexual identity as clear-cut and fixed was a critical part of the reform argument — if a group have a clearly delineated identity, then the justification for acceptance and rights becomes easier.

As mentioned earlier, the gay liberation movement was about more than just legal reform. Gaining individual rights was important, but for many the acceptance and even celebration of homosexuality was also critical: 'the problem was not just the laws but societal attitudes' (Guy, 2002, p. 94). The protest was against the hegemony of heterosexuality and the 'patriarchal family', and the movement was characterised by defiance and pride. An important part of that defiance was encouraging gays to come out. Coming out was an act of protest, not just an individual act but the joining of a community, which provided a sense of solidarity and, importantly, a visibility that would allow the community's voices to be heard. It is a potent example of how the act of protest shapes and in some cases forms a collective identity (Polletta & Jasper, 2001). As Australian academic and gay rights activist Dennis Altman (1983) explains, shifting the debate from behaviour to identity was a powerful move that forced opponents 'into a position where they can be seen as attacking the civil rights of homosexual citizens rather than attacking . . . antisocial behaviour' (p. 9).

The gay liberation movement, and associated legislative reform protests, spanned decades and is not yet a closed chapter. The first official meeting took place on the University of Auckland campus in 1972, followed by the first of many 'public and provocative' events (Guy, 2002, p. 96) — for example, a Gay Day in Albert Park. This event took place at the site of a statue of Queen Victoria, with 'Will Victorian morality ever die' as one of the key catchphrases.

While legislative change was only one part of the agenda, Fran Wilde's Homosexual Law Reform Bill was a critical, and arguably the most memorable, part of the fight. The 18 months leading up to the Bill's final success were characterised by fierce debate and protest by both sides, inside and outside of Parliament. The oppositional forces were formidable, and many of them saw the fight as being against more than just homosexual law reform. It was a fight against what was seen by many conservative or Christian people as the broad decline of moral standards in society (Guy, 2002). Homosexual law reform was representative of a range of other liberal issues, such as abortion. The final parliamentary vote was 49 in favour and 44 against, with the age of consent (set in the Bill at 16, the same as for heterosexual sex) considered to be one of the primary reasons for the closeness of the vote.

While a defining moment in the history of gay pride, this legislative change was not the end of the political and public protests and successes. Another important achievement was the new Human Rights Act of 1993, which extended its protection against discrimination to include sexual orientation. But, in 1994, the first Hero Parade through the streets of Auckland triggered protest from conservative Christians, among other groups; clearly, the question of whether homosexuality was normal and acceptable was still not settled (Guy, 2002). The next legislative landmark was the passing of the Civil Union Act by the Labour Government in 2004, which enabled same-sex couples to register their unions and thus gain some of the rights of heterosexual couples.

However, marriage was still the preserve of heterosexual relationships and, for many, the Civil Union Act labelled homosexuals, once again, as second-class citizens (Baker & Elizabeth, 2012). The most recent achievement for the gay movement in New Zealand has been the passing of the Marriage (Definition of Marriage) Amendment Act 2013, which redefined marriage as the union of '2 people, regardless of their sex, sexual orientation, or gender identity' (section 4). Once again, a range of Christian groups (although by no means all Christians) vigorously protested against the legislative change, but the legislation passed with a clear majority of 77 to 44 votes.

 See a video of the passing of the Marriage (Definition of Marriage) Amendment Act, and the ensuing waiata: https://www.youtube.com/watch?v=KlVaPHdTWMk

So is there no longer a need for a gay protest movement? Have we reached a point where homosexuality is not merely tolerated but accepted by society? Or have the battle lines simply changed? Certainly this has been a successful movement. In the 50 years since members of the LGBT community first started raising their voice in protest, they have gained much in terms of removing the barriers to equal legislative rights based on sexuality. Alongside those political changes, they have achieved increased acceptance of their identities by at least the majority of the population. In many circles, homosexuality is no longer something to be hidden, and pride in that identity is increasingly possible.

But more is needed. For instance, gay Muslim men in New Zealand still live dual lives — out in mainstream areas of society, but living a life of pretence when in the context of their Muslim families and communities (Anonymous, 2015). 'Muslim' and 'gay' continue to be incompatible identity threads. In addition, the focus until recently has been predominantly on sexuality rather than gender, and a growing concern is the rights of people who do not conform to the strongly held binary gender norms. The evolving and expanding acronym LGBTQIA+ (lesbian, gay, bisexual, trans, queer/questioning, intersex, asexual, plus others) is testament to this widening focus. Theoretically, discrimination against people on the basis of their gender identity is prohibited by the Human Rights Act 1993; however, a report by the Human Rights Commission (2008) found that transgender people in New Zealand experience considerable discrimination and face numerous barriers in their daily lives. One of the recommendations of that report is that gender identity be explicitly included in the Human Rights Act.

This issue is starting to trigger protest. In 2016, the Pride Parade was disrupted by protests from a group called No Pride in Prisons. The specific concern was the inclusion of police and corrections officers in the parade, with protesters arguing that this was inappropriate, given allegations of abuse against transgender inmates in prisons (Yeoman, 2016). In a more local example, a transgender teenager attending a girls' college in Blenheim was asked not to use the girls' toilet (Eder, 2016). This triggered media coverage and an online petition that, in part, led to the school changing its policy to allow students to use the bathroom of whichever gender they identified with. These examples highlight that sexuality and gender are still matters of protest. The details of the identities at stake may have shifted, but the basic cause — to be treated as equal citizens — remains the same.

The 1981 Springbok Tour

The gay liberation movement is an ongoing protest movement centred on personal identity threads, and focused on achieving change for a specific community in New Zealand. In contrast, the 1981 Springbok Tour protests were triggered by a political event, and centred on our national identity, what it means to be a New Zealander. The questions of why people protested, the struggles they faced, and the nature of the consequences are therefore quite different.

The fierce rivalry on the rugby field between New Zealand and South Africa, which operated a separatist political and social system known as apartheid, was long tainted by racial divides. Historically, only whites could play for South Africa's national rugby team, the Springboks, while their counterparts, the All Blacks, were multiracial. However, in the 1960s Māori players were excluded from All Black tours of South Africa, a discrimination that triggered protest in New Zealand and resulted in the cancellation of a planned tour here in 1967. Worldwide condemnation of South Africa's apartheid regime was growing, and in 1968 the United Nations (UN) declared a sports boycott of South Africa. Despite this, All Black teams toured South

The winter of discontent

The 1981 Springbok tour was one of the most
sustained, ugly and divisive periods of protest ever
experienced in New Zealand. Tense and violent
encounters between police, and their specially
formed Red Squad, and protestors — as shown here
in Wellington in August — were common.

Africa in 1970 and 1976, with the South African government deeming Māori players to be 'honorary whites'. Following the 1976 tour, 28 African nations boycotted the Olympic Games in protest. In 1981, Prime Minister Robert Muldoon, despite having endorsed the Gleneagles Agreement in which Commonwealth governments agreed to discourage sporting contact with South Africa, supported the New Zealand Rugby Union's decision to invite the Springboks to New Zealand.

The resulting protests have been described as 'a defining point in contemporary New Zealand history' (Lacey, 2015, p. 505). Continuing for 56 days, the demonstrations were widespread, involving groups such as students, women's groups, churches, sports clubs and trade unions joining anti-racist groups, such as HART (Halt All Racist Tours). The country was split roughly equally between supporters and protesters. But there were intersections with other threads of identity: protesters included more women, city dwellers and Labour Party supporters (Fougere, 1989). As photographer Marti Friedlander (2013) said, 'The tour gathered New Zealanders together as never before, but it also divided them' (p. 224). The level of protest and civic unrest, and the intensity of the police response, were unparalleled. But why? What was it about this event that polarised and galvanised such a response?

View Merata Mita's film *Patu!*: https://www.nzonscreen.com/title/patu-1983

On the surface, for protesters, it was about racism: welcoming a racially selected team was supporting apartheid. For tour supporters, it was about individual freedom: there was no place for politics in sport, and sportspeople should have the right to play who they wanted. But at a deeper level this was a protest about what it meant to be a New Zealander: were we a nation of rugby players and fans, or a nation that stood against injustice in the world? It was a protest, a dispute, about identity.

Two aspects of New Zealand identity were challenged: the role of sport, and rugby in particular, and our race relations. According to Fougere (1989), to understand the response to the tour, we have to understand how rugby has shaped our individual and national identity. Sport is central to New Zealand life and, although its central role in the national identity is waning, no sport is more central than rugby. Sport, through local, regional, franchise and national team support, enables a collective identity that can integrate and unify a diverse nation (ibid.). And rugby aligned well with New Zealand's masculine, frontier culture — a place of raw but controlled physical violence. Rugby enabled masculine friendship, and its appeal to all classes and ethnicities fitted well with the narrative of New Zealand as an egalitarian, classless society. (This idea is also explored by David in Chapter 9.) Rugby's strong link with the rural way of life, central to New Zealand's view of itself as a nation, was also critical (MacLean, 2003). Given these strong alignments between rugby and New Zealand identity, it is perhaps unsurprising that tour supporters saw the protests as a challenge to their way of life.

The second aspect of New Zealand identity central to the protests was what journalist Geoff Chapple (1984) has described as 'New Zealand's sublime secret' (p. 9): that despite our reputation and view of ourselves as a country with excellent race relations, this was not a nation with racial harmony and tolerance. According to the myth, it was particularly heinous for New Zealand, of all countries, to be supporting apartheid by welcoming the Springboks. In reality, however, the 1970s had seen a rapid increase in Māori protest, including the 1975 hīkoi — the Māori Land March — and the occupation of Bastion Point in 1977–78. Historical breaches of the Treaty of Waitangi were starting to be examined, and there was growing recognition of the impacts of colonisation and the embedded racism within New Zealand's political, economic and social structures (Pollock, 2004). For Māori, therefore, protesting against the tour was also about recognising and protesting about the problems closer to home. For Pākehā on both sides of the protest, the link the tour showed between black South Africans and Māori, coming at the end of a decade of challenges to our race relations, was a cause of anxiety (Pollock, 2004).

The tour and protests had wide-ranging consequences in terms of identity and citizenship. In an immediate sense, the protests were largely unsuccessful: except for the Hamilton match, the tour progressed until the end. But the impacts of the protests were far-reaching. Sociologist Geoffrey Fougere (1989) argues that it marked the end of rugby's role as the mirror of New Zealand society. However, the protests did not occur in isolation. This was a time of considerable social change in Aotearoa New Zealand. Historian Malcolm MacLean (2003) identifies three layers of political discontent: Māori land rights, feminism and dissatisfaction with the National Government. Fougere (1989) also points out that Britain joining the European Union had weakened New Zealand's colonial ties. These social movements, all issues of identity and citizenship, were illustrated and magnified by the tour, and ultimately meant that rugby and its values and practices were increasingly 'at odds with patterns newly emerging in New Zealand culture' (p. 120).

The protests also had an impact on race relations in New Zealand and South Africa. As part of the wider social movement challenging our race relations, the protests helped New Zealand recognise the myth of racial harmony and begin to address structural racism. Over the next few years, important changes included extending the jurisdiction of the Waitangi Tribunal, te reo Māori becoming an official language, and immigration laws emphasising skills rather than country of origin. In South Africa, the protests were a small part of the momentous change that occurred over the following decades, including the release from prison of Nelson Mandela in 1990 and the end of apartheid in 1994 with South Africa's first full vote. Leanne Pooley's (2006) excellent documentary *Try Revolution* portrays the tour from a South African perspective, and offers insight into its importance. In the words of Desmond Tutu, the black Anglican archbishop in South Africa who was a major figure in the anti-apartheid movement: 'You can't even compute its value, it said the world has not forgotten us, we are not alone'. It is a tragedy that the tour had to go ahead, with its accompanying division of New Zealand, for that profound message to be communicated.

A short extract from Leanne Pooley's documentary *Try Revolution* is available here: https://www.nzonscreen.com/title/try-revolution-2006

Digital protest

Large numbers of New Zealanders have been involved in the two case study events examined here. In the case of the Springbok Tour protests, other than talkback radio, protest actions were primarily physical — people gathering and marching in places of significance. The early stages of the gay protest movement were also largely physical, although more recent events have included greater elements of online protest. In this final section of the chapter, we come back to the first aim of the voices section of the book: understanding the different ways that people give voice. Advances in technology and changes in the social world mean that recent protests often have a different flavour, with voice being expressed through digital methods. In particular, digital media and social networking tools are seen as having considerable potential to engage youth in political and social issues (Tawhai, 2015). There is, however, considerable debate around digital activism. Here, I just touch on some of the key issues. Sy picks up this topic and adds more depth in Chapter 8 as part of his examination of digital places.

Digital protest is often described by such derogatory terms as 'clicktivism' or even 'slacktivism': 'feel good online activism that has zero political or social impact'

(Morozov, 2009). The strongest critics argue that it is not just an inferior form of activism, but that it is motivated by self-interest and instant gratification (Halupka, 2014). Actions such as 'liking' or 'sharing' a political post, changing a profile picture, or signing a digital petition can be seen as spontaneous reactions to content, rather than sustained and premeditated civic engagement. For instance, the Kony 2012 online activist campaign — featuring a video revealing the activities of Ugandan warlord Joseph Kony, leader of the Lord Resistance Army (LRA) — went viral, with the video viewed 100 million times in its first week. Despite this success, the associated physical protests were not well attended (Meikle, 2014).

Digital technologies do, however, enable different forms of activism. Alongside more traditional collective action, based on shared identities and membership of overarching organisations, an emerging alternative — termed 'connective action' — replaces those group ties with fluid social networks and activism that is personal and individualised (Bennett & Segerberg, 2012). Connective action has the scope to include a range of different personal reasons for protesting a situation, and relies in part on the use of digital tools to enable quick sharing through personal networks. There has been a proliferation of new tools of protest, including online petitions and blogs, and social networking tools such as Twitter and Facebook get messages out quickly to large numbers of people and groups. The speed and breadth of this communication can effect quick change. A recent, small-scale example of the impact of social networking was the inclusion of the Red Peak option in our flag choices in the 2015 referendum on flag change, the late inclusion driven by online protest.

As is often the case, it is not a matter of either physical *or* digital methods being best; street protest is also not without its critics. Rather, it is about people drawing on the strengths of both. Digital tools, used as part of a suite of tactics including traditional protest activities, can be valuable (Karpf, 2010). For example, the Black Lives Matter movement started as a social media hashtag in 2013, but has grown into a widespread community of activists who protest offline (Hunt, 2016). The balance must be right. One of the founders of that movement, Alicia Garza, has spoken out about the challenges of online protest alongside embodied protest, and the dangers of too much attention being given to the online conversation ahead of the real-world activism. The internet and the increasing use of digital tools have undoubtedly changed how people connect in order to raise their shared voices in protest. And, as with all change, this comes with both benefits and challenges.

 See this interesting debate in *The Guardian*: https://www.theguardian.com/commentisfree/2015/oct/10/debate-should-we-still-bother-with-street-protests-ed-vulliamy-anne-mcelvoy-air-france-cereal-killer

Conclusion

Protest, be it face-to-face or digital, is a critical form of participation, and an important right in a thriving democratic society. Freedom of expression and the right to peaceful assembly are enshrined in the New Zealand Bill of Rights Act 1990. Whether motivated by the rights accorded to a shared identity thread, as in the example of the gay rights movement, or by disagreement with a political event or action, as in the Springbok Tour example, protest is a way for groups of people to come together to join their voices and to effect change. Throughout history, various groups have struggled to have their voices heard through formal political channels. The two examples discussed here serve as illustrations of the importance of protest, the diverse motivations that drive protest, and the wide-ranging consequences, particularly in terms of identity. While linked to individual identity, protest is also a function of the socio-political context in which it occurs. Both the gay rights movement and the tour protests were part of a wider period of social change during which the New Zealand identity has evolved from a rural, rugby-playing, masculine culture to a more liberal and inclusive society, with a wider recognition of the importance of equality of rights and recognition for different identities.

Zeynep Tufekci (2014), a sociologist working in this field, argues that we need effective social movements to deal with the world's large social and ecological issues, but the movements need to move beyond large-scale, fast expression of voice — clicktivism — and instead focus on consensus decision-making to establish policy proposals that can effect real change. Tufekci ends her TED talk by highlighting new digital tools that can facilitate this process. One of these, Loomio, is a collaborative decision-making tool developed by social activists here in Aotearoa New Zealand. Loomio's byline is a fitting end to this topic: 'When we hear all voices, we make better decisions.'

Watch Zeynep Tufekci's TED talk here: https://www.ted.com/talks/zeynep_tufekci_how_the_internet_has_made_social_change_easy_to_organize_hard_to_win

Chapter 4 — Shout it out: Participation and protest in public life: http://turangawaewae.massey.ac.nz/chapter4.html

Recommended reading/viewing

Friedlander, M. (2013). *Self-portrait.* Auckland, New Zealand: Auckland University Press.

Guy, L. (2002). *Worlds in collision: The gay debate in New Zealand, 1960–1986.* Wellington, New Zealand: Victoria University Press.

Pollock, J. (2004). 'We don't want your racist tour': The 1981 Springbok Tour and the anxiety of settlement in Aotearoa/New Zealand. *Graduate Journal of Asia-Pacific Studies, 2*(1), 32–43.

Pooley, L. (Writer). (2006). *Try revolution* [Television documentary]. New Zealand: Spacific Films.

Watson, G. (2017). Sport and citizenship in New Zealand. In A. Brown & J. Griffiths (Eds.), *The citizen: Past and present* (pp. 197–221). Auckland, New Zealand: Massey University Press.

References

Altman, D. (1983). *The homosexualization of America: The Americanization of the homosexual.* Boston, IL: Beacon Press.

Anonymous. (2015). Muslim and gay: Seeking identity coherence in New Zealand. *Culture, Health & Sexuality, 18*(3), 280–293. doi:10.1080/13691058.2015.1079927

Baker, M., & Elizabeth, V. (2012). Second-class marriage? Civil union in New Zealand. *Journal of Comparative Family Studies, 43*(5), 633–645.

Bennett, W. L., & Segerberg, A. (2012). The logic of connective action. *Information, Communication and Society, 15*(5), 739–768. doi:10.1080/1369118X.2012.670661

Bill of Rights Act. (1990). Retrieved from http://www.legislation.govt.nz/act/public/1990/0109/latest/DLM224792.html website

Chapple, G. (1984). *1981: The tour.* Wellington, New Zealand: Reed.

Civil Union Act. (2004). Retrieved from http://www.legislation.govt.nz/act/public/2004/0102/latest/DLM323385.html website

Drury, J., Cocking, C., Beale, J., Hanson, C., & Rapley, F. (2005). The phenomenology of empowerment in collective action. *British Journal of Social Psychology, 44*(3), 309–328. doi:10.1348/014466604X18523

Dunstall, G. (1992). The social pattern. In G. W. Rice (Ed.), *The Oxford history of New Zealand* (2nd ed., pp. 451–481). Auckland, New Zealand: Oxford University Press.

Eder, J. (2016, June 16). Transgender student Stefani Muollo-Gray: I was told to use the boys' toilets. *The Marlborough Express.* Retrieved from www.stuff.co.nz

Fougere, G. (1989). Sport, culture and identity: The case of rugby football. In D. Novitz &

B. Willmott (Eds.), *Culture and identity in New Zealand* (pp. 110–122). Wellington, New Zealand: GP Books.

Friedlander, M. (2013). *Self-portrait*. Auckland, New Zealand: Auckland University Press.

Grey, S. (2015). Citizen engagement. In J. Hayward (Ed.), *New Zealand government and politics* (6th ed., pp. 496–498). Melbourne, Australia: Oxford University Press.

Guy, L. (2002). *Worlds in collision: The gay debate in New Zealand, 1960–1986*. Wellington, New Zealand: Victoria University Press.

Halupka, M. (2014). Clicktivism: A systematic heuristic. *Policy and Internet, 6*(2), 115–132. doi:10.1002/1944-2866.POI355

Hansen, D. A. (1968). Social institutions. In A. L. McLeod (Ed.), *The pattern of New Zealand culture* (pp. 49–67). Melbourne, Australia: Oxford University Press.

Human Rights Act. (1993). Retrieved from http://www.legislation.govt.nz/act/public/1993/0082/latest/DLM304475.html

Human Rights Commission. (2008). *To be who I am: Report of the inquiry into the discrimination experienced by transgender people*. Wellington, New Zealand: Human Rights Commission.

Hunt, E. (2016, September 2). Alicia Garza on the beauty and burden of Black Lives Matter. *The Guardian*. Retrieved from https://www.theguardian.com/us-news/2016/sep/02/alicia-garza-on-the-beauty-and-the-burden-of-black-lives-matter

Kaase, M. (2011). Participation. In B. Badie, D. Berg-Schlosser, & L. Morlino (Eds.), *International encyclopedia of political science* (pp. 1778–1789). Thousand Oaks, CA: Sage.

Karpf, D. (2010). Online political mobilization from the advocacy group's perspective: Looking beyond clicktivism. *Policy and Internet, 2*(4), 7–41. doi:10.2202/1944-2866.1098

Lacey, A. (2015). Activism and social movements. In J. Hayward (Ed.), *New Zealand government and politics* (6th ed., pp. 499–510). Melbourne, Australia: Oxford University Press.

MacLean, M. (2003). Making strange the country and making strange the countryside: Spatialized clashes in the affective economies of Aotearoa/New Zealand during the 1981 Springbok rugby tour. In M. Cronin & J. Bale (Eds.), *Sport and postcolonialism* (pp. 57–72). Oxford, England: Bloomsbury Publishing.

Marriage (Definition of Marriage) Amendment Act. (2013). Retrieved from www.legislation.govt.nz/act/public/2013/0020/latest/DLM4505003.html website

Marx, A. W. (1995). Contested citizenship: The dynamics of racial identity and social movements. *International Review of Social History, 40*, 159–183. doi:10.1017/S002085900011363X

Meikle, G. (2014). Social media, visibility, and activism: The Kony 2012 campaign.

In M. Ratto & M. Boler (Eds.), *DIY citizenship: Critical making and social media* (pp. 373–384). Cambridge, MA: MIT Press.

Morozov, E. (2009, May 19). The brave new world of slactivism. *Foreign Policy*. Retrieved from http://www.npr.org/templates/story/story.php?storyId=104302141 website

Parker, W. C. (2005). Teaching against idiocy. *Phi Delta Kappan, 5*, 344–351.

Polletta, F., & Jasper, J. M. (2001). Collective identity and social movements. *Annual Review of Sociology, 27*, 283–305. doi:10.1146/annurev.soc.27.1.283

Pollock, J. (2004). 'We don't want your racist tour': The 1981 Springbok Tour and the anxiety of settlement in Aotearoa/New Zealand. *Graduate Journal of Asia-Pacific Studies, 2*(1), 32–43.

Pooley, L. (Writer). (2006). *Try revolution* [Television documentary]. New Zealand: Spacific Films.

Roggeband, C., & Klandermans, B. (2010). Introduction. In B. Klandermans & C. Roggeband (Eds.), *Handbook of social movements across disciplines* (pp. 1–12). New York, NY: Springer.

Tawhai, V. M. H. (2015). Youth engagement. In J. Hayward (Ed.), *New Zealand government and politics* (6th ed., pp. 511–522). Melbourne, Australia: Oxford University Press.

Tufekci, Z. (2014, October). *Online social change: Easy to organise, hard to win.* Retrieved from https://www.ted.com/talks/zeynep_tufekci_how_the_internet_has_made_social_change_easy_to_organize_hard_to_win

van Stekelenburg, J., & Klandermans, B. (2013). The social psychology of protest. *Current Sociology, 61*(5–6), 886–905. doi:10.1177/0011392113479314

Yeoman, S. (2016, Feb 20). Protesters bring Pride Parade to a halt. *The New Zealand Herald.* Retrieved from http://www.nzherald.co.nz/nz/news/article.cfm?c_id=1&objectid=11592972

CHAPTER FIVE:

Express yourself
Voice through the arts

Trudie Cain

Introduction

At the time of writing, the Auckland Art Gallery Toi o Tāmaki was holding a photographic exhibition that tells the story of the 1981 Springbok Tour. It is a poignant collection of images from a number of photographers, each speaking to a powerful and defining moment in New Zealand's history. When I look at this collection, the recurring theme for me is the tension between the power of the collective and the complexity of the individual. Some of the photographs have been modified by adding text or colour — often used to represent blood — to otherwise black-and-white images. This serves to underline the extent to which the Springbok Tour was experienced by so many as a war zone, with fiercely held beliefs about what this country should stand for as a nation. When I first saw this exhibition, I already knew about the Springbok Tour. And yet these images made me reflect on the tour in a way that I hadn't before; these images spoke to me with a powerful, reverberating voice.

This chapter is the final chapter of three on what it means to have a voice in Aotearoa New Zealand. The preceding chapters have considered, first, the role of political participation and representation in ensuring that both individual and group interests are accounted for, and, second, how political protest can bring about social, political or economic change. In these two chapters, civic participation and political protest were introduced as key features of Aotearoa's political landscape with the power to amplify the voices of citizens. This chapter moves beyond the overtly political sphere, and considers instead how the arts might be used to ensure that the viewpoints, experiences and realities of those who might be marginalised, disenfranchised or otherwise silenced can be recognised.

But why do the arts even matter? Creative New Zealand, the government's arts funding agency, states (2016) that the arts 'contribute to New Zealand's economic, cultural and social well-being', and empirical research supports this claim. The arts are shown to improve individual health and wellbeing outcomes (Staricoff, 2004), rejuvenate cities (Markusen & Gadwa, 2010), support democracy and social inclusion (Stern & Seifert, 2010) and contribute a sense of belonging, connectedness and place (Hall & Robertson, 2001). The arts also contribute to the construction of individual, community and national identity (Pound, 2009; Johnson, 2005), and illuminate key issues facing contemporary society, fostering dialogue about those issues, and potentially contributing to social change (Clammer, 2015). Contemplating the United Kingdom without the arts, Arts Council chief Peter Bazalgette (2014) writes:

> Take the collective memory from our museums; remove the bands from our schools and choirs from our communities; lose the empathetic plays and dance from our theatres or the books from our libraries; expunge our festivals, literature and painting, and you're left with a society bereft of a national conversation . . . about its identity or anything else.

Undoubtedly, art is an important contributor to individual and collective identity, both here in Aotearoa New Zealand and elsewhere around the world. As such, in a book on identity and belonging in this country, it is vital that the arts' role is considered. In the remainder of this chapter, I work through three key ideas, providing case studies of each. First, I consider the power of the arts to represent and construct both national and individual identity. An example is provided of young female Bhutanese refugees shaping their ethnic and gendered identity through dance. Second, I discuss how art can challenge and contest dominant ideas and histories. I use Lynda Chanwai-Earle's play *Ka Shue* (*Letters Home*) to illustrate how creative practice can tell an alternative history of New Zealand's early Chinese settlers. Finally, I consider the community development and place-making role of the arts, and the way both formal and informal art can speak for a community. Christchurch's community-based initiative, Gap Filler, is used as an example.

Art and the shaping of identity

There is a wealth of scholarly literature outlining the role of the arts in shaping national identity (Pound, 2009; Johnson, 2005). New Zealand artists, particularly in the mid-twentieth century, often referenced the scale and grandeur of the New Zealand landscape, but in ways that are very distinct from other influential artists around the world. Colin McCahon's *Six Days in Nelson and Canterbury* is a good example. Rita Angus's *Cass* also features the South Island landscape, but underlines the sense of isolation and seclusion arguably associated with life in the most remote parts of the South Island. Literature produced around the same time also speaks to powerful imagery of Kiwi rugged masculinity that is grounded in an equally rugged New Zealand landscape (see, for example, John Mulgan's classic 1939 novel *Man Alone*). Although these works don't speak for all of our lives, especially those of us who live in New Zealand's cities, the narrative still resonates as uniquely New Zealand.

Many artists have drawn on both Māori and European influences to tell the story of New Zealand's place in the world. Shane Cotton (Ngāpuhi) has used a combination of European painting techniques and Māori symbolism to explore cultural identity and New Zealand's colonial past. And, over half a century ago, Gordon Walters created *Painting No. 1*, which brought together two strands of his cultural identity. The stylised koru motif was revisited throughout much of his career, and has since become an important reference point for the art world and a prominent symbol of biculturalism in Aotearoa. Interestingly, Walters — who was Pākehā — has received some criticism for appropriating Māori symbolism and using it out of context. Others, however, have applauded his use, suggesting instead that his work is an 'act of homage from the outside, so acknowledging the truth of his historical, ethnic and cultural circumstance' (Pound, 2009, p. 317).

These examples demonstrate the power of the arts to tell stories of national identity. They generate a collective voice of this place, and provide ways of thinking and talking about what it means to be a New Zealander. But we need to take care that this isn't overstated. These examples demonstrate that both art and artist raise important questions about culture, ethnic identity, power and voice. If art has the capacity to 'unify the nation, to construct it as one place' (Bell, 2011, p. 91), questions must always be asked about whose version of unified place is being represented.

Expressing oneself creatively also provides an opportunity for exploring and constructing individual identity. At a psychological level, the arts have therapeutic benefits, providing a way to 'further a person's emotional growth, self-esteem, psychological and social integration ... provid[ing] the basis for self-understanding'

(Edwards, 2014, pp. 7, 12). Ultimately, the arts provide a vehicle for thinking about, and shaping, a sense of identity, belonging and citizenship.

Constructing identity through performance — a case study

The arts are used to both represent identity and construct identity. In the following, I provide an example of four women engaging with a creative process and performance to construct ethnic and gendered identity. In 2014, then Massey University student Jessica Halley carried out a research project aimed at better understanding the experiences of Bhutanese refugees who had settled in Palmerston North. Refugees first began to arrive in Aotearoa from Bhutan in 2008 as part of New Zealand's agreement with the United Nations High Commissioner for Refugees. The New Zealand government recognised that very specific settlement support was necessary for recently arrived refugees — who, unlike migrants, had not chosen to leave their homeland — and developed strategies to ensure that:

> Refugees are participating fully and integrated socially and economically as
> soon as possible so that they are living independently, undertaking the same
> responsibilities and exercising the same rights as other New Zealanders
> and have a strong sense of belonging to their own community and to New
> Zealand. (Labour and Immigration Research Centre, 2013, p. 122)

Developing a sense of identity, belonging and citizenship with this country is clearly underlined in the strategic document. However, many refugees arrive in New Zealand having faced extreme hostility, hardship and, in some cases, brutality in their home country. Most have also had to leave behind family members, often in uncertain political environments. Although refugees' experiences are varied, they often share specific settlement challenges, most notably 'communication difficulties, using money and modern technologies, lack of transportation, and feelings of loneliness and isolation' (Ferguson, 2011, p. vi). Material needs relating to employment and housing (Nash, Wong, & Trlin, 2006) and finding appropriate primary healthcare services can also prove challenging (Lawrence & Kearns, 2005). Many refugees do not have the economic, social and cultural capital to support themselves and their families as they settle, and there is evidence to suggest that refugees often 'join the poor and oppressed in an ongoing struggle for genuine inclusion and participation in order to exercise their civic rights as well as duties' (Nash, Wong, & Trlin, 2006, p. 345). These very specific and very real difficulties can be overlooked by policy and service delivery agencies, leaving some refugees multiply marginalised or

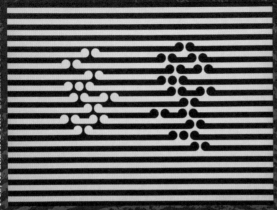

Art with multicultural roots

Gordon Walters was born in Wellington in 1919. Between 1935 and 1939 he trained and worked as a commercial artist, and studied part-time at the art department of Wellington Technical College. In 1941 he met Theo Schoon, an Indonesian-born Dutch artist and photographer who encouraged his growing interest in the abstraction of painters Paul Klee, Joan Miró, Jean Arp and Piet Mondrian. In 1946 he paid a visit to Schoon, who was in South Canterbury recording Māori rock art near the Opihi River. This encouraged Walters to introduce ideas and motifs from indigenous art into his own work. By 1956 Walters was experimenting with the koru motif, a curving bulb-like form on a stem found in moko (tattoo) and kōwhaiwhai (rafter painting). He looked at the paintings of Giuseppe Capogrossi and Victor Vasarely to provide guidelines for making a series of compositions limited to a few formal elements. By 1958–59 he had evolved his own version of the koru as a geometric motif in which positive and negative elements mirror one another in a taut dynamic relationship.

By 1964 he was making large paintings in PVA (polyvinyl acetate) and acrylic media, the first of which was entitled *Te Whiti*. This work in dramatic black and white contrast was executed on hardboard in a style of uncompromising hard-edged abstraction never seen before in New Zealand. It was the first of a series of paintings restricted to the koru motif and a few geometric forms such as the triangle and circle. The painting above is entitled *Painting No. 1* and was completed in 1965.

By using Māori titles, Walters acknowledged the inspiration he received from the koru and related motifs such as rauponga. He created a new kind of painting in which Māori motifs and European abstract painting were drawn together. He was criticised in the 1980s for appropriating these motifs, but Walters himself saw it as a positive response to being an artist with bicultural roots. ABRIDGED FROM silenced as they attempt to forge a life for themselves in New Zealand.

This is important social and political context for understanding Halley's (2014) research, a vital aspect of which focused on how four young refugee sisters negotiated the 'performative process of "growing up" in a new country' (p. ii). Halley spent many hours with the young women, talking with them about their experiences. During this time, she recorded on her phone a dance they performed (with a friend) at a Bhutanese cultural festival.

 Watch the performance at the Bhutanese cultural festival here: http://www.youtube.com/watch?v=3oQj7QlSlfU&feature= youtu.be

The performance is helpful for thinking about voice, identity and belonging. It provided an opportunity for the young women to negotiate complex understandings of their ethnic and gendered identity. Like many young women living in New Zealand (whether they were born here or not), they appreciate American hip-hop. But the fusion of Bollywood music and dance in their performance simultaneously references their love of the Bollywood films they watched while living in the Bhutanese refugee camp. By bringing these two aspects of their life together in this performance, the women bridge their past and present lives, creating what might be described by Jonathan Rutherford (1990) as a *hybrid* identity — a new ethnic identity that emerges from belonging in both worlds.

The performance is also an active construction of their gendered identity in a Western context. In the introduction, Ella wrote about the cultural norms that shape identity. Bhutan has very specific and restrictive ideas about how women should act in public places. In the performance, however, we see the women challenge these restrictions and, instead, embrace Western norms that are far more permissive and, at times, overtly sexualised. The women 'play' with their gendered identity by borrowing from contemporary music videos and celebrity culture, and creatively expressing themselves in a way that reflects their new life in New Zealand. Indeed, the young women consider their performance an expression of empowered feminist identity, in that they demonstrate a positive relationship with their bodies, and they take control over how their bodies might be viewed by others.

One of the key ideas of this book is that identity (ethnic, gendered or otherwise) is constructed through interactions with others, and that many of these encounters are not benign. Rather, they are embedded within relations of power that determine who might be included or excluded, and to what effect. What might it mean to participate within a given community, such as the Bhutanese refugee community in Palmerston North? The performance is located in a network of relationships, including those with other young Bhutanese refugees, their Bhutanese family and friends, and perhaps others who were born locally. Throughout the performance, it is possible to hear the applause, cheers and encouragement from other young people in the audience. As Jessica explained to me, however, what it is not possible to detect in the recording is the silence of the Bhutanese community elders. The women's performance challenges Bhutanese tradition and embraces Western ideals, and, in doing so, contributes to a generational and cultural divide within the community. The women's desire to embrace New Zealand life, and all that it entails for the young people who live here, creates enormous tension within the Bhutanese community.

In all likelihood, this performance is very similar to many others that have taken place across New Zealand — young women embodying and embracing the influences of pop culture icons. What makes this performance different is that it speaks to the power of creative expression to craft a new identity that makes sense of a complex set of experiences both in New Zealand and elsewhere. Through this performance, the women try out new identities to make sense of who they are in a new place. In doing so, they highlight the fluidity of identity — identity is always changing — and the extent to which identity is shaped by the social, cultural and temporal context in which we find ourselves. What we see in this performance is the active construction and reconstruction of identity: young women embracing artistic expression as a way of making sense of their past and present lives, and their newly emerging ethnic and gendered identity in this particular time and place.

Contestation and the arts

A recurring theme throughout this book (and this section in particular) is that having a voice is rarely natural or inevitable; many people resident in New Zealand do not feel that they have a legitimate place from which to speak and be heard. People or groups are socially, culturally and politically excluded on the basis of a range of identity threads, including ethnicity, sexuality, body size and ability, gender and class. When you are different from the 'norm', it can be difficult to ensure that your experience and viewpoint are accounted for. In the preceding chapter, Ella considered political protest as a form of voice. Here, I consider how the arts might also be used as a form of protest that ensures the dissenting voices of this country are heard.

New Zealand has a history of using the arts to challenge ideas, and speak up and speak out against social and political injustices. For example, *The Power of Community* was part of a 2013 global initiative called *Inside Out: The people's art project*.

 The photos of Christchurch children taken after the earthquake for Inside Out are here: http://www.insideoutproject.net/en

The project featured a series of black-and-white photographs of children who attended a Brighton, Christchurch, school prior to the Canterbury earthquakes. The collection of photographs, which were pasted on the streets of Christchurch, was about challenging the government to keep their school — the place they considered the centre of their community — open after it was threatened with closure. While this collection of photographs has the power to speak for a local community that is geographically located, the unapologetically feminist photography of New Zealand-born artist Alexis Hunter speaks for the broader community of women. Her subversive collection of photographs, titled *The Model's Revenge*, examines and critiques the politics of gender and sexuality.

Other examples of art activism include the poetry of Brian Turner, who has written of the degradation of New Zealand's environment (see, for example, 'River Wind'), and a piece of art provocatively titled *Tuhoe Never Signed the Fucking Treaty*, which was collectively created by 'Concerned Citizens', a group of artists in support of Tūhoe activists. Perhaps one of the most well-known protest art works is Ralph Hotere's painting *Vive Aramoana*, which was created in the early 1980s as part of the protest movement to stop an aluminium smelter being built at the entrance to Otago Harbour. The work sold in 2012 for $183,000, arguably demonstrating its 'lasting voice and presence' (Booth, 2013). Undoubtedly, the arts have been used to raise political consciousness, foster dialogue about contemporary issues, and promote social change, especially in support of those who are disenfranchised (Clammer, 2015; Beasley & Hager, 2014).

Some art revisits history and ensures we do not forget. During the Anzac 100-year commemorations in 2016, a series of sculptures appeared across Wellington's central city. The sculptures were installed by 'guerrilla artists' thought to be associated with Peace Action Wellington. They depicted New Zealand's most well-known conscientious objector, Archibald Baxter. During the First World War, Baxter was among a number of soldiers who refused to fight and was consequently punished by

River Wind

The wind may let us down,
but it never fails. The wind
carries dark clouds
on its shoulders and totters down
from the mountains.

And there comes a time
when all hills are mountains. Now is the time.
If rain is to fall
let it fall gently on the shoulders of the mountains,
and let it run quietly
and quickly
into the river that feels the light in the sky
and prizes the light.

Instinctively
you know what the river is saying
without being told. You hear
what the river is singing
without knowing the words
to the song. You know where
the river is going
and that it doesn't know
what you know, that it tempts you
to envy
and the feeling returns and returns.

BRIAN TURNER. PUBLISHED IN *ELEMENTAL:
CENTRAL OTAGO POEMS*. GODWIT, 2012.

being tied for long periods in the 'field punishment No. 1' position, including on the Western Front. The sculptures were designed to challenge what the artists viewed as the 'romanticisation of war and the militarisation of Anzac Day', and they certainly achieved great interest and media attention during the time of their installation. (Rhys and Carl discuss the political stance of conscientious objectors in greater detail in Chapter 11.) Interestingly, Wellington City Council was not in a hurry to remove the sculptures. A council spokesperson at the time stated: 'Wellington is a political and creative city and we are not in the business of stifling political expression. We'll make sure the sculptures are secure and we'll seek discussions with Peace Action Wellington about their future' (Hunt, 2016).

People who were interviewed by media during this time reported finding the installations a powerful reminder of the atrocities and complexities of war. The installations certainly started a conversation about New Zealand's war history. But they also bridged the past with the present, encouraging people to reflect on New Zealand's current contributions to war.

The arts are clearly important for contesting how New Zealand is and how it ought to be. While protest art, sometimes referred to as 'artivism', is a powerful example of how this operates, other examples are not as overt. The following case study provides an example of the arts — in this case, theatre — being used to tell an alternative version of New Zealand history.

Contesting history through theatre — a case study

The first wave of Chinese immigrants to New Zealand arrived mostly from the Guangdong province following an invitation from the Otago goldmining region. In 1871, the number of Chinese living in the region peaked at 4300 (mostly men). Amid concerns expressed by local residents about the increasing Chinese population, the Chinese Immigrants Act was passed by Parliament in 1881. The Act imposed a poll tax of £10 (approximately $1640 in today's currency) on Chinese immigrants, and limited the number of Chinese passengers permitted to land in the country to just one passenger for every 10 tonnes of a vessel's cargo. In 1896, the tax was increased to £100, and the ratio of Chinese immigrants to cargo increased to one person for every 200 tonnes of cargo (Ip, 2015). In addition, Chinese arrivals were subject to literacy tests and thumb-printing, and were denied the right to naturalisation and access to social welfare benefits. Most, too, were ineligible to vote in national elections. In sum, Chinese migrants were considered 'undesirable aliens' (Ip & Pang, 2005, p. 177).

Without doubt, the poll tax was discriminatory; no other ethnic group was subjected to the same treatment. From 1934 the poll tax was waived, but it was not officially repealed until 1944, after other countries had abandoned similar discriminatory practices. And it was not until 2002 that the prime minister, Helen Clark, offered an official apology to the Chinese community for the suffering caused. Despite contributing to the economic and social fabric of the region, and the country more broadly, these early immigrants to New Zealand had no voice. They were socially silenced through the extreme hardship, harassment and discrimination they often faced from non-Chinese goldminers, who did not appreciate the competition. Their physical isolation on the margins of European settlements further exacerbated their social silencing. With most ineligible to vote, they were also politically silenced.

Although there are many historical accounts of the Chinese poll tax, these accounts do little to depict the long-term emotional and material implications of such a policy. Many descendants of the poll tax have shared familial stories *within* the Chinese community. Although vital to a Chinese–New Zealander identity-building project, this kind of storytelling fails to contribute to a wider understanding of the impact of the poll tax on Chinese and national identity, but in 1996, playwright Lynda Chanwai-Earle wrote a play titled *Ka Shue (Letters Home)*. The play was created to give voice to the political, social and cultural aspects of this largely untold story. In the playwright's note that precedes the written text of the play, the author writes:

> I am Eurasian by ethnicity, a fourth generation New Zealander. I am also a descendant of the 'Poll Tax'. Based on the Chinese side of my family (the Dong clan of Bak-Chuen), *Ka Shue* uncovers some of the last 150 years of a buried history in New Zealand. There has been a noticeable absence of a Chinese voice in this country. (Chanwai-Earle, 2003, p. 46)

In these words the author clearly articulates her familial and ethnic identity, and the historical context that has shaped those identities; it is from her understanding of who she is as a Chinese–New Zealander descended from poll tax immigrants that she is able to write this play and bring to the surface the 'buried history'.

The play tells the story of a single family across three generations, and weaves together individual and familial identities, locating them in specific historical encounters and contexts (in addition to the Chinese poll tax, Tiananmen Square also plays a pivotal role). It is multi-lingual, employing a mix of Mandarin, Cantonese and English, which illustrates the challenges of straddling linguistic, class and cultural boundaries as a migrant. The play captures in performance the myriad ways in which identity in the present is grounded in very specific historical events in the past. It

A cruel punishment

In 2016 sculptures of conscientious objectors, including Archibald Baxter, were erected in Wellington by the organisation Peace Action. Baxter was one of over 2000 New Zealanders who resisted conscription following its introduction in October 1916. Baxter was a Christian socialist and committed pacifist, but these were not grounds for avoidance of service. Along with 272 others, he was imprisoned. It was then decided to send 14 resisters overseas for service. Baxter continued to resist, and in the company of two others he suffered field punishment No. 1 in October 1917. The men were tied to a post in the open with their hands bound tightly behind their backs for up to four hours in all weathers. The poles were tipped forward, and the ropes cut into the flesh, cutting off blood flow. This painful experience did not break Baxter's determination that he would not assist the war, and he was finally sent home in August 1918, one of only two men to resist service until the end. Baxter described his experiences in a classic account, *We Will Not Cease*. ABRIDGED FROM TE ARA — THE ENCYCLOPEDIA OF NEW ZEALAND was first performed in 1996, a time that was marked by anti-immigration sentiment, resulting in a perceived threat of New Zealand's 'asianisation' (Chung, 2014, p. 178). This timing underlines further the extent to which ethnic identity is constructed in particular political, historical and social contexts.

Through writing and theatre, Chanwai-Earle's work placed Chinese identity firmly in the public arena. It told a very New Zealand story that had previously not been told, and it did so in a way that was accessible to both Chinese and non-Chinese audiences. This was a human story that was both personal and political in the way it depicted how historical moments of racial discrimination continue to be realised in the present. However, it is not only a play about Chinese identity. It is also a play about national identity, in the way it fundamentally challenges the perception that New Zealand is an egalitarian society where every citizen is treated equally and provided with the same opportunities. (David considers this idea in Chapter 9.) As such, *Ka Shue* (*Letters Home*) demands audiences think critically about what it means to be a New Zealander in such a diverse country.

This example uses theatre to tell a story of the Chinese poll tax that moves beyond an historical account and seeks instead to capture the profound long-term implications of this moment in New Zealand's past. It tells the story of how people are silenced, and how the arts have played a role in representing their collective stories and ensuring that their voices are heard. In the play (and its performance to a large, diverse audience), history is rewritten, and identity is articulated as a fluid concept that is grounded in particular socio-historical contexts and encounters.

Place-making, community development and the arts

'Place-making' is a term used in the social sciences to describe the ways in which people consciously engage in activities to make places meaningful to them. The term is also used to describe the range of activities undertaken by planners, designers and managers of public spaces in order to produce places that meet the cultural, economic, social and ecological needs and preferences of specific groups of people.

The arts are a vital feature of healthy and connected communities; art contributes to a sense of belonging, connectedness and place (Hall & Robertson, 2001; Pollock & Paddison, 2014). The next part of this book considers place explicitly, but I want to briefly introduce place here, because the arts play such an important role in supporting place-making in both formal and informal ways. Formalised art includes commissioned public art, such as Max Patté's *Solace in the Wind* in Wellington (also known informally as 'The leaning man'), and Michael Parekowhai's *Lighthouse* on Queens Wharf in Auckland (also known as 'The state house'). The 'nicknames' are indicative of the familiarity and connection residents develop with the works and, irrespective of whether we like or approve of the art, both of these pieces are uniquely New Zealand. While Patté's work speaks to Wellington's reputation as the 'windy city', Parekowhai's work references the heritage of state housing in New Zealand.

Cultural festivals such as Matariki, Diwali, Pasifika and the Chinese Lantern Festival perform an important role in promoting and celebrating ethnic diversity and in negotiating identity and belonging in Aotearoa. Writing about the origins of the Pasifika Festival, Jared Mackley-Crump (2016a) argued that 'Pasifika festivals are highly public community events, in which diverse displays of material culture are offered up for consumption by both cultural tourists and Pacific communities alike' (pp. 33–34). This is an important point. Cultural festivals create opportunities to perform identity to multicultural audiences (Mackley-Crump, 2016b), but they also help to create strong, inclusive and cohesive communities (Laing & Mair, 2015). These kinds of events are important features of New Zealand's place-making, and provide a platform for telling our richly diverse ethnic and cultural stories.

Alongside formal arts-based events, such as art installations and cultural festivals, there are many informal initiatives. Informal arts include: street performers who might busk, dance or throw fire in some of New Zealand's larger cities; guerrilla knitters, also referred to as 'yarn bombers', who personalise, beautify or reclaim public places (Farinosi & Fortunati, 2013); or graffiti artists who respond to the existing built environment, creating more interesting, political and engaging public spaces. Such forms of artistic expression are important contributors to the vitality, sociality and conviviality of street life (Simpson, 2011).

Of course, informal and formal expressions of art are not created equally; they are embedded within relations of power that legitimate their presence in public places. Informal expressions of art are constrained, for example, by by-laws that govern what can and can't be done in a public space, and formal expressions of art are often the result of arts committees and local government determining what art and which artists will represent a given community. While I have argued that the arts provide a voice for those citizens who might be marginalised or excluded, the social, political and economic context will always shape the way a voice might be heard.

Regional place-making — a case study

An interesting case study with regard to place-making and voice is the community initiative Gap Filler in Christchurch. The devastating earthquake of 22 February 2011 left the inner city empty and bereft, as people deserted the city and its remnants of

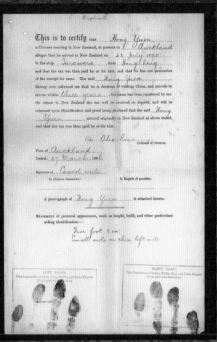

Discrimination by tax

The poll tax was a cruel imposition on the few Chinese who wished to settle in New Zealand. The image above is of a receipt of Hong Yuen's poll tax document, from one of the many poll tax books which are housed by Archives New Zealand. Along with the name of the immigrant, most receipts contain a formal photograph or fingerprints, their age, place of origin, the date they were receipted and the name of the ship on which they arrived.

Pasifika celebrates

The first Pasifika Festival was held in Auckland in 1992, and it is now one of the largest annual events in the Auckland area. It includes a fashion show, theatre performances, concerts, stalls, competitions and many other activities. Pasifika attracts over 225,000 visitors and encompasses the majority of Pacific cultures, including Samoan, Cook Islands, Fijian, Hawaiian, Niuean, Tahitian and Tongan.

buildings. As the Canterbury Earthquake Recovery Authority (CERA) concentrated on co-ordinating response and recovery efforts, others concentrated on filling the gap created by the exodus. Gap Filler was born from a belief that the citizens of Christchurch desperately needed to come together and socialise in *their city* — a city that was now barely recognisable to them. The initiative began with the creation of a gathering space that could host a temporary garden café, pétanque, live music, poetry readings and an outdoor cinema (Gap Filler, 2016). The gathering space was no more than a small block of land in the middle of Colombo Street, with some fake grass and a few pieces of furniture. But in creating this place, the gap was filled with social connection, fun and a sense of community. Since then, more than 70 events or installations have been created across Christchurch, each designed to contribute to a sense of community, ranging from a Dance-O-Mat to a book exchange.

 Follow the link to see the kind of work Gap Filler does in the community: http://www.gapfiller.org.nz/

The plans for the Christchurch rebuild are impressive. Shiny brochures with high-production values and high-tech promotional videos illustrate the various zones that are intended for central Christchurch: zones for eating, zones for shopping, and zones for doing business, for example. But when I see the plans I don't feel anything. And feeling — feeling connected, feeling a sense of belonging, feeling part of the community — is an important part of living in a community, a part that the Gap Filler contributors clearly understand. American anthropologist Dorinne Kondo (1995) writes that the arts engage all the senses, 'producing a more visceral impact than does textual prose and hence eliciting greater intellectual/emotional response' (p. 62). To put this simply, art helps us to get out of our thinking minds and into our feeling bodies. The grass-roots, collaborative and creative foundation of Gap Filler is the key to its success. Although its organic charm sits uneasily alongside the orderly gloss of the official city plan (the film *The Art of Recovery* captures beautifully the tension between the city's economic and community development), the initiative is about Christchurch citizens actively creating the kind of place they want to live. Without doubt, this initiative is about identity, belonging and place-making.

 You can watch a trailer of the documentary *The Art of Recovery* here: http://artofrecoveryfilm.com/

Conclusion

The arts provide a powerful voice for the nation, for communities and for individuals. Art serves as a nation-building project, telling a unique story of this land and the people who live here. Art serves as a community-building project, with artists using creative expression and action to generate communities and neighbourhoods that are designed for the people who want to live, work and play there. And art serves as a self-building project, offering possibilities for the expression, representation and construction of individual identity.

The arts are used in countless ways to tell the many diverse stories of this country. In doing so, creative practice provides a voice for those who are silenced, whether they are socially silenced through discriminatory practices, or politically silenced through inadequate representation in the political sphere; art can tell their stories in powerful and authoritative ways. The arts are perfectly positioned to contest and challenge dominant ideas about this land, or revisit limited and reductionist histories that offer only a partial historical truth. Although the arts cannot stand in for political representation and participation, artivism speaks an alternative truth from beyond the edges of mainstream society that can reach people in ways that support, challenge and complicate identity, culture and belonging in Aotearoa New Zealand.

 Chapter 5 — Express yourself: Voice through the arts: http://turangawaewae.massey.ac.nz/chapter5.html

Recommended reading

Hall, T., & Robertson, I. (2001). Public art and urban regeneration: Advocacy, claims and critical debates. *Landscape Research, 26*(1), 5–26. doi: 10.1080/01426390120024457

Johnson, H. (2005). Dancing with lions: (Per)forming Chinese cultural identity at a New Zealand secondary school. *New Zealand Journal of Asian Studies, 7*(2), 171–186.

Mackley-Crump, J. (2016a). *The Pacific festivals of Aotearoa New Zealand: Negotiating place and identity in a new homeland* [e-book]. Honolulu, HI: University of Hawaii Press.

Pound, F. (2009). *The invention of New Zealand: Art and national identity, 1930–1970.* Auckland, New Zealand: Auckland University Press.

Filling the gap

Gap Filler was initially formed in response to the September 2010 earthquake
in Christchurch, then expanded after the February 2011 quake. It is supported
by the Gap Filler Trust and is a registered charity. Its first project ran from late
November until early December 2010, transforming an empty site on Colombo
Street into a temporary garden café, with pétanque, live music, poetry readings,
outdoor cinema and more. The project was incredibly well-received and utilised,
leading to further projects including art installations, concerts, workshop spaces
and eventually semi-permanent structures such as the Pallet Pavilion, RAD Bikes
and the Dance-O-Mat (shown above). Gap Filler continues to operate, describing
itself as 'a creative urban regeneration initiative that facilitates a wide range of
temporary projects, events, installations and amenities in the city. These short-
term and comparatively small-scale projects are far less risky than new permanent
developments — and consequently open up opportunities for experimentation:
trying new ideas, pushing social boundaries, adopting participatory processes to
get everyday people involved in creating their city. Working with local community
groups, artists, architects, landowners, librarians, designers, students, engineers,
dancers — anyone with an idea and initiative — they activate city spaces for
temporary, creative, people-centred purposes.

'By recycling materials, teaming up with suppliers, harnessing volunteer power
and being creative, Gap Filler proves that the regeneration of the city does not
rely solely on large-scale developments by the private or public sectors. Great
things can be achieved with community power and resourcefulness; we can be
flexible and swift in adapting to our changing city, meaning our projects will
always provide contemporary reflection on the state of society.' ABRIDGED FROM
GAPFILLER.ORG.NZ

References

Bazalgette, P. (2014, April 27). *We have to recognise the huge value of arts and culture to society*. Retrieved from https://www.theguardian.com/culture/2014/apr/27/value-of-arts-and-culture-to-society-peter-bazalgette

Beasley, M. M., & Hager, P. M. (2014). Intervention, instigation, interruption: Art, activism, and social policy. *Journal of Poverty, 18*, 1–4.

Bell, A. (2011). That strange fissure opened by discovery/invention: The invention of New Zealand in art. *New Zealand Sociology, 26*(2), 88–102.

Booth, C. (2013, January 23). *Art speaks action*. Retreived from https://artspeaksaction.wordpress.com/page/2/

Chanwai-Earle, L. (2003). *Ka-shue* (letters home). *Manoa, 15*(1), 46–69.

Chung, H. (2014). Chineseness in (a) New Zealand life: Lynda Chanwai-Earle. *New Zealand Journal of Asian Studies, 16*(2), 173–194.

Clammer, J. (2015). *Art, culture and international development: Humanizing social transformation*. New York, NY: Routledge.

Creative New Zealand. (2016). *The evidence to support your advocacy*. Retrieved from http://www.creativenz.govt.nz/

Edwards, D. (2014). *Art therapy: Creative therapies in practice* (2nd ed.). London, England: Sage.

Farinosi, M., & Fortunati, L. (2013). A new fashion: Dressing up the cities. *Textile: The Journal of Cloth and Culture, 11*(3), 282–299.

Ferguson, B. (2011). *The Bhutanese refugee resettlement journey: Settlement*. Wellington, New Zealand: Ministry of Business, Innovation and Employment.

Gap Filler. (2016). *Gap Filler*. Retrieved from http://gapfiller.org.nz/

Hall, T., & Robertson, I. (2001). Public art and urban regeneration: Advocacy, claims and critical debates. *Landscape Research, 26*(1), 5–26. doi: 10.1080/01426390120024457

Halley, J. (2014). *Performing identities on Facebook: Young Bhutanese women becoming 'kiwi'* (Unpublished dissertation). Massey University, Palmerston North, New Zealand.

Hunt, T. (2016, April 26). *Conscientious objector Archie Baxter remembered in guerrilla sculpture*. Retrieved from http://www.stuff.co.nz/national/last-post-first-light/79299545/Conscientious-objector-Archie-Baxter-remembered-in-guerrilla-sculpture

Ip, M. (2015, February 8). Chinese: Recent developments. In *Te Ara: The Encyclopedia of New Zealand*. Retrieved from http://www.teara.govt.nz/en/chinese/page-1

Ip, M., & Pang, D. (2005). New Zealand Chinese identity: Sojourners, model minority and multiple identities. In J. Liu, T. McCreanor, T. McIntosh, & T. Teaiwa (Eds.), *New Zealand identities: Departures and destinations* (pp. 174–190). Wellington, New Zealand: Victoria University Press.

Johnson, H. (2005). Dancing with lions: (Per)forming Chinese cultural identity at a New Zealand secondary school. *New Zealand Journal of Asian Studies, 7*(2), 171–186.

Kondo, D. (1995). Bad girls: Theatre, women of color, and the politics of representation. In R. Behar & D. A. Gordan (Eds.), *Women: Writing culture* (pp. 49–64). Berkeley CA: University of California Press.

Labour and Immigration Research Centre. (2013). *New land, new life: Long-term settlement of refugees in New Zealand* (Main Report). Wellington, New Zealand: Ministry of Business, Innovation and Employment.

Laing, J., & Mair, J. (2015). Music festivals and social inclusion: The festival organizers' perspective. *Leisure Sciences, 37*(3), 252–268.

Lawrence, J., & Kearns, R. (2005). Exploring the 'fit' between people and providers: Refugee health needs and health care services in Mt Roskill, Auckland, New Zealand. *Health and Social Care in the Community, 13*(5), 451–461.

Mackley-Crump, J. (2016a). *The Pacific festivals of Aotearoa New Zealand: Negotiating place and identity in a new homeland* [e-book]. Honolulu, HI: University of Hawaii Press.

Mackley-Crump, J. (2016b). From private performance to the public stage: Reconsidering 'staged authenticity' and 'traditional' performances at the Pasifika Festival. *Anthropological Forum, 26*(2), 155–176.

Markusen, A., & Gadwa, A. (2010). *Creative place-making* (White Paper). Washington, NY: National Endowment for the Arts.

Nash, M., Wong, J., & Trlin, A. (2006). Civic and social integration: A new field of social work practice with immigrants, refugees and asylum seekers. *International Social Work, 49*(3), 345–363.

Pollock, V. L., & Paddison, R. (2014). On place-making, participation and public art: The Gorbals, Glasgow. *Journal of Urbanism, 7*(1), 85–105.

Pound, F. (2009). *The invention of New Zealand: Art and national identity, 1930–1970.* Auckland, New Zealand: Auckland University Press.

Rutherford, J. (1990). The third space: Interview with Homi Bhabha. *Identity, community, culture, difference* (pp. 207–221). London, England: Lawrence & Wishart.

Simpson, P. (2011). Street performance and the city: Public space, sociality, and intervening in the everyday. *Space and Culture, 14*, 415–430.

Staricoff, R. L. (2004). *Arts in health: A review of the medical literature* (Research report 36). London, England: Arts Council England.

Stern, M. J., & Seifert, S. C. (2010). *Arts-based social inclusion: An investigation of existing assets and innovative strategies to engage immigrant communities in Philadelphia.* Philadelphia, PA: William Penn Foundation.

PART THREE: PLACES IN AOTEAROA NEW ZEALAND

Places: Introduction

Trudie Cain and
Juliana Mansvelt

The title of this book is *Tūrangawaewae: Identity and belonging in Aotearoa New Zealand*. As Te Rina, Margaret and Veronica discussed in Chapter 2, 'tūrangawaewae' means 'one's sacred or special place of belonging', and as such we ask those who read this book to reflect on the place on which they stand, whether it is here in Aotearoa New Zealand or elsewhere. The first two parts of this book support such an endeavour: Part 1 considered the identities of the people who live here, and Part 2 explored how voice might be expressed in different ways and in different contexts. A key theme running through these sections was that identity threads shape experience in multiple and powerful ways. This third section of the book is titled 'Places in Aotearoa New Zealand', and considers more explicitly how identity might be shaped by the places we inhabit and the people we might encounter, and, conversely, how places might be informed by the people who inhabit them.

About Part 3

Human geographers define 'place' as a space which is given social meaning by human activity and/or imagination. With this fairly all-encompassing definition as a starting point, it is easy to see how places provide the contexts through which the sociality and materiality of life manifests. Places are a key source of belonging and identity as sites of inclusion, security, comfort, freedom, and material and social wellbeing. But they are also sites of exclusion, marginalisation, alienation, fear and anxiety. Relatedly, places are where the communities to which we belong (or to which we aspire) come together to address matters of mutual concern; and equally, they can provide a refuge (or a place of disengagement) from such collective interactions. Undoubtedly, place matters.

One of the most powerful ways of creating a sense of place is through shared understandings of the conventions and norms enacted *in situ*. Conventions can be thought of as typical or common ways of interacting in a given place. For example, it is fairly accepted and conventional that in a dining room we might eat, read at the table, drink coffee, or chat with friends. But sometimes conventions become norms which comprise the traditions, customs and practices that govern behaviour. Norms might include queuing to be served at the supermarket rather than pushing in, and not talking on your phone at the movies, although it is important to note that norms and rules may vary across cultures, time and place. Although some norms are explicit, they are often based on tacit knowledge which is learned through experience. This means that those who are unfamiliar with a place may find themselves experiencing discomfort, unease or even censure or punishment if they behave in a way that is beyond the norm. Norms tend to be associated with moral values, and are powerful because they become indicative of how people *ought* to behave in a given place.

The idea that norms dictate behaviour is important, because it underlines the ways in which power is embedded in place. There is a tendency to think of places as neutral, but they rarely are, because how they are structured, organised and understood influences the social relationships and encounters that might occur. Some places — private gyms and golf clubs, for example — are quite literally exclusive, and have restrictions about access and participation. Importantly, inclusion and exclusion often reflect specific identity threads, such as being of a certain age or gender, or having the disposable income to pay membership fees. The extent to which an individual is included and able to fully participate has significant consequences for identity, citizenship and a sense of belonging.

The three chapters comprising this section consider the extent to which place matters for the construction of identity in different place-based contexts. Each of these chapters considers a different kind of place, and ultimately argues that place matters very much indeed. Like the preceding sections of this book, this section has a conceptual template which binds the contributing chapters together and links the section to the overall themes of the book. The conceptual template underpinning Part 3 has four key elements:

1. Interactions with others: We consider the ways in which our presence and engagement with others in different places helps shape identity. Importantly, we think about this as a reciprocal process, so we also

consider the extent to which such interactions shape the very places in which they occur.

2. Structuring relations: We recognise that places are shaped by formal and informal norms, conventions or regulations that shape interactions between people that occur in different contexts.

3. Place and power: Power is the capacity to bring about consequences for others, whether negative or positive. We examine how power is exercised in different places and to different effects.

4. The consequences of place for citizenship: Finally, we look at the extent to which the places we inhabit, whether they are physical or digital places, hinder or facilitate our membership of different social and political communities.

Overview of chapters

It is not easy to choose just three places to include in a book about identity and belonging when all of social life happens 'in place'. Our final decision reflected a desire to consider a balance between private and public, digital and non-digital, and regulated and non-regulated places. In providing a range of places, we hoped to illuminate how each operates and, more specifically, the ways in which interactions between people in these different places shape individual and collective identities.

In Chapter 6, 'Physical places — home as place', we consider the importance of house and home in creating a sense of place, identity and belonging. We consider the symbolic attachments associated with home — not just the physical materiality of a building we might call home, but also the more ephemeral sense of a location we associate with home. We argue that understandings of home are shaped by the context in which we live as well as the encounters we share with others there. We focus, in particular, on the gendered ways of 'doing' home life, and the implications of this for identity and citizenship. We also consider the role of home ownership in contemporary New Zealand, and the extent to which it provides a sense of security to occupants. Underpinning this chapter is an understanding that this most private of places provides profound opportunities for developing a sense of identity, belonging and citizenship.

Chapter 7, 'Institutional places — the university', focuses on the university as an institutional place that provides a very specific and regulated context in which identity is shaped. Written by Richard Shaw, this chapter comments on the social norms, conventions and regulatory practices that exist in universities, and the impact they have on notions of identity, belonging and citizenship. Relatedly, he explores some of the social encounters through which students' identity is formed, and considers how power is exercised in order to illustrate the links between universities and wider citizenship considerations. In doing so, Richard interrogates the role and function of the university, and how it is located within normative political debates that stress the need for a work-ready graduate. Richard's chapter creates a space for considering the significant consequences of universities for an individual's sense of self as well as the wellbeing of the wider community.

The final chapter in this section, Chapter 8, is called 'Digital places — globalising identity and citizenship'. In this chapter, Sy Taffel considers the multitude of ways in which digital places create opportunities for new identities to emerge in new digital spaces, and similarly create opportunities for a sense of belonging and citizenship. Although this book focuses primarily on what it means to be a citizen of Aotearoa New Zealand, Sy's chapter necessarily moves beyond the borders of this place to reflect on the implications of digital identities for understandings of global citizenship. He achieves this by moving beyond the realm of social media, laying bare the exploitative production and consumption practices of the digital world. In doing so, he challenges us to consider the extent to which we contribute to these injustices through our identities as consumers.

Conclusion

The key message of this section of the book is that our sense of self, and our understanding of what it means to be a citizen of this country, is intimately connected to different places and the relationships that we have in them. In each of the following chapters, we consider the role of place in shaping identity and, in some cases, the impact that identity might have on places. In other words, we emphasise the importance of different sorts of places and, more specifically, the importance of the interactions between people in those places in shaping individual and collective identities. These chapters are closely connected with citizenship. The power structures that underpin specific places can provide an economic, political and socio-cultural context in which inclusion or exclusion can be determined. Such power structures can manifest in different ways that are both formal (e.g. policy documents which outline eligibility for membership to a given place) and informal (e.g. the tacitly understood knowledge about appropriate interactions in a given place). Undoubtedly, these structures, which occur in both digital and physical places, have implications for notions of identity, belonging and citizenship.

CHAPTER SIX:

Physical places
Home as place

Juliana Mansvelt, Trudie Cain
and Ann Dupuis

Introduction — the meaning of 'home'

The introduction to this section of the book defined 'place' as 'a space which is given social meaning by human activity and/or imagination'. This necessarily broad definition accounts for all manner of places, but one of the most important places in many of our lives, and one to which we attribute great meaning, is undoubtedly 'home'.

Over the past two decades much has been written about home. This is not surprising, as home is a multidimensional concept and used in a range of humanities and social sciences disciplines, including psychology, sociology, anthropology, geography, history, architecture, philosophy and planning. But it is notoriously difficult to pin down. What does home mean to you? Your answer, we're sure, will depend on the context in which you find yourself — who is asking the question and where you are at the time of being asked. For example, if you are travelling overseas, you will likely reply 'New Zealand'. But if you are holidaying in Queenstown and are asked the same question, your response will be more geographically specific. Depending on who is asking the question, you might respond with the place where you were born or grew up. In other contexts, your answer might be a specific house that you associate with home — perhaps the house you lived in as a child, or the house where you currently live.

Those of us who have migrated between one country and another might feel we have two homes — our country of birth and our adopted country. And let's not muddy the waters even further by thinking about those places we might visit and just *feel* as though we are home. As we said, 'home' is complicated!

In the broadest of terms, home can refer to both a place and a physical, material structure. But both are socially constructed. Home (either as place or dwelling) is shaped through our memories (good or bad, accurate or not) and is the site of our most intimate encounters — both within ourselves and with those we care about. It is the site in which we are first socialised into the roles we perform in public places that inform our way of 'being' in the world. Home is the site in which we enact our everyday habits and routines that shape who we are. And home is the site of our past, present and future; it is where many of our memories reside, where we live in the present and where we make plans for our future. This most private of places provides the setting in which the very 'socialness' and the material 'stuff' of life is made.

Meanings of home are geographically, culturally and temporally specific. Home is variously described as a site of the conspicuous display of material goods that both represent and construct identity (Hurdley, 2006), and a place where identity and a sense of belonging can be shaped (Case, 1996). Our nostalgia for home might conjure up romanticised ideas of family life and home: home is where the heart is. This reflects the idea that home is a relational place, but, like other places, home is also the site of unevenly distributed power relations (Blunt & Dowling, 2006). Home is a complex space that is multidimensional and possesses both objectively and subjectively shaped meanings.

In this chapter, we explore the meaning of 'home', and reflect on the many ways in which identity can be represented and constructed through home. Throughout, we scrutinise common and sometimes taken-for-granted meanings, and consider how having a place we call home might be important to our sense of self, belonging and tūrangawaewae. We begin by discussing home as one's origins in a geographical or spatial sense. We then turn to home ownership and the normative underpinnings of the home-ownership narrative in Aotearoa New Zealand, including the way gendered identity is played out. Finally, we draw on British sociologist Anthony Giddens' (1990) notion of ontological security to explore the extent to which both home ownership and renting offer occupants a sense of security and stability. Too often the notion of home is swathed with romantic and idealistic connotations. It is intended that this chapter move away from such an uncritical representation of home to show that meanings of home are socially constructed, historically contingent and strongly debated, and that they have political implications.

Places as home: where are you from?

The traditional Māori way of formally introducing oneself to others is through a mihimihi, a greeting which introduces the speaker, their connections to others via waka, iwi and hapū, their whakapapa, and their place of origin. This is a powerful way of anchoring oneself in place and sharing understandings of place and home with others. A pepeha is part of a mihimihi, and helps frame the ways in which the person's identity is connected to whenua and the significant features of place where one comes from. As Te Rina, Veronica and Margaret discussed in Chapter 2, this will typically incorporate geographical features such as maunga, awa and moana. This description makes it sound little more than a list of geographical and familial associations. But mihimihi and pepeha are so much more than this. They represent the ways in which one's spiritual, emotional and physical sense of self is deeply and intimately connected to place and people, present and past, and provide those listening with a sense of the standing place or tūrangawaewae of the speaker, as well as giving an opportunity to recognise and acknowledge connections through shared whakapapa.

Notions of place incorporated in pepeha speak to the emotional, spiritual and affective attachments people have to home, and the ways in which home provides meaning in people's lives. We can also see such attachments to place and home in numerous spheres of social and cultural life. For example, Dave Dobbyn's 2006 song 'Welcome Home' contains profoundly New Zealand imagery that speaks to *this* place: 'there's a woman with her hands trembling, and she sings with a mountain's memory'. This line is a clear reference to wiri — the shaking of hands during waiata that is performed by Māori to demonstrate a deep affinity to Nature. The song and the accompanying video, which features a number of migrants — including then asylum-seeker Ahmed Zaoui — were inspired by anti-racism protests in Christchurch, and have become synonymous with powerful discourses of unity and inclusion that shape what it means to call New Zealand home. (Part 4 considers the stories of New Zealand in greater detail.)

Watch the video for Dave Dobbyn's song 'Welcome Home' here: https://www.youtube.com/watch?v=hQlVmvXAGLI

Maurice Gee, one of New Zealand's most celebrated writers of children's and adults' fiction, draws strongly on elements of place as home, particularly his experiences of growing up in the 1940s and spending time around Henderson Creek in West Auckland. In the following, Gee describes powerfully the ways in which the places we come from can become a core part of our identity:

> If you live in one place all through your childhood that place grows around you like a skin and it can never be put off. It also gets deep into your mind, into the darkest recesses. It's where those most important things happened — not the best or worst things necessarily, although possibly those, but the original happenings that make the mark on us we can never erase. It's where we learn to see, to name, and suspect the thing behind the thing. (Barrowman, 2015, pp. 14–15).

Social constructions of place as 'homes where we come from' are significant in everyday speech — perhaps most obvious when we are away from our home countries. As health researcher Janine Wiles (2008) argues, when people live away from home, they may develop a renewed sense of what home is, and an appreciation of how their current dwelling place differs from what and where they consider home to be. For many New Zealanders who are living outside the country, speaking of home involves drawing upon the beauty and diversity of Aotearoa New Zealand's landscapes. This is of particular importance in New Zealand because of our histories of migration and settlement, the way the environment has been transformed and the 'strong connections between the land and cultural identity in our politics, economy, and art' (Ballantyne & Bennett, 2005, p. 9).

New Zealand-based historians Ballantyne and Bennett (2005) argue that landscapes are made and remade, and point to the debates and conflict around land and landscape, and the vexed question of the relationship between land and national identity. But social, political, economic and landscape change can alter one's sense of home and place; this is particularly the case when such changes are abrupt, as in the case of the Christchurch earthquakes. A large body of scholarly literature is emerging that focuses on the changing meaning of home in post-earthquake Christchurch, especially for those whose homes have been 'red-zoned' and are unable to be rebuilt. Many Cantabrians experienced terrible tragedy and loss, but remained deeply committed to the city; their emotional connection and resonance with Christchurch did not waver. Stories that capture the loss of all that Christchurch represented can be found on the government-supported website Quakestories. For example, in her story, Sarah from Fendalton writes:

> They say that what doesn't kill us only makes us stronger. For most of us

A city in ruins

A scene of devastation in Christchurch the morning after the magnitude 6.3 earthquake in February 2011, which killed 185 people and injured several thousand. Since then Christchurch has experienced thousands of aftershocks. The ruined central city is gradually being rebuilt.

it hasn't killed us but it has made us face our fears, face depression, face anxiety, face uncertainty, face an unwanted rollercoaster ride that never stops . . . and face losing our beloved city. . . . They say that Cantabrians are tough, stoic and resilient. I just think that whether we recognise it or not, our hearts are so entrenched in this very special city that we CAN'T let Mother Nature beat us, for if we do then the very soul of Christchurch is broken and THAT is unthinkable. (Quakestories, 2011)

Sarah's story, and many more like it, remind us that it is essential to recognise that constructions of home are fluid, rather than fixed and unchanging. For many of the Cantabrians whose homes were destroyed and whose lives were turned upside down, a sense of place and home in Christchurch was cemented rather than torn apart. This speaks to the deep connection we create with place, and the capacity of this connection to overcome seemingly insuperable challenges.

Home ownership, identity and belonging

In the previous section we explored the emotional attachments and meanings which might derive from understanding places as a symbol of home. Here, we examine homes as particular dwelling places, and ask critical questions about how the norm of home ownership in Aotearoa New Zealand might influence identity and belonging. For much of the twentieth century, meanings of home in this country have been connected to the phenomenon of home ownership. Historically, this country had some of the highest home-ownership rates in the world. As early as 1911, over half of New Zealand's households were owner-occupied, compared with only 10 per cent of households in the United Kingdom. Although these rates experienced a temporary decline during the Depression, rates steadily increased to reach a high of 73.8 per cent in 1991. Since then, we have seen a downward trend as income levels have failed to keep pace with property prices, leading to a new generation of renters (Eaqub & Eaqub, 2015). The 2013 census recorded that just 50 per cent of households owned their own homes (with or without a mortgage), and a further 14.8 per cent were held in a family trust — 64.8 per cent overall (Statistics New Zealand, 2013a).

 For a graphical representation of the decline in housing ownership and future projections, see: http://www. tradingeconomics.com/new-zealand/home-ownership-rate

Both the high rates of home ownership experienced in the twentieth century, and the more recent decline in this century, have much to do with context: the policies and practices in place. State support for home ownership began in the nineteenth century. However, mass ownership was established with three major initiatives in the 1950s and 1960s: 3 per cent loans; the capitalisation of the family benefit, which allowed for future family support payments to be taken as a lump sum and used as a deposit on a home; and the Group Building scheme, which stimulated housing supply by supporting private builders. These factors provided a perfect policy context in which to encourage home ownership.

Social conventions which normalised private spaces of home developed alongside state encouragement of home ownership. British social commentator Austin Mitchell (1972) characterised New Zealanders' obsession with home and garden in the title of his book, for example, as the 'half-gallon, quarter-acre pavlova paradise'. For much of the twentieth century, homes were sites for the establishment of conventions and norms around forms of gendered domesticity. For men, this included a culture of do-it-yourself (DIY) enshrined in notions of frontier masculinity. For women, gendered domesticity centred on home provisioning through baking, bottling and cooking. The 'ladies, a plate' culture, as well as the scientific management of families and households, further strengthened understandings of gendered norms in the home (Park, 1991).

These observations are not benign; they speak to relations of power in domestic life that have material effects. Historian Jock Phillips (1996) noted:

> But what if he spent the weekend at home, then what? Was not the home the woman's world? The man's response was to cordon off from the domestic environment certain exclusive male territories. Fences of sexual segregation were erected at home. The man would not cook unless it was over a campfire; he would not clean unless it was the car; he was prepared to garden so long as it was always vegetables and not the herbaceous border; he was prepared to mend things so long as it was a washer and not socks, and he was ready to cut wood. The jobs that were acceptable were those that generally involved heavy physical work or mechanical skills — outside tasks which allowed him to relive the fantasy of the pioneering life. (p. 243)

We can see from Phillips's quote how homes are riven with gendered meaning. From this perspective, for much of the twentieth century 'home-making' might be viewed as a largely feminine act of caring, involving the use of domestic

Housed by the state

In 1937, Prime Minister Michael Savage lifted
a dining table through the door of the first
state house in New Zealand in Wellington.
Although there had been various previous
attempts at social housing, it wasn't until the
Great Depression of the 1930s that the Labour
Government began a concerted building effort
to provide people with homes of their own with
state backing. This image is of neighbourhood
children in a state housing street in Mount
Albert, Auckland.

appliances, decoration, consumption and filling one's house with material objects. These acts can be considered as distinct from 'making home', a practice which relied primarily on masculine ingenuity, an emphasis on DIY improvement and repairs using tools, and productive outdoor pursuits such as vegetable gardening. Increasingly limited access to homes with gardens has certainly contributed to changes in gendered domestic practices. Perhaps more important, however, are changes to gendered norms that promote more egalitarian relationship structures. At least in part this has been produced through a rise in dual-income households and men's increased involvement in childcare.

Investment in home, both economically and culturally, has historically been an essential element of identity and belonging for generations of New Zealanders. Home ownership has long been integral to the New Zealand ethos (Ferguson, 1994). One journalist went as far as to suggest that 'Becoming a home owner is a rite of passage; anybody who reaches 40 without buying a house is decidedly suspect, not fully adult' (McLeod, 1989, p. 11). Written in 1989, this would be an absurd proposition today. Yet despite the current housing crisis and the prospect of owning one's own home moving beyond the reach of so many of us, home ownership remains a key element of New Zealand's national story.

Running alongside this ideological and normative view is the popular wisdom that property has always been a good investment. It would be entirely incorrect to suggest that somehow New Zealanders have been duped into believing this, given that the economic rewards of home ownership can be spectacular — Auckland house prices increased by 85 per cent between 2012 and 2016 (Real Estate Institute of New Zealand, 2016). Moreover, economic benefits can be passed on to the next generation via housing wealth inheritance (Dupuis, 2012a). But economic benefits are dependent on a range of factors, including the length of ownership and the location of the property; the economic benefits for home owners in New Zealand's urban centres are very different from New Zealand's small rural towns.

While declining home-ownership rates, urban intensification and issues of affordability are now challenging the home-ownership model, owning your own home remains, at least to some degree, a normative rite of passage and a key source of belonging, wealth and identity. But what does this say of those who cannot access the private housing market? It is important to understand the impact of home ownership on broader patterns of wealth distribution, social stratification and inequality. (Chapter 9 considers the unequal distribution of wealth in this country in greater detail.) This points to the unanticipated consequences of policy, in that supporting some but not others into home ownership can have long-term consequences. In 2016, New Zealand topped global rankings for rises in house prices (Radio New Zealand, 2016). With house price inflation, stringent restrictions on bank lending, little sign of state intervention in housing, and regional disparities in access to and opportunities for employment (which impacts on home ownership), in many parts of New Zealand a new generational divide is appearing whereby the possibility of ever becoming home owners is rapidly diminishing (including students who may be burdened with sizeable loans to repay). Another aspect of this is the long-term disparity between Pākehā, and Māori and Pasifika owner-occupation rates.

Home as a site of ontological security . . . and insecurity

The previous section alluded to the stability and security that the home, and home ownership in particular, can bring. We want to unpack this idea by drawing on a concept introduced by British sociologist Anthony Giddens. Giddens (1990) coined the term 'ontological security' to describe an individual's state of 'being-in-the-world' — a state of being that is 'emotional . . . and rooted in the unconscious' (p. 92). If a person is ontologically secure, he argues, they have a sense of order that arises from being in a world that offers them certainty, stability and continuity.

Ontological security is a useful concept for thinking about the home. In engaging with Giddens' work, the housing theorist Saunders (1989) suggested that home ownership provided a means of securing ontological security as '[t]he home is where people are off-stage, free from surveillance, in control of their immediate environment. It is their castle. It is where they belong' (p. 184). A more systematic elaboration of ontological security as it relates to housing was put forward by Dupuis and Thorns (1998), and breaks the concept down into four themes:

1. constancy of home ownership
2. a site of familial routines
3. a site of control and freedom from surveillance, and
4. a site where identities are constructed.

In the following, we examine each of these themes in turn, and consider the extent to which home ownership can lead to both ontological security and insecurity. We also consider whether renting is equally capable of providing ontological security.

Constancy of home ownership

The first theme proposed by Dupuis and Thorns (1998) is that home ownership

Domestic demarcation

The man of the house digs in the garden while his wife looks on in this scene from a typical New Zealand front yard of the 1950s.

creates constancy and stability for those who live there, which, in turn, provides ontological security. However, the housing and home-ownership context in Aotearoa New Zealand has changed dramatically: first, home ownership is now beyond the reach of many New Zealanders, and second, many New Zealanders have large mortgages that can foster financial stress, anxiety and, ultimately, ontological insecurity.

Financial security and stability is an important contributor to ontological security, and yet in 2014 over one-quarter (27 per cent) of New Zealand households spent more than 30 per cent of their income on housing, 15 per cent of households spent more than 40 per cent, and 8 per cent spent more than half their household income (Ministry of Social Development, 2016). (Note that housing is considered unaffordable if servicing the mortgage requires more than 30 per cent of the household's gross income.) Those who are least able to afford it are spending the greatest percentage of their income on housing: again in 2014, 41 per cent of those in the lowest household-income quintile spent more than 30 per cent of their income on housing costs, compared with just 10 per cent of those in the top income quintile (Ministry of Social Development, 2016). For the poorest citizens of this country, little is left to meet other basic needs, such as food, transport, clothing, medical care and education. Irrespective of whether someone owns or rents their home, it would seem that housing is becoming increasingly unable to provide ontological security for inhabitants and, indeed, could be more likely to generate ontological insecurity.

Long-term renting is not part of this country's national narrative. Renting is considered to be a risky business generating great vulnerability for tenants, who are arguably subject to the whims of a landlord and face the constant fear of eviction. But the number of people renting is certainly rising as home ownership is increasingly concentrated in the hands of a few. In Auckland, for example, the percentage of households who rent their home increased by 18.5 per cent between 2006 and 2013. Children are most likely to live in rented accommodation; 46.5 per cent of children under the age of four live in rented accommodation, and the percentage of children under 15 years of age living in rented accommodation increased from 39.8 per cent in 2006 to 43.7 per cent in 2013 (Goodyear & Fabian, 2014).

We are not suggesting that renting in and of itself generates ontological insecurity. However, renting is correlated with greater transience: in 2013, over a third (35.0 per cent) of people in households who rented had lived there for less than one year (compared with 14.4 per cent of those in households who owned their home or held it in a family trust) (ibid.). Transience has negative impacts on health and education outcomes for New Zealand's young people, but moving around a lot also hinders the development of friendships and a sense of community connectedness. All of these things are vital for creating ontological security.

A lack of access to the rental housing market can create an even greater degree of instability and insecurity in people's lives. The high turnover of rental properties, short tenancies and an inability to afford adequate rental housing means many more New Zealanders are disconnected from home as a source of ontological security. There has been much publicity in recent times about crowding in houses, as well as families living in garages, makeshift accommodation and cars. It is estimated from the 2013 census that one in 100 New Zealanders is now in severe housing deprivation (defined as those living in housing without adequate security of tenure, privacy and/or control, or in structurally inadequate properties). This compares with one in 120 New Zealanders at the 2006 census (Amore, 2016). Researchers suggest 70 per cent of the housing-deprived are staying with extended family or friends in severely crowded houses, 20 per cent are staying in a motel, boarding house or camping ground, and 10 per cent are living on the street, in cars, or in other improvised dwellings (ibid.). It is clear that for these New Zealanders 'house' and 'home' are not synonymous terms, with their dwelling places lacking the qualities which might provide ontological security in an uncertain world.

A site of familial routines

The second point made by Dupuis and Thorns (1998) is that the home provides a site for the establishment of family routines. In other words, home is where we learn how to 'do' family life. Take a moment to reflect on the kinds of routines you have in your own home. It might be difficult to think of any at first, because our norms become so embedded in our everyday lives that we largely take them for granted. But do you do any of the following: take off your shoes when you arrive home; take turns to cook dinner for the household; have a roster around cleaning responsibilities; watch a particular TV programme; or go to bed at the same time each night? All of these things are indicative of the everyday routines we establish that shape our domestic lives. Although not practised every day (and certainly not practised by everyone), annual events such as birthdays, Matariki, Christmas and Easter are also occasions for the display of family practices that signify how your family celebrates, acknowledges each other and functions overall.

Whether we realise it or not, many of our quotidian and celebratory practices in the home reflect our identity threads: our religious beliefs will shape whether we say grace before a meal; our ethnicity might determine whether it is appropriate to sit on the kitchen bench; and our culture might shape whether dinner guests bring a contribution or not. The home is also the site in which gendered norms are performed and shaped (Gorman-Murray, 2007). Through the encounters we have with others in the home, and the behaviours we perform there, we are socialised into appropriate ways of being male and female, masculine and feminine, in the public sphere.

The 2009/2010 time use survey measured the time parents spend on a range of activities, including childcare, in the home (Statistics New Zealand, 2013b). The survey shows that among partnered heterosexual couples, mothers continue to undertake the majority of parental childcare during the week. This was especially the case when couples had at least one child aged less than five years: 59 per cent of childcare was provided by the mother only, compared with just 6 per cent by the father only (ibid.). Even when both parents worked full-time, mothers still spent more time caring for the children: 48 per cent of all childcare was solely provided by the mother, compared with just 14 per cent of childcare provided by the father (ibid.).

The discrepancy in time spent in a hands-on childcare role illustrates empirically that the things we do in the home are shaped by our identity threads, in this case our gender, and the social norms that dictate how those identity threads will be performed. The gendered division of labour illustrates the relations of power that are embedded in familial practices, and in doing so troubles the idea that ontological security can be found in the routines of domestic life.

A site of control and freedom from surveillance

Reference to gendered power dynamics in the home brings us to the third point made by Dupuis and Thorns (1998): the home is a site where people feel in control of their lives and free from the surveillance of the outside world. This theme has much in common with the longstanding view of home as a haven or refuge from the outside world, where people can relax, be themselves, be free from public scrutiny, be creative, and especially engage in close, caring and enduring family relationships. To paraphrase sociologist Erving Goffman (1990, p. 115), on walking through the front door it is possible to relax, drop our front, forgo speaking our lines, and step out of character. With these words, Goffman creates a clear distinction between our public and private worlds (or front stage and back stage).

This is a powerful idea and one that has some traction — home *feels* private; it is readily distinguishable from other kinds of public places, such as the shopping mall, the park or the university. But the distinction between private and public is far more fluid than ever before. New technologies mean we communicate across the borders of the home every day, inviting people into our personal places, sometimes without having met them in person. Our use of social media is harnessed by corporations keen to capitalise on their understanding of who we are (you can read more about this in Sy Taffel's chapter on digital identity). Smart technology means we, too, can cross the physical borders of the home; we can turn on our lights and air conditioning, for example, well in advance of arriving home by using our smartphones. But this information is also captured by the very corporations that manufacture these products. Digital technologies have certainly called into question the extent to which the home provides a site of ontological security resulting from greater control and freedom from surveillance.

The idea that the home (and home ownership, in particular) provides a site of ontological security has also been criticised by a number of feminist academics in particular, who focus on the negative and darker side of home, where home can be experienced as a place of brutality. Domestic violence has reached epidemic proportions in Aotearoa New Zealand, and examining police records makes for a sobering read. Around half of all homicides in New Zealand are committed by a family member (Family Violence Death Review Committee, 2014), 76 per cent of intimate-partner violence-related deaths were perpetrated by men between 2009 and 2012 (ibid.), and every five and a half minutes, a family violence investigation is recorded in this country (Statistics New Zealand, 2015) — shocking when you consider that over three-quarters of family violence incidents are not reported to police at all. Over three-quarters of recorded assaults against women are committed by an offender who is identified as family (New Zealand Family Violence Clearinghouse, 2016), and one in three women will experience physical and/or sexual violence from a partner in their lifetime (ibid.). And with regard to Aotearoa New Zealand's young people, 14 per cent report being hit or physically harmed by an adult at home (Clark et al., 2013).

These figures are staggering, and paint a powerful picture of the vulnerability of women and young people in particular. For those who experience domestic violence of any kind, the home offers little in the way of protection or safety, given that it is the primary site where such abuse occurs. Indeed, the very fact that the home is a private space outside the surveillance of others offers the abuser free rein to operate (Dupuis, 2012b). What is clear is that for these people the home has little to do with the ontological security of inhabitants.

A site where identities are constructed

The final theme identified by Dupuis and Thorns (1998) is the idea that home is where identities are constructed — where we become who we are. From the moment we are born, we are socialised into particular ways of being. Our identities are acquired through the everyday things that we do in the physical space of the home, and the everyday encounters we have with people there. We have already touched on some of the ways that gendered and ethnic identity is constructed in the home through the practices we perform. But the home is also intimately tied to practices of consumption, providing the site for the conspicuous display of material goods, purchased and utilised as a tool for self-representation (Pink, 2004). Social–cultural anthropologist Arjun Appadurai (1986) suggests that material objects have their own life story. An object begins its 'life' as a commodity (something that is purchased), but is quickly de-commodified as we start to grow attached to it for one reason or another and attribute it with symbolic significance.

For example, you might have a collection of china plates given to you when your grandmother died, or a special piece of art that you received for your twenty-first birthday, or a box set of Milly-Molly-Mandy books from your childhood. The symbolic meaning of these kinds of items is primarily nostalgic, but meaning might also be economic — like the home itself, things have multiple meanings. The display of these things is deeply personal, and they become powerful markers of identity; they speak to who you are (Miller, 2010). Whether your home is rented or owned, constructing identity in the home through the display of material goods provides a possible pathway to ontological security.

Conclusion

In this chapter we have explored the centrality of the home in the shaping of identity and belonging. Exploring notions of places as homes, and homes as places, has enabled us to reflect on the ways in which places are intimately connected with our sense of self and our relations to others. Importantly, we have shown that our identity threads — gender and ethnicity, for example — play an important role in shaping how domestic life will be enacted through a range of conventions and norms. Everyday practices that are informed by identity demonstrate the extent to which home and 'place as home' are not neutral spaces, but are sites in which power is expressed and produced.

It has been argued that home, and home ownership in particular, is an important source of ontological security, a sense of being, coping and feeling secure in the world. But such security is increasingly tenuous, and this chapter has challenged this assumption, raising questions about the effects of norms within homes, and of norms of home ownership themselves. In a context of housing and income insecurity, rising prices, and shortages of suitable dwellings in parts of New Zealand, for many New Zealanders owning one's home is no longer a rite of passage, and renting produces a different set of challenges. Housing policy has resulted in economic and social inequalities between owners and non-owners, and such changes not only challenge constructions of home, but also provoke questions about the extent to which all citizens can access places of dwelling which provide a key source of ontological security.

 Chapter 6 — Physical places: Home as place: http://turangawaewae.massey.ac.nz/chapter6.html

Recommended reading

Ballantyne, T., & Bennett, J. (Eds.). (2005). *Landscape/community: Perspectives from New Zealand*. Dunedin, New Zealand: University of Otago Press.

Eaqub, S., & Eaqub, S. (2015). *Generation rent: Rethinking New Zealand's priorities*. Wellington, New Zealand: Bridget Williams Books.

Goodyear, R., & Fabian, A. (2014). *Housing in Auckland: Trends in housing from the census of population and dwellings 1991 to 2013*. Wellington, New Zealand: Statistics New Zealand.

Wiles, J. (2008). Sense of home in a transnational social space: New Zealanders in London. *Global Networks, 8*(1), 116–137. doi: 10.1111/j.1471-0374.2008.00188

References

Amore, K. (2016, June 3). Homelessness accelerates between censuses. Wellington, New Zealand: University of Otago. Retrieved from http://www.otago.ac.nz/news/news/otago613529.html

Appadurai, A. (1986). *The social life of things: Commodities in cultural perspective*. Cambridge, England: Cambridge University Press.

Ballantyne, T., & Bennett, J. (Eds.). (2005). *Landscape/community: Perspectives from New Zealand*. Dunedin, New Zealand: University of Otago Press.

Barrowman, R. (2015). *Maurice Gee: Life and work*. Wellington, New Zealand: Victoria University Press.

Blunt, A., & Dowling, R. M. (2006). *Home*. New York, NY: Routledge.

Case, D. (1996). Contributions of journeys away to the definition of home: An empirical study of a dialectical process. *Journal of Environmental Psychology, 16*, 1–15.

Clark, T. C., et al. (2013). *Youth '12 overview: The health and wellbeing of New Zealand secondary school students in 2012*. Auckland, New Zealand: The University of

Auckland. Retrieved from https://www.fmhs.auckland.ac.nz/assets/fmhs/faculty/ahrg/docs/2012prevalence-tables-report.pdf

Dupuis, A. (2012a). Home as inheritance. In S. Smith, M. Elsinga, L. Fox, O'Mahony, O. S. Eng, S. Wachter, & R. Dowling (Eds.), *International encyclopedia of housing and home* (Vol. 2, pp. 399–403). Oxford, England: Elsevier.

Dupuis, A. (2012b). Ontological security. In S. J. Smith, M. Elsinga, L. Fox O'Mahony, O. S. Eng, S. Wachter, & R. Dowling (Eds.), *International encyclopedia of housing and home* (Vol. 5, pp. 156–160). Oxford, England: Elsevier.

Dupuis, A., & Thorns, D. (1998). Home, home ownership and the search for ontological security. *Sociological Review, 46*(1), 24–47.

Eaqub, S., & Eaqub, S. (2015). *Generation rent: Rethinking New Zealand's priorities.* Wellington, New Zealand: Bridget Williams Books.

Family Violence Death Review Committee. (2014, June 26). *Fourth annual report: January 2013 to December 2013.* Wellington, New Zealand: Health Quality and Safety Commission. Retrieved from http://www.hqsc.govt.nz/our-programmes/mrc/fvdrc/publications-and-resources/publication/1600/

Ferguson, G. (1994). *Building the New Zealand dream.* Palmerston North, New Zealand: Dunmore Press.

Giddens, A. (1990). *The consequences of modernity.* Stanford, CA: Stanford University Press.

Goffman, E. (1990). *The presentation of self in everyday life.* Garden City, NY: Doubleday.

Goodyear, R., & Fabian, A. (2014). *Housing in Auckland: Trends in housing from the census of population and dwellings 1991 to 2013.* Wellington, New Zealand: Statistics New Zealand.

Gorman-Murray, A. (2007). Contesting domestic ideals: Queering the Australian home. *Australian Geographer, 38*(2), 195–213.

Hurdley, R. (2006). Dismantling mantelpieces: Narrating identities and materializing culture in the home. *Sociology, 40*(4), 717–733.

McLeod, M. (1989, December 18). A home of your own. *The New Zealand Listener.*

Miller, D. (2010). *Stuff.* Cambridge, England: Polity Press.

Ministry of Social Development. (2016). *The social report 2015: Te purongo oranga tangata.* Wellington, New Zealand: Ministry of Social Development.

Mitchell, A. (1972). *The half-gallon quarter-acre pavlova paradise.* Christchurch, New Zealand: Whitcombe and Tombs.

New Zealand Family Violence Clearinghouse. (2016, July). *Data summary: Violence against women.* Auckland, New Zealand: University of Auckland. Retrieved from https://nzfvc.org.nz/data-summaries/violence-against-women

Park, J. (Ed.). (1991). *Ladies a plate: Change and continuity in the lives of New Zealand women*. Auckland, New Zealand: Auckland University Press.

Phillips, J. (1996). *A man's country? The image of the Pakeha male, a history*. Auckland, New Zealand: Penguin.

Pink, S. (2004). *Home truths: Gender, domestic objects and everyday life*. Oxford, England: Berg.

Quakestories. (2011). Retrieved from http://www.quakestories.govt.nz/111/story/

Radio New Zealand. (2016, September 8; 2.23 pm). New Zealand tops global list for house price rises. Retrieved from http://www.radionz.co.nz/news/national/312817/new-zealand-tops-global-list-for-house-price-rises

Real Estate Institute of New Zealand. (2016). *REINZ Auckland region analysis for October 2016*. Retrieved from https://www.reinz.co.nz

Saunders, P. (1989). The meaning of home in contemporary English culture. *Housing Studies 4*(3), 177–192.

Statistics New Zealand. (2013a). *Home ownership continues to fall*. Retrieved from http://www.stats.govt.nz/Census/2013-census/profile-and-summary-reports/quickstats-about-national-highlights/home-ownership.aspx

Statistics New Zealand. (2013b). *Caring for children: Findings from the 2009/10 time use survey*. Wellington, New Zealand: Statistics New Zealand.

Statistics New Zealand. (2015). *New Zealand Police recorded crime and apprehension tables*. Retrieved from http://nzdotstat.stats.govt.nz/wbos/Index.aspx?DataSet Code=TABLECODE740

Wiles, J. (2008). Sense of home in a transnational social space: New Zealanders in London. *Global Networks, 8*(1), 116–137. doi: 10.1111/j.1471-0374.2008.00188

Institutional places
The university

Richard Shaw

Introduction

Institutions are assemblages of physical places, overlaid by the conventions, norms and rules that regulate social relationships within those environs. They are a particular type of place, and a university is a specific example of the genre (as is a museum, a hospital, a cinema or an art gallery).

Universities matter. In a powerful defence of the critical importance of the social sciences and humanities in the twenty-first century, American journalist and author Fareed Zakira (2015) cites Wilson's concern that we are drowning in information while starving for wisdom. Zakira's point — which is that what the world needs now are people who can think critically and act wisely — seems as good a place as any to start this chapter, given that one of the historic raisons d'être of universities is to transform information into knowledge in the hope that this will lead to wisdom. It is one thing, for example, to know that at the 2014 general election in New Zealand only 75 per cent of eligible voters aged 18–24 enrolled, but another to parse that data into knowledge of the complex causes of political disengagement (and thus to avoid making the mistake of blaming low voter turnout on lazy, apathetic individuals).

In universities — and to a greater or lesser extent this also applies in other tertiary institutions, such as whare wānanga and polytechnics — the processes of shifting from information (or data) to knowledge and wisdom can have significant consequences for both individuals' sense of self and the wellbeing of the wider community. In short, universities provide perfect examples of the ways in which institutions shape people's sense of identity (and vice versa). In this chapter, therefore, I explore some of the identity encounters through which students' identity is formed, examine the rules that structure interactions in a university, look at the ways in which power is exercised, and tease out some of the links between universities and wider citizenship considerations.

Being at uni: identity threads and encounters

In the introduction to this section of the book, you encountered the notion that places comprise the contexts in which we interact with others and, in so doing, shape our sense of identity. In turn, the ebb and flow of such exchanges have consequences for the rules, whether formal or informal, which structure the ways in which people interact in those places. Let's begin by reflecting, then, on the sorts of identity encounters people have in the different communities that make up their lives as students.

When we meet someone for the first time, one of the questions we commonly ask is 'What do you do?' The answer helps us locate our new acquaintance in some sort of context, and establish ourselves in relation to them. A student might respond to that query with 'I'm a student' or 'I'm studying'. What does it mean to be a student? What does that particular identity mean for the way someone goes about their daily life?

The *Concise Oxford Dictionary* defines a student as a 'person studying in order to qualify himself for some occupation, or devoting himself to some branch of learning or investigation' (Sykes, 1982, p. 1058). But the singular category 'student' has many different hues. Any student's experience will reflect not only the specifics of their university, campus and mode of study, but also their own history and circumstances. The choice of a particular degree and specific papers, decisions made regarding which other students to associate with, and the sense that is made of the books, chapters and articles encountered along the way: these and countless other elements of a student's life will be influenced by the threads — age, socio-economic class, sexuality, ethnicity and so forth — that 'produce the fabric of a person's identity' (Burr, 2015, pp. 123–124). In short, 'student' is not a unitary category.

Nor is being a student an homogeneous experience. Rather, it plays out in contrasting ways for different people, as is illustrated by considering how a person's identity as a student intersects with their living arrangements. Some students live on campus; some in flats; some in homes that are far from the university at which they are studying. Let's reflect on the rituals, routines and behaviours that occur in these different contexts. The lives of students living in hostels are to some degree regulated by institutional rules: when and where they eat, the times of the year during which they must vacate 'their' rooms, the standards of behaviour expected in the hostel and so on — all of these reflect the rules in place at any given time. Some of these rules are formal and the consequences of breaking them are made blindingly clear, but others are tacit.

As to life in student flats, there is typically an expectation that flatmates will engage in the communal life of the flat. Indeed, the very term 'flatmate' tells you something about the relationships you are expected to have with the others you share a flat with. It carries a normative expectation of amiability that is missing, for instance, from the French term *colocateur*, which simply suggests an arrangement in which people share a living space. The advent of digital technologies is shifting the practices associated with this normative rule; for instance, anecdotally, at least, it appears to be much more common now than it used to be for people to spend time alone streaming content. However, the expectation that as a member of a flat you will contribute to the shopping and cook for your flatmates appears to continue to exert a significant influence over student life in this country. It operates with the force of a rule, yet it isn't codified anywhere.

 Check out this episode from one of New Zealand's early reality TV shows, *Flatmates*: https://www.nzonscreen.com/title/flatmates-episode-one-1997

For distance students, that part of their identity labelled 'student' typically demands balancing multiple family, work, community, study and other responsibilities. (In fact, these days the requirement to juggle competing demands is probably a fact of life for virtually all students, wherever they live.) To put this differently, managing the interplay, if not outright tension, between one's different identity threads can be highly challenging for students who, having perhaps spent the day looking after children or in an office, have to hit the books once dinner has been prepared and served and the kids have been put to bed.

The wider point is these identity encounters occur in social, physical and online contexts — halls of residence, flats, homes, social networks, pubs and so forth — and are negotiated with others, including family members, other students, university staff, government officials at StudyLink or the Inland Revenue Department, and miscellaneous others (banks, landlords, retailers, the police and so on). In these interactions, some activities will be sanctioned because they are perceived as appropriate behaviour (even though they might not be all that well received in other contexts), while other forms of conduct will be proscribed because they are felt to be inappropriate. For example, the same students who might (at a stretch) be indulged when they take both the supermarket trolley and the shopping home would probably not be granted the same leeway as working professionals.

The rules of the university game

Students have other encounters, particularly in the context of the formal environment of the university, which are also structured by certain 'rules of the game'. The rules in question might be explicit: for instance, a student cannot hand in an assignment that has been plagiarised (at least, not without running the risk of being detected and punished). Others are tacit and informal. The following claim from Arran Stibbe (2010), who teaches English and Creative Writing at the University of Gloucester, provides a clear sense of just how broad the scope of these formal and informal rules of the game really is:

> [A]ll the rules — explicit and implicit — which guide students in how they should talk and act in the classroom, how they should write their essays, how they should give presentations, all the assessment briefs, assessment criteria, regulations for assessment, referencing guides [and] feedback on written work, are guiding them into particular disciplinary identities. (p. 91)

Stibbe's point about students' disciplines is something I will turn to shortly, but his references to talking and acting are particularly relevant. The general point is that such interactivity is structured by expectations of appropriate behaviour. That expectation is most marked in the relationship between academics and students, in which context talking and acting tends to reflect clearly defined roles and accepted ways of doing things. Thus, it is generally considered poor form (by academics, at least) for students to routinely check their Facebook feed in lectures or to talk audibly in a lecture about something that is not relevant to the topic du jour. There are also conventions around engaging with people whose views you do not agree with: for instance, launching personal attacks on other students in online discussion forums or tutorials is well and truly out of bounds.

Mortar board and gown

A graduation day procession at Massey
University in 2015. It's far too happy a day to
be worrying about the size of their student
loans, but no doubt some of these students are.
Since the introduction of fees, the meaning of
a university education in New Zealand, and the
value we place on such an education as a society,
have shifted: the private dimension of taking
a degree has become more prominent, and the
case for a public education has correspondingly
diminished (although it is far from dead).

Designing rules into the furniture

These rules and roles are even designed into the architecture of universities' learning environments. Think of a traditional lecture theatre comprising banked rows of seats facing a lectern. This particular built environment — which is nothing if not a secular interpretation of a sacred space — encourages certain kinds of interactions between staff and students, and makes others a little tricky. Students do not sit facing each other — they face the front of the room. *A priori* that physical arrangement does not encourage discussion amongst students; rather, it is expressly intended to focus their attention on the person delivering the lecture.

Such arrangements also embody clear messages about the possession of knowledge and the respective roles of students and staff. Information may well be everywhere, as Wilson argues, but knowledge, which is the core currency of a university, is a little harder to find. The fundamental assumption literally built into a lecture hall is that this is a place where intellectual novices come to learn from acknowledged experts. The layout of the theatre — and lecturing does have a performative or theatrical dimension to it — privileges certain types of knowledge (those acquired through rigorous, disciplined study) and specific ways of learning (by listening and asking questions).

The divide, or, to put it differently, the 'authority structure' of the lecture theatre, is emphasised by the physical distance that exists between students' seats and the space the lecturer inhabits. It is not much of an exaggeration to suggest that this space is intended to represent the boundary between knowledge and ignorance, and between those who are members of an academic club and those who are not. Entrance to this exclusive club is by invitation only, and demands of aspiring members that they demonstrate — generally, through the completion of a doctorate — that they have understood and incorporated the relevant disciplinary and institutional rules of the game.

To a degree, traditional authority structures within universities are evolving. The use of digital learning technologies, recourse to more interactive teaching methods, and the gradual replacement of the traditional banked lecture theatre with flat-floored teaching spaces — these and other changes alter the dynamic between academics and students. Established ways of doing things are remarkably resilient, however, and it is far from clear that these new developments will ever wholly disrupt a relationship based upon the unequal possession of knowledge.

Disciplining students

There is one defining feature of studying at a university that may be central to a student's identity even if, at least at first, they are barely aware of it. 'Student' is a broad category which can be broken down into various sub-categories: there are undergraduate students, international students, returning students, internal and distance students, part-time or full-time students, and so on.

But one central and unavoidable element of all students' identity is the part that is defined by their discipline. This person is a Politics student; that one is majoring in Sociology; and those three over there are English, French and Media Studies students, respectively. Each is a student, but the preceding qualifiers clearly distinguish one from the other. And that qualifier matters a great deal, because the signal characteristic of a discipline is the ways of explaining the world that are shared by members of that disciplinary community. In quite a literal sense, a discipline uses theories, concepts and research methods to teach someone to see and understand the world in a particular way: the phenomena studied, the language used to explain those phenomena, the methods used to collect and analyse empirical data, and so on, combine to socialise students into the ways and conventions of a very specific intellectual community.

In the quote referred to a page or two back, Stibbe (2010) suggests that this process of socialisation is 'implicit and unquestioned'. I don't entirely agree. Rather, being a student (and an academic for that matter) requires explicit reflection on the ways in which we make sense of things. For example, as a political scientist I am aware that the theories I draw on to explain voting behaviour emphasise the influence of societal factors (ethnicity, social class, etc.) on people's choices. An academic psychologist, however, might offer explanations of the very same behaviour that focus on a person's cognitive and emotional responses to external political stimuli. Neither is inherently superior; both contribute to our understanding of the phenomenon in question.

The growing popularity of inter-disciplinary courses, in which students engage with several disciplines, tends to bring these discipline-specific ways of making sense out into the open. Disciplines play a central role in crafting students' intellectual identities. But they also shape the professional identities people take into their lives after graduating. When students leave university, they carry with them these disciplined, structured ways of making sense of things, and use them to navigate their way in the world beyond university. Making sense of literature, language, society, art, politics, events in the wider world and so on is, after all, one of the reasons many of us seek a university education.

One-way traffic?

So much for the influence a university and its disciplines has on students' identities. To some extent the traffic heads in the other direction, too, insofar as students' individual and collective identity has consequences for the way things are done within the university. An initiative recently undertaken at Massey University provides an example of how this happens. In 2016, the university introduced a series of changes to the Bachelor of Arts (BA) degree, one of the most significant of which was the implementation of a core curriculum. There were several reasons for the creation of this bespoke set of compulsory papers, one of which was that it would enable all BA students to learn the social and emotional skills and intelligence that will be central to the jobs of the future (Frey & Osborne, 2013). A second was that the current and former BA students surveyed as part of the process indicated clearly that a core would help construct a positive sense of identity and belonging among BA students.

On the basis of these views, the university revised the BA in ways which have had significant and positive consequences for the deployment of resources. New staff have been employed; original learning resources have been created; the working practices and routines of academics have altered; and physical space in the university has been redeployed to accommodate changes in class sizes. The changes were designed with various aspects of students' identity in mind: as members of a community of BA students, as intellectually curious people, and as future employees and employers.

We're all equal here. Aren't we?

Well, no, we're not all equal. By now it should be clear that universities are innately hierarchical institutions in which power — that is, the capacity to bring about consequences for others — is unequally distributed. Those imbalances take different forms, not all of which will be visible to students. There are, for example, hierarchies of power that structure relationships between academics. Professors wield more power than lecturers or tutors. In the context of a New Zealand university, the word 'professor' is generally attached to someone whose research is internationally recognised and whose qualities as an educator may or may not be of an equivalent standard. The title is symbolic and sends a very clear signal of authority, one which may be met by other inhabitants of the institution with a certain measure of deference.

Gender is one of the identity threads discussed throughout this book, and is another basis on which power is unequally distributed across the university. Gender and formal authority tend to be interwoven in universities. Women comprise a little over 50 per cent of all academic staff in New Zealand's eight universities, but account for just 19 per cent of all professors (and this at a time when around 60 per cent of all university graduates are women). Moreover, an investigation by *The New Zealand Herald* found that, across the board, women academics earn some $13,000 less per annum than their male counterparts who do the same work.

There are also relations of power based on research performance (measured in publications and research grants): star researchers typically enjoy higher status and greater influence than star teachers. A division between the academic and professional staff also exists, with the activities of the former usually accorded greater status (and money) than those of the latter.

See *The New Zealand Herald*'s Insights section on the gender pay gap: http://insights.nzherald.co.nz/article/gender-pay-gap

Inequalities also apply in what is arguably the most fundamental relationship within a university: that between academic staff and students. You have already read about some of the ways in which the architecture of the classroom reflects and reinforces unequal relationships: what goes on in a lecture is fundamentally a relationship of power in which academics command centre-stage and talk while students listen. But the imbalance is perhaps most obvious in the gatekeeping role academics play. Bluntly, academics decide whether students pass or fail their courses. There are, of course, procedural means for seeking redress, but in the final instance the determination of whether or not a student has learned what an academic has asked them to learn is the academic's to make (and this may be entirely appropriate, given that academics are, or should be, subject specialists).

The fact that students contribute to the cost of that learning does not render the staff–student relationship one of equals. There is a view that the advent of student fees has reinvented the student as a consumer. In other words, some might argue that a student who pays fees for a course of academic study is purchasing a commodity, and as such is entitled to the same levels of responsive service as attached to the consumption of other goods and services. The issue of exactly *what*, if anything, is being purchased is not moot. A student may believe she is buying her certificate, diploma or degree, but an academic is likely to counter that what is being purchased is the opportunity to learn, not an outcome on an essay or exam.

The latter view is buttressed by the fact that, in this country, a tertiary education remains substantially publicly funded. The precise balance of public funding

Campus life

Students at Massey's Manawatu campus. When students leave university, they carry with them disciplined, structured ways of making sense of things, and use them to navigate their way in the world beyond university.

versus private contribution (in the form of fees) varies from year to year and from course to course, but in the humanities and social sciences students generally meet around 20 per cent of the total cost of their degree. Put differently, the rights and obligations of students are not equivalent to those of consumers of commodities that are not publicly subsidised to the tune of 80 per cent or so.

That is not to gainsay the impact of fees, or of the challenges students face meeting the costs of living and course-related expenses (which are discussed shortly). And nor is it to ignore that, in the quasi-market that is New Zealand's tertiary education sector, students choose where they take their academic custom (albeit increasingly within economic constraints). The point, however, is that debates about how the burden of paying for tertiary students' education is allocated do not substantially detract from the fundamental basis of the relationship between academics and students. That has to do with the authority academics possess grounded in their membership of both an institution and a discipline.

The university and citizenship

Finally, let's address the citizenship dimensions to all this: in other words, let's shift gears and reflect on the place of universities in — and the contributions they make to — the wider national community. One aspect of this discussion concerns the policy context that shapes the experience of being a student.

A key feature of that wider environment concerns the level of public subsidy which tertiary courses attract. Briefly, notwithstanding the costs which individuals incur in attending university, a significant portion of the cost of someone's degree remains publicly subsidised. Tellingly, however, in this respect all students are not treated equally: the public subsidy for those studying in the disciplines of the social sciences and humanities has (at the time of writing) been static since 2013, while support for those studying the so-called STEM subjects (Science, Technology, Engineering and Maths) has steadily increased. This has significant consequences for the distribution of resources within universities, most of which are not visible to students. More important is that it reflects political choices about where priorities for public investment are. Specifically, it reflects a set of assumptions about both the purpose of a tertiary education (the generation of economic growth) and the sources of such growth (innovation in the sciences) that are — as we shall shortly see — contestable.

A second and related feature of the policy context concerns the costs people incur when they take on tertiary study. Some of these are opportunity costs (e.g. forgone income), which are nigh on impossible to quantify. Other costs are easier to capture. Data regarding student loans, which for many students provide the key means of meeting the course-related and living costs associated with studying, are one important measure. In 2015, the median student loan was $14,421 (although only 37 per cent of all borrowers had a loan of less than $10,000), and the median repayment period sat at seven years (this varies, depending on variables such as the size of the loan, gender, ethnicity, whether repayments are made in New Zealand or from overseas, and so on) (Ministry of Education, 2015).

Some of the risks associated with these figures, such as the cost of providing students with interest-free loans totalling $14.8 billion, are publicly borne. However, debt can also influence the choices graduates make about their futures. For instance, it appears to have a bearing on whether or not people move overseas and, if so, when or even if they return, where they can afford to live, and plans for having families (ibid.). In short, the policy context that has emerged from political choices made over recent years has material consequences for people who choose to take on tertiary study, some but far from all of which are positive.

Perhaps even more importantly, cost deters some people from taking on tertiary education in the first instance. In what feels like another country now, Clarence Beeby (1983), the visionary educationalist and one-time director of the Department of Education, argued that 'every New Zealander, whatever his or her level of academic ability, whether she be rich or poor, whether she live in the town or country, will, at least, have a free education, absolutely free, of the kind for which she is best fitted and to the fullest extent of her powers' (p. 110). Beeby was talking about the primary and secondary sectors, but today many of those who argue against charging fees for tertiary study (which began in 1989) invoke his compelling case that a free education is a fundamental right of citizenship.

It's about the economy, stupid

These and other consequences demand that we reflect on the extent to which a university education facilitates membership of, and participation in, various communities post-study. Indeed, they also invite us to consider the potential consequences of *not* having a tertiary degree. In Aotearoa New Zealand, this issue is almost always framed as the impact a university degree has on someone's employment and earnings prospects. Bluntly, the instrumental question that is nearly always asked is: What's the likely return on your (and the public's) investment in your degree? By most measures, a person's income and employment prospects are enhanced by the completion of a degree. Universities New Zealand suggest that a typical university graduate will earn $1.6 million more over their working life than someone who has not graduated with a degree, while the Ministry of Education (2015) found that five years after graduating the median earnings of Bachelor's degree graduates are 46 per cent higher than those of people earning the national median income.

Universities New Zealand — Te Pōkai Tara reports on the benefits of gaining a degree: http://www.universitiesnz.ac.nz/node/854

It is perfectly reasonable to focus on employment outcomes, not least because of the costs borne by many graduates. However, to *only* do this is to assume that there is just one answer to the question: What is the purpose of a university degree? I think that is a mistake. Instead, different explanations of and for that purpose should be considered.

Some of these lie in the reasons individuals give for having enrolled at a university. Hong Kong education researchers David Kember, Amber Ho and Celina Hong (2010) found that people's motives for attending university can be organised into a series of categories, including compliance with the expectations of family and teachers, the perceived attractions of a university lifestyle (including the sense of belonging to a community), a wish to enhance career prospects, and an interest in pursuing learning in particular subjects.

Public debate in this country about the value of universities is substantially shaped by the last two of these categories. The dominant story is the employability narrative alluded to above, in which context the function of a degree — and of universities in general — is to produce a suitably credentialled supply of labour in response to employers' demands (Grey & Sedgwick, 2014). In addition to the funding increases denied to disciplines in the humanities and social sciences noted above, other recent government initiatives demonstrate the pre-eminence of the employability narrative. One is the Rate My Qualification project that the Tertiary Education Commission rolled out in 2016, inviting employers and graduates to express their views on the relative merits of different institutions' qualifications. Another is the requirement (since 2017) for all tertiary institutions to publish information regarding the employment status and earnings of their graduates, broken down by specific degrees and diplomas.

These policies reflect a particular view of the nature of university degrees (which is that they are primarily about helping graduates find work), and the sorts of things that should be taught in them (technical skills rather than broader intellectual and cognitive competencies). There are three clear problems with this story. First, individuals' employment outcomes are influenced by things universities have little or no control over, including how hard students work while studying, how diligently they apply themselves to searching for work, and the level of demand for labour in the wider economy. The clear inference in much government policy, however, is that tertiary providers are primarily responsible for employment outcomes, which seems more than a little unfair.

Second, it is not immediately clear why the interests of employers should be privileged in this particular way. There may well be other sections of society for whom a university education should be about something other than (or additional to) finding work, but those views are not strongly reflected in present government policy.

Third, the 'universities-should-respond-to-the-requirements-of-employers' lobby assumes that the skills employers need both now and in the future can be predicted and subsequently designed into university courses. It is notoriously difficult, however, to forecast these sorts of things. Moreover, it is now clear that the twin influences of globalisation and automation will ensure that the future world of work will be quite different to the present one. For instance, a recently published report (Chartered Accountants Australia New Zealand, 2015) examined the possible impact of disruptive technologies on the ways in which we work and interact socially in Aotearoa New Zealand. Recycling data generated by Carl Frey and Michael Osborne (2013) from Oxford University, the report's authors predict that 46 per cent of the jobs presently carried out in this country — both blue- and white-collar — are at risk of automation within the next two decades.

It is important not to overreact to such figures. For one thing, as these innovations displace or reshape some jobs, they will also create new ones. The point, however, is that specific technical skills will not be enough in this new world of work. Instead, people will need transferable skills, such as critical thinking, problem-solving and social intelligence, that will help them navigate a working life likely to contain many jobs (some of which do not yet exist) rather than a single career. It is worth noting that the original Frey and Osborne (2013) report concluded that, as automation speeds up, workers 'will reallocate to tasks that are non-susceptible to computerisation — i.e., tasks requiring creative and social intelligence. For workers to win the race, however, they will have to acquire creative and social skills' (p. 45). You wouldn't think so on the basis of current government policy.

But it's not just about the economy, stupid

Frey and Osborne's (2013) conclusion is precisely why it is important to consider a second answer to the question: 'What is the purpose of a degree?' This response stems from the statutory definition of a university. Section 162 of the Education Act 1989 states that the principal aim of universities is 'to develop intellectual independence'; further, it requires universities to 'accept a role as critic and conscience of society'. In other words, the students and staff who make up our universities have the right (if not a legal obligation) to ask awkward questions, question received wisdoms and poke at sacred cows, and voice controversial or unpopular opinions. That *doesn't* mean they get to rant. These statutory rights and requirements have to be exercised ethically, transparently and within the law. All the same, the law makes it clear that universities are required to do more than prepare people for work.

These contests over the meaning and purpose of universities are not just academic (pun intended). For one thing, they have direct consequences for what is deemed to count as knowledge. The employability narrative tends to emphasise skills and attributes with direct application to the job market. This can marginalise knowledge that is important even though it may not be directly applicable to the (current) world of work, and produce a university experience that more closely resembles training than education. It can also have a chilling effect on the capacity of academics to teach, and students to learn, about perspectives on the world that challenge the status quo. In the end this is likely to serve only the interests of those already in positions of political and economic power.

Debates about the purpose of universities also have material consequences for what is held to be acceptable (or, indeed, required) behaviour within those institutions. In Chapter 4, you read that students at our universities were amongst those who took to the streets to protest against the Vietnam War, apartheid in South Africa and inequality in Aotearoa New Zealand. Student voice — expressed through protest and student radio and newspapers — was once a vibrant element of public life both on campuses and well beyond, and was frequently directed at issues of broad social, economic and political importance. Indeed, the student voice was considered an important part of the foundations of a 'vibrant, informed and participatory democracy' (Bridgman, 2007, p. 128). Not so much these days, perhaps. Writing for the online *Bloomberg View*, columnist Megan McArdle (2015) captures the spirit of our times:

> Cultural and economic shifts have pushed students towards behaving more like consumers in a straight commercial transaction and less like people who were being inducted into a non-market institution. The rise of [universities] as labour market gate-keepers has transformed [them]

The life of the mind

The heritage precinct of the Massey University
campus in Palmerston North. The university's
original building, which dates from its origins as
an agricultural college, is at left.

from a place to be imbued with the intangible qualities of character and education . . . into a place where you go to buy a ticket to a good job. A university education is supposed to accomplish two things: expose you to a wide variety of ideas and help you navigate your way through them; and turn you into an adult, which is to say, someone who can cope with people, and ideas, you don't like.

In effect, what is happening is that students' future identity as workers is squeezing out their present identity as students (Daniels & Brooker, 2014). One of the great things about a university education is that it requires you to learn things you did not previously know. That experience can be challenging, stimulating and sometimes uncomfortable, and it requires that you identify and question the limits of your own existing knowledge. But if all we want from our universities these days are job-ready students, we risk producing people who may be fine at working but poorly equipped to live in a world full of people who do not look, think or behave as they do. Not what is required, you might think, at a time when the faces, voices and stories of this country — much less the wider world — are as rich, diverse and connected as they have ever been.

Conclusion

Michael Sandel (2012), a professor of government theory at Harvard, argues that, when a price is attached to something, that thing is transformed and becomes other than what it once was. In New Zealand, as a consequence of the introduction of fees, the meaning of a university education, and the value we place on such an education as a society, have shifted: the private dimension of taking a degree has become more prominent, and the case for a public education has correspondingly diminished (although it is far from dead). In turn, what is expected of both students and staff has also shifted, as have the identities of those within universities. We are all a lot more market-oriented these days, and some would argue less publicly inclined as a result.

I wonder if this reflects something deeper in our national psyche. Here in Aotearoa New Zealand, some of the assumptions we make about students, and about the value of tertiary learning more generally, reflect a certain distrust of (or outright disdain for) the life of the mind. Intellectual endeavour is not in and of itself something we routinely put on a pedestal. Rather, we tend to privilege work. More than that, we privilege a particular understanding of what counts as work. The word 'work', and this perhaps reflects that New Zealand's economic roots lie in the land, is often reserved for things requiring physical activity and the production of tangible artefacts or services that, when sold, directly contribute to economic activity. Conversely, intellectual activity (and the reading and talking that accompanies it), particularly if it takes place in non-market contexts, is sometimes felt to be somehow not quite *real* work. Hence the criticisms of ivory towers and regular calls for universities' staff and students to join the 'real world'. (Quite which world those people presently inhabit is never specified.)

There is clearly an important economic role for the universities to play. Beyond that, however, they also have a critical part to play in fostering and promoting public as well as market (or private) values. And these things matter. As Australian geographer Iain Hay (2016) has persuasively argued, we inhabit a point in history when it is crucial that we are able to distinguish information from knowledge, interpret and learn from the lives of others, and ask sharp questions of those in positions of economic and political power. More than anything else, we need to know how to disagree with others (and to do that well), and how to live alongside those with values and ways of living that differ to our own. These things are central to a society that is inclusive (rather than one which excludes) and accepting of different identities (rather than one which routinely rejects those who are somehow marked as different). And they are at the core of what it is to be a university student. Being invited to learn about people, knowledge and ideas that may at first seem new, alien and uncomfortable is perhaps what Wilson had in mind when he bemoaned that we are drowning in information while starving for wisdom.

 Chapter 7 — Institutional places: The university: http://turangawaewae.massey.ac.nz/chapter7.html

Recommended reading

Grey, S., & Sedgwick, C. (2014). Go study for the economy. In D. Cooke, C. Hill, P. Baskett, & R. Irwin (Eds.), *Beyond the free market: Rebuilding a just society in New Zealand* (pp. 113–120). Wellington, New Zealand: Dunmore Press.

Hay, I. (2016). Defending letters: A pragmatic response to assaults on the humanities. *Journal of Higher Education Policy and Management*. doi: 10.1080/1360080X.2016.1196963

Sandel, M. (2012). *What money can't buy: The moral limits of markets*. New York, NY: Farrar, Straus and Giroux.

References

Beeby, C. (1983). Centennial address. *National Education, 65*(3), 106–110.

Bridgman, T. (2007). Assassins in academia? New Zealand academics as 'critic and conscience of society'. *New Zealand Sociology, 22*(1), 126–144.

Burr, V. (2015). *Social constructionism* (3rd ed.). London, England: Routledge.

Chartered Accountants Australia New Zealand. (2015). *Disruptive technologies: Risks, opportunities — can New Zealand make the most of them?* Retrieved from http://tinyurl.com/podgr6m

Daniels, J., & Brooker, J. (2014). Student identity development in higher education: Implications for graduate attributes and work-readiness. *Educational Research, 56*(1), 65–76.

Frey, C., & Osborne, M. (2013, September). The future of employment: How susceptible are jobs to computerisation? Paper presented at the *Machines and Employment Workshop/Oxford Martin Programme on the Impacts of Future Technology*, Oxford University, England.

Grey, S., & Sedgwick, C. (2014). Go study for the economy. In D. Cooke, C. Hill, P. Baskett, & R. Irwin (Eds.), *Beyond the free market: Rebuilding a just society in New Zealand* (pp. 113–120). Wellington, New Zealand: Dunmore Press.

Hay, I. (2016). Defending letters: A pragmatic response to assaults on the humanities. *Journal of Higher Education Policy and Management.* doi: 10.1080/1360080X .2016.1196963

Kember, D., Ho, A., & Hong, C. (2010). Initial motivation orientation of students enrolling in undergraduate degrees. *Studies in Higher Education, 35*(3), 263–276.

McCardle, M. (2015, August 13). *Sheltered students go to college, avoid education.* Retrieved from http://tinyurl.com/p7jhynl

Ministry of Education. (2015). *Student loan scheme* (annual report). Wellington, New Zealand: Ministry of Education.

Sandel, M. (2012). *What money can't buy: The moral limits of markets.* New York, NY: Farrar, Straus and Giroux.

Stibbe, A. (2010). Identity reflection: Students and societies in transition. *Learning and Teaching in Higher Education, 5*, 86–95.

Sykes, J. (Ed.). (1982). *Concise Oxford Dictionary.* Oxford, England: Clarendon Press.

Zakira, F. (2015). *In defense of a liberal education.* New York, NY: W. W. Norton.

CHAPTER EIGHT:
Digital places
Globalising identity and citizenship
Sy Taffel

Introduction

Thinking about digital places can often be rather confusing as a consequence of the way that we commonly talk about digital technologies. Terminology such as 'virtual' spaces and communities, and 'immaterial' labour, suggests that digital spaces are somehow removed from everyday material reality and physical spaces. Indeed, if we think about the structure of this part of the book, it may at first glance appear that digital places are somehow separate from physical places, hence their location within a separate chapter. Consequently, this chapter begins by examining the networked spaces and flows of digital production to contextualise the international spaces and material impacts of digital technologies as a way of situating some of the physical dimensions of digital places which are often ignored. An important point raised in this section is the extent to which we are implicated in the exploitative nature of the industry through our consumption of digital technology.

The chapter then moves on to explore some of the ways that digital technologies have altered the ways of producing and consuming culture, thereby shaping the ways that citizens form and perform identities. Following the famous aphorism 'We shape our tools and thereafter they shape us' (Culkin, 1967, p. 70), we should note that technological systems play a constructive role in identity formation. While this should not be understood as technology strictly determining the way society functions, it does advocate that technologies can permit, suggest, afford, offer, block, prohibit, deny or otherwise exert pressures and set limitations upon how culture, communication and identity operate within any particular society.

In a contemporary context, this means considering the ways that pervasive wireless access to networked social media platforms change certain ways in which we behave towards one another. Importantly, social media and digital culture have involved the convergence of the previously distinct realms of mass and interpersonal communication. This means that most of us now actively produce mediated content that is publicly or semi-publicly available online, be it Facebook conversations, photos posted to Instagram and Snapchat, or YouTube videos. The production of these mediated communications, using corporate social media platforms, are an important part of how we perform and curate our sense of identity and belonging.

The chapter concludes by moving away from identity and towards citizenship and democracy, considering some of the claims surrounding how digital technologies impact on political debates, organisations and actions, and contemplating what this might mean for twenty-first century citizenship in Aotearoa New Zealand.

Digital places and digital infrastructures

From Aotearoa New Zealand, engaging with digital places necessarily requires us to move beyond national boundaries. Aotearoa New Zealand doesn't manufacture microprocessors, RAM, capacitive touchscreens or other components associated with contemporary information and communications devices, such as smartphones, tablets and laptops, and nor are many of the metals and minerals used to produce digital devices mined here. Indeed, the term 'internet' is a portmanteau composed of the words 'inter'(-national) and 'net'(-work), denoting that the internet is a network of computer networks which are distributed across nation states. These networks are connected via a global network of undersea fibre-optic cables, which then connect with the national-level fixed-line telephone networks that run to your home, allowing you to send and receive information from computers located elsewhere on the internet. At the level of materials, infrastructure and labour, then, thinking about digital systems and how we engage them from within Aotearoa New Zealand requires a focus which goes beyond national boundaries and examines transnational networks of trade and production.

 For a regularly updated and interactive map of the global network of submarine cables go to: http://www.submarinecablemap.com/

The three images shown on page 189 depict equipment located in Massey University's IT Services server room. Image A shows rack-mounted servers, which provide the computation necessary to manage access to the university's online learning environment, university websites, shared storage and other services. Image B shows rack-mounted storage. The 48 hard disk drives seen here store 192 terabytes of data, including all of the data for the university's online learning environment. Image C shows some of the wired fibre-optic connections through which this data travels from the servers to the university intranet and the external internet. The blue fibres can accommodate 40,000 Megabits per second (Mb/s) of data, while the yellow fibres allow for 10,000 Mb/s. We can contrast these speeds with the fact that only 23 per cent of broadband internet connections in Aotearoa New Zealand are faster than 24 Mb/s (Statistics New Zealand, 2015a).

Examining these material networks brings a range of political and ethical issues into focus. These issues begin with the extraction of the raw materials used in microelectronics, such as tantalum, the main global application of which is producing electrolytic capacitors for digital devices. Tantalum has been a key mineral in the conflict within the Democratic Republic of Congo (DRC), where international and civil wars are thought to have been responsible for around 5.4 million deaths over the past 15 years (Coghlan et al., 2007). While tantalum and other conflict minerals were not the root cause of the Congolese conflict, they have been important factors in sustaining and aggravating the conflict, as the various warring factions turned to the DRC's mineral wealth to finance their ongoing military campaigns (Nest, 2011).

Alongside the human costs of producing digital technologies, there are considerable environmental impacts wrought by mining and refining materials. For example, rare earth elements — which aren't actually that rare, but are very hard to separate from one another, and often are found in extremely low concentrations — are vital to the production of microelectronic devices ranging from hard disk drives to headphones. These elements are almost exclusively mined in China. Every tonne of rare earth metals produced also produces 12,000 cubic metres of acidic waste gas, 75 cubic metres of acidic wastewater and around a ton of radioactive waste, as rare earths tend to be found alongside radioactive elements such as thorium and radium. The lake which holds the toxic wastewater tailings at Bayan Obo, China's largest rare earth mine, is 11 square kilometres in size, and is thought to hold over 180 million tonnes of waste from the facility. Since 2009, Baotau Steel, which owns and operates the mine, have been relocating farmers away from the lake following a sharp rise in cancers among the human population and growth defects among livestock. This land is now effectively unsuitable for life because of the impacts of producing materials used to manufacture digital technologies (Taffel, 2016).

After extraction, materials are refined into ores, alloys and components, before being assembled within gargantuan (primarily) Chinese factories, which can have hundreds of thousands of workers. Workers in these places are often paid poorly and forced to work unpaid overtime, and have been filmed by non-government organisations falling asleep from exhaustion during their gruelling 12-hour shifts. These poor working conditions rose to international prominence in 2010 when 14 young migrant workers committed suicide by jumping off the roof of the Foxconn factory in Shenzhen. While Foxconn might not be a brand you are familiar with, it manufactures devices for corporations such as Apple, Lenovo, Dell, Hewlett-Packard, Nintendo and Microsoft. These corporations largely outsource manufacturing to regions where labour is cheap, and where regulation to protect the environment and labourers is minimal.

This global context is important for understanding the ethical issues raised by the consumption of digital products in Aotearoa New Zealand. As purchasers of these products, to what extent are we implicated in the exploitative labour relations and environmental devastation which occurs from the production of digital technologies? These actions certainly would not be permitted on legal or ethical grounds were they to occur within Aotearoa New Zealand, but in a globalised world are we happy to support them happening to other people in other places? What does this say about what it means to be a global citizen, especially when the telecommunications technologies which help foster a sense of being globally connected in real time are themselves built upon such inequitable social and ecological practices? Finally, understanding this global context encourages us to think about how we might engage with these issues and the power relations they point towards.

Creating content in digital culture

A very different understanding of the links between digital techno-culture, identity and citizenship arises from thinking about the roles that digital environments play in the constant construction and performance of our sense of self and identity. We use social media to interact, share, connect, plan and socialise with our whānau, hapū and wider communities. These digital encounters can be globally distributed (but organised around a particular social network or shared point of interest) or very tightly tied to specific places. Recent research indicates that, among school students in New Zealand, the use of digital technologies takes up a vast amount

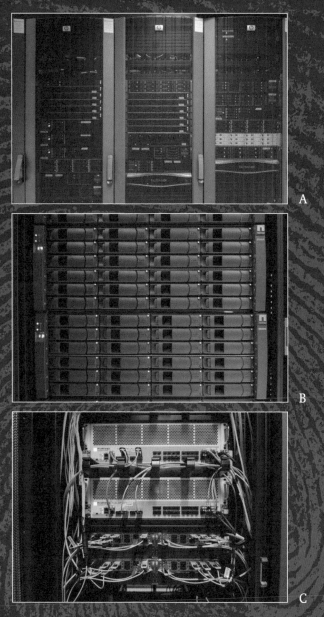

A

B

C

Material networks

Equipment in Massey University's IT services
server room.

of many people's everyday lives. Thirty-five per cent of students spend over three hours every day on the internet, 30 per cent spend at least three hours a day texting, and 25 per cent spend at least three hours a day playing computer games (Clark et al., 2013). Consequently, if we are interested in examining how identities are being constructed and performed, it is important to engage with these digital spaces, and to think about the many ways they contribute to identity and belonging.

It is easy to assume that everyone is equally connected to digital spaces. However, we should remember that there are inequalities in terms of access and speed (bandwidth). As of October 2015, Aotearoa New Zealand had 3.9 million internet-connected mobile phones (Statistics New Zealand, 2015a) and an estimated population of 4.6 million (Statistics New Zealand, 2015b). Given that many individuals have more than one smartphone (commonly one for personal use and one for work), we can estimate that around 20 per cent of the population does not have an internet-enabled mobile device. Importantly, we should recognise that there is a correlation between those who lack connectivity and economic disadvantage, ethnicity and geographical isolation. Whereas 96 per cent of households with an annual income of over $100,000 have internet access, only 55 per cent of households whose income is between $10,000 and $20,000 do. While 85 per cent of Auckland and Wellington households have internet access, only 65 per cent of those in Northland do. Although 86 per cent of Pākehā New Zealanders have internet access, only 68 per cent of Māori and 65 per cent of Pasifika people living in New Zealand do (Statistics New Zealand, 2013).

Furthermore, we should remember that not all forms of access are equal. In 2015, there were 100,000 high-speed fibre-optic internet connections in Aotearoa New Zealand, offering speeds over a thousand times faster than the 55,000 dial-up connections (Statistics New Zealand, 2015a). This has real implications for the way people can participate in digital spaces. While those with fibre can stream ultra-high-definition video in real time and upload huge amounts of media-rich content, those with the slowest internet connections cannot even stream low-definition YouTube videos or music from services such as Spotify.

One of the big changes within the media environment, which has occurred alongside the move to digital technologies, has been the transition from a mass media culture towards a networked and interactive one. Throughout the mid- and late twentieth century, industries such as film, television and radio tended to be quite limited in terms of breadth, with only a few channels available and content being delivered via a few-to-many model of broadcasting that targeted a broad cross-section of the imagined national public. We should, however, note that much of New Zealand's television was imported from the United Kingdom, the United States and Australia; indeed, Aotearoa New Zealand has one of the lowest percentages of domestically produced television in an OECD country. As a consequence, the type of national identity shaped by the mass media, and by television in particular, in Aotearoa New Zealand was heavily influenced by the United States, the United Kingdom and Australia. This is quite different to many other countries, which produced the overwhelming majority of their own national television content and so developed a more distinctive national media culture.

Digital culture, by contrast, has seen the proliferation of vast amounts of mediated content, catering for all kinds of niche communities and tastes. Whether you are interested in guerrilla gardening, League of Legends, cosplay or cute cat videos, there is a huge amount of material online to suit your particular interests, and a community of like-minded people, distributed in different places across the globe, who are eager to discuss, debate, remix, like, comment, share and otherwise engage. Consequently, the scale of contemporary global media production and consumption has increased dramatically: in 2015, every minute, over 100 hours' worth of video content was uploaded to YouTube and 5 million videos were viewed.

These figures highlight a second big shift between mass and digital culture: from content being exclusively produced by professionals for the public, whose engagement was limited to watching and/or listening, to a situation where users themselves generate a large volume of the mediated content being consumed. This is partially attributable to the dramatic fall in the financial costs associated with accessing the technology required to produce media, but it is also due to the growth of broadband internet and 3/4G cellular networks as a means of distributing high-bandwidth media content (such as high-definition video) and the broadening of access to the social, cultural and technical knowledge of how to effectively use these tools and technologies. In 1995, a time when the internet was still relatively new, making a video not only required access to expensive production and editing equipment, but learning how to operate that equipment also usually entailed taking a tertiary education or professional training course. Today, by contrast, you can use a smartphone and consult YouTube tutorials for the requisite skills and knowledge to produce high-quality videos, audio, designs, artwork or other endeavours.

One way of conceptualising these changes has been through the framework of convergence and fragmentation (Jenkins, 2006). While content has broadened and audiences have (in many cases) fragmented, there has also been the convergence of media producers and consumers, professionals and amateurs. We should, however, bear in mind that a large proportion of the most heavily viewed, liked and shared media is still professionally produced. While early utopian approaches to the digital culture predicted the collapse of the boundaries between professional and amateur productions, and there are now far more media producers who are able to derive at least some financial revenue from advertisements or referral links, high-budget productions are able to purchase, promote and otherwise act to ensure that their material becomes visible online. Frequently, this includes paying social media marketing teams to generate online discussion, which appears to emanate from public discourse rather than traditional forms of advertisement (Holiday, 2012). Rather than a binary opposition between mass and digital culture, then, it may make more sense to explore ways that digital technologies have altered, but not entirely replaced, elements of mass culture.

Another approach is to consider these changes through a broader structural framework, which contends that mass media was produced within a system of industrial capitalism, whereas digital culture is produced within neoliberal capitalism. Industrial capitalism was dominated by techniques of standardised mass production and consumption, and is often referred to as 'Fordism', referring to the technological model of mechanised assembly lines which produced identical end-products, a process which was introduced in Henry Ford's motorcar factories in the United States. Unlike the uniform, standardised cars emblematic of industrial production and mass culture, the cultural logic of neoliberalism (which is also referred to as 'post-Fordism') addresses consumers as unique individuals, whose identities are shaped by their personal consumption choices (Amin, 2011). This is not to suggest that broader economic and social structures precisely determine cultural activity and identity or vice versa, but rather that we should consider how these mutually constitutive relations operate within a given society.

Some early twenty-first-century accounts of the internet, Web 2.0 and participatory culture celebrated the rise of the active citizen-creator as heralding the democratisation of the media, but we should note that the contemporary, social-media-dominated online environment does not equate to an equitable playing field. In many cases, there now exists a single, for-profit platform which is dominant across much of the globe. Whether it is Facebook for social networking, Google for searching, Twitter for microblogging, Amazon for online shopping or YouTube for online video-streaming, we find a similar pattern of near-monopolistic control within the various domains of social media.

Interestingly, this distribution is marked by extreme inequality, with a handful of websites having hundreds of millions of daily users, while the majority of the internet has few if any hits. It has been posited that this inequality is partially due to the structure of the world wide web as a scale-free network. In research into a variety of scale-free systems, from citation patterns in science through to web linking and popularity, Albert-László Barabási and Réka Albert (1999) found that a common pattern within these disparate networks is an inverse power–law distribution, meaning that unlike a normal distribution (also known as a 'bell curve'), which sees points equally distributed around a mean point, there are a handful of extremely popular nodes and a long tail with a large number of very unpopular nodes.

Rather than a structure for equity and democracy, this work suggests that a powerful structural force relating to the web pushes distributions towards inequality. The online platforms we use are not just the result of personal choices made by individuals; their popularity and utility also arise from network dynamics, which in part function through peer pressure to inhabit the same digital spaces as our friends and loved ones. Consequently, already popular sites with a critical mass draw in more users, whereas those with few users remain unpopular.

With the notable exception of Wikipedia, the user-generated online encyclopaedia which is a not-for-profit organisation, the giants of social media are all profit-generating corporations whose market values are typically measured in hundreds of billions of dollars. Indeed, in 2016 the world's top five companies in terms of their market capitalisation were all US-based tech companies: Apple, Alphabet (Google), Microsoft, Amazon and Facebook (Ovide & Molla, 2016). It is worth considering how and why platforms such as Facebook and YouTube, which are free at the point of use and which have enormous costs in terms of the technological overheads of maintaining vast server farms, as well as the employee costs associated with software development, can be so highly valued. The answer to this question lies in the revenue which is generated by advertising, a model which was previously popularised within mass media forms such as newspapers, television and radio.

What changes with social media is that, rather than standardised adverts which are sent to all viewers, users are sent highly targeted advertising which utilises the data provided by your past activities: profile details, likes, comments, photographs, GPS and IP address locational data, purchase histories and so on. Being able to carefully tailor both the adverts you see and the content you receive is seen as being key to the success of social media platforms. Personally tailored content and advertising again resonates with the broader cultural logic of individualised and unique consumers, but algorithmic personalisation has been criticised for commodifying social interactions and for creating filter bubbles, which refers to showing users content that reinforces pre-existing beliefs and biases rather than contesting them (Pariser, 2011). Whereas traditional, location-based communities included difference and contestation, the algorithms that govern social media feeds can easily create echo chambers of like-minded individuals who do not have to be aware of, or engage with, alternative perspectives.

Digital environments and social media platforms form spaces in which there are contested power relations between users, advertisers and platform owners. People continuously construct elements of their persona within digital spaces, which are used for socialising, pursuing hobbies, consuming and creating media content. At the same time, however, many of the platforms are simultaneously using the users, harvesting data to target advertising and content towards them, which contributes towards shaping the identities of those users whose interactions also shape other individuals' experiences of the platform.

While there is obviously a huge disparity in the power relations between multibillion-dollar global corporations and individual users, we should not assume that users do not engage in acts of playful everyday resistance against systems of corporate control and capture. Changing profile details to falsify your gender, age or other personal details, or clicking on links you are uninterested in to alter the advertising a platform thinks will be relevant to you, sits alongside employing technically sophisticated tools, such as ad-blockers and virtual private networks (VPNs), as examples of what French scholar Michel de Certeau (1984) described as the tactics of the weak, which stand in contrast to the strategies of the powerful.

Social media and digital identities

Another key change surrounding the digital communications environment has been the way that the previously distinct realms of interpersonal and mass communications have converged. Throughout the twentieth century these existed as separate technological infrastructures for mass communications, such as film, television and radio, and for mediated interpersonal telecommunications, such as telephone and postal networks, or the 35-millimetre photographic cameras that were used to take family photos. Whereas the mass media used a centre-to-periphery model of broadcasting, which was prohibitively expensive for most people to be able to engage with except as an audience, huge numbers of individuals were able to write letters, make telephone calls and take photographs. These forms of communication, however, were limited in terms of their distribution, with telephone calls and letters only reaching a single individual, whereas showing photographic images to others required their physical proximity to the photographic print.

The internet changes this situation, by enabling a mode of communication which is not one-to-one (like the telephone) or one-to-many (like television), but can be understood as a many-to-many model of communication. Furthermore, the convergence of multiple media, which previously had required different chemical and/or electrical means for communication, within the single medium of binary-encoded digital information allows for a range of still and moving images, sounds and text to be incorporated together in these mediated conversations.

We should note, however, that digital infrastructures are not singular and fixed, but are constantly expanding and changing, so the types of connectivity and communications that use the internet today are very different to those that existed 10 years ago. One major shift has been away from wired connections to desktop computers, towards the type of high-bandwidth wireless connectivity that is now fairly ubiquitous within urban areas, and which is primarily accessed through mobile computational technologies, particularly smartphones. Mobile internet access offers an important departure, in that it means many of us now carry computational devices with us all of the time, allowing us to not only access information, but also to connect, communicate and share mediated content with our family, whānau and friends at any time.

The immediate connectivity allowed by smartphones and photo-sharing forms of social media allows loved ones to see moments of our lives — but does this mean that we now spend more time than ever before on editing the so-called 'present' and curating a branded online identity? Being constantly connected has many obvious benefits: we can share messages of support, solidarity and care at a moment's notice, let people know that we will be late to meet them, share our latest selfies, or allow our friends to see funny pictures of the cat. There are, however, also a number of concerns that emerge from the risks associated with this communications environment: that being 'always on' is having a negative effect on the attentional capacities of young people; that people used to digitally mediated communications struggle with real-time face-to-face conversations where they cannot edit their words; that people publicly share material which will detrimentally impact on their job prospects later in life; that these tools enable new forms of antisocial behaviour, such as cyberbullying; that they open up vulnerable people to various forms of online predation through financial scams, identity theft and sexual harassment; and that as we become more intimate with our digital devices we become less attuned to being intimate with other people.

 For a more in-depth discussion of these issues see Sherry Turkle's TED talk drawn from her book *Alone Together*: http://www.ted.com/talks/sherry_turkle_alone_together?language=en#

While the technology industries advertise mobile communication technologies as a way of enhancing our freedom and agency, they can also mean that we are always available for work, receiving email and other forms of work-related communications throughout what used to be considered leisure time. Paradoxically, these tools enhance particular forms of freedom, while constraining others. Rather than simply being a force for good or bad behaviours, we can conclude that digital spaces offer the possibility for various forms of social activity, which covers a spectrum ranging from highly desirable to highly undesirable actions, with the precise balance of actions which eventuate largely depending on the ways that people engage and interact with these technologies.

Digital politics and digital activism

One usage of digital technologies that is of particular relevance to contemporary forms of citizenship (briefly discussed in Chapter 4) is the ways that digital platforms impact on political activism, organisation and mobilisation. The capacity of digital forums to provide spaces for interaction, deliberation, debate and dialogue between citizens generated a lot of excitement surrounding claims that digital platforms would provide a renewed model of the public sphere.

The concept of the 'public sphere' was developed by German social theorist Habermas (1991), who was interested in how democracy — a term whose literal translation indicates the rule of the people — does not merely include voting for elected representatives once every few years, but is also characterised by deliberative exchanges between informed citizens in spaces separated from both commercial and governmental domains. Habermas points towards the bourgeois European coffee-shop culture in the eighteenth and nineteenth centuries as an example of spaces where citizens debated how and why laws should be enacted in fledgling democracies — although there are serious issues with this proposed normative model of the public sphere, given that non-Europeans, women and the working classes were entirely excluded from these deliberative exchanges.

Subsequently, Habermas explores how the public sphere in the twentieth century was altered by the introduction of the mass media, which effectively shaped debates in advance of any public discussion. Proprietors of newspapers, radio stations and television networks were placed in positions of communicative power, whereby their voices and political perspectives were amplified above those of most members of the public, thereby stifling genuine democratic dialogue by shaping the opinions and identities of audiences.

During the 1990s and early 2000s, optimistic commentators argued that the participatory mode of exchange afforded by the internet would bring about a fundamental change in the orientation of the public sphere, and would consequently create a more inclusive and democratic culture and society (e.g. Kellner, 1999). What has transpired is, however, rather more complex than the straightforward declarations of cyber-democracy suggested. Digital environments do provide spaces for citizens to engage in debates, share ideas, sign petitions and participate in other forms of online political action. Additionally, social movements and activist groups which have risen to prominence since the 1990s, from the Zapatistas and alter-globalisation movements through to Occupy and the Arab Spring, have all utilised the internet as a pivotal tool for practically organising political action, as well as adopting organisational forms which parallel the structural model of the distributed network that underpins the internet (Hardt & Negri, 2005).

It should be noted that the internet and the world wide web are not the same thing, with a crucial distinction existing between the network of peers (equal nodes) which comprises the internet, and the server/client distinction that characterises the web, and which structurally forms a hierarchical centre-to-periphery model.

While some commentators have celebrated activists embracing (primarily

Occupy

The Occupy movement is an international socio-political movement against social inequality and lack of 'real democracy' around the world, its primary goal being to advance social and economic justice and new forms of democracy. The movement has many different scopes; local groups often have different focuses, but among the movement's prime concerns are how large corporations (and the global financial system) control the world in a way that disproportionately benefits a minority, undermines democracy and is unstable. The first Occupy protest to receive widespread attention was Occupy Wall Street in New York City, which began on 17 September 2011. By 9 October, Occupy protests had taken place or were ongoing in over 951 cities across 82 countries, including New Zealand. Initially overt police repression was minimal, but by the end of 2011 authorities had cleared most of the major camps. The last remaining high-profile sites — in Washington, DC and London — were evicted by February 2012.

The movement commonly uses the slogan 'We are the 99%', the #Occupy hashtag format, and organises through websites such as Occupy Together. According to *The Washington Post*, the movement, which has been described as a 'democratic awakening' by Cornel West, is difficult to distil to a few demands. In October 2011, Los Angeles City Council became one of the first governmental bodies in the United States to adopt a resolution stating its informal support of the Occupy movement. In October 2012 the Executive Director of Financial Stability at the Bank of England stated the protesters were right to criticise and had persuaded bankers and politicians 'to behave in a more moral way'. ABRIDGED FROM WIKIPEDIA

American, often corporate) digital technologies as a way of spreading forms of Western freedom and democracy, especially when these tools have been utilised in places such as Egypt and Hong Kong (e.g. Shirky, 2011), others have been rather more sceptical about the impacts of digital technology on politics and activism (e.g. Morozov, 2012). Although social media and campaigning websites such as Avaaz make it very easy for individuals to demonstrate support for particular causes through clicking 'like' or signing online petitions, this communicative action, characterised by weak social bonds and a brief temporal engagement, is quite different from the type of community which is formed through participating in direct or industrial action, where interpersonal connections tend to be much stronger.

Indeed, one argument positing why movements such as the Arab Spring and Occupy have failed to fulfil their initial promise — with Occupy having largely dissolved into internal disputes, and the revolutionary movements in Egypt and Libya leading to military rule in the former and a protracted civil war in the latter — is that social media provide powerful tools for mobilising large numbers of people quickly, but without forming the necessary organisational infrastructure to meet longer-term goals, these swarm-like, leaderless social movements are poorly suited to the practicalities and complexities of governing.

Another important critique of digital activism is foregrounded by considering the global attention, energy and enthusiasm generated by the Kony 2012 viral video and campaign, as noted in Chapter 4, which sought to mobilise social media to assist in capturing the Lord's Resistance Army (LRA) commander Joseph Kony, who was indicted for committing war crimes, including forcibly recruiting child soldiers, by the International Criminal Court in 2005, but has evaded capture since then. While the video gained over 100 million views, and provoked a huge amount of sentiment and sympathy for Kony's victims, this did little to actually curtail the reign of Kony or the LRA within central Africa, and as of December 2016 he is still at large.

Similarly, we could point towards the #BringBackOurGirls campaign surrounding 276 female students kidnapped by Jihadist militants Boko Haram in Nigeria during 2014. Again, a huge amount of online awareness-raising occurred, and in some cases this even spurred declarations of support from foreign governments, but in terms of actually returning all the kidnapped students, nothing tangible was achieved.

These two cases exemplify what American political theorist Jodi Dean (2009) has described as the fantasy of the internet as a space of global citizenship and democracy. Citizens in Aotearoa New Zealand, the United States and Western

Europe are not able to meaningfully effect political change by signing petitions, liking social media posts or sharing videos about conflicts in far-flung nations, where in many cases the English language is unlikely to be understood. While the internet offers the promise of a global democracy able to match the scope and scale of globalised capitalism, in practice what kind of rational-critical democratic dialogue could you maintain with individuals who speak only Farsi, Mandarin or Xhosa? Dean argues that our contemporary context can be understood as a novel mode of communicative capitalism, where the real-time circulation of enormous volumes of user-generated content on corporate digital platforms is a key driver of contemporary economies, and which instils contributors with a misplaced feeling of meaningfully contributing to global political action.

That is not to say that online communications are not useful in generating political change, and even the most ardent critics of digital democracy readily state this, but digital technologies do not necessitate the spread of freedom, democracy or other solely positive attributes. While technologies, digital or otherwise, have been, and will continue to be, important tools with which citizens can organise, mobilise and effect social change, we should bear in mind that the same technologies are also employed by repressive governments, autocratic dictators and other hierarchically privileged figures to surveil, locate and control resistance.

As the cache of documents leaked by Edward Snowden in 2013 dramatically revealed, corporate- and state-based systems of digital surveillance are thoroughly entangled. The Snowden materials are also useful in foregrounding New Zealand's role within the Five Eyes global surveillance network alongside the United Kingdom, the United States, Canada and Australia. From rhetorics of digital democracy and globalised public spheres, this asks us to return to thinking about how the geographical location of Aotearoa New Zealand plays a role in global systems of state-led surveillance and control which are predicated upon the digital systems that are often rather simplistically equated to enhancing freedom and autonomous actions.

Conclusion

Thinking about digital place requires us to move beyond national boundaries in certain ways, while also requiring us to consider how our technologically mediated activities affect our ongoing performances of identity and sense of belonging. Digital technologies require us to think beyond nation states in terms of material systems of production, global telecommunications systems and international surveillance networks. Examining these systems raises a number of important questions around the ethics of global citizenship, given that socially and environmentally destructive practices surround the production of digital technologies. There are also questions about the ways in which digital technologies allow novel modes of state and corporate surveillance to penetrate into aspects of our lives that were previously deemed to be private and personal, and how doing so has an impact on the way we construct ourselves as individuals.

Indeed, the way that highly targeted social-media advertising affects our consumer behaviours demonstrates one way in which unequal power relations permeate digital spaces, and exemplifies how technological structures affect the types of identity-forming consumer choices that we make. These commercial technological systems are not neutral, and the algorithms which suggest content you may like, or show particular materials on newsfeeds while excluding others, play an active but often unseen role in shaping identities. This does not, however, claim that technology strictly determines identity, but rather that identity is something that is constantly being negotiated between personal choices and social, cultural and technological infrastructures.

We have seen how wireless, networked, digital platforms have blended the realms of interpersonal communication and mass media, how they have created the notion of being 'always on', and how this fairly new mode of social and technological connection has both positive and negative consequences. Digital spaces potentially offer unparalleled possibilities for connecting with others, sharing culture and knowledge, and becoming active citizens. However, they also create the risk of forming echo chambers where individuals carefully craft narcissistic representations of themselves while avoiding alternative perspectives and becoming less adept at real-time interactions with other people.

Finally, we have explored the ways in which digital platforms are widely used for contemporary civic and activist interventions. Some thinking around digital politics equates particular tools and technologies with freedom and democracy, but there is considerable evidence to suggest that they are equally useful for surveillance and curtailing political dissent. Digital places and technologies, then, are important sites for understanding key elements of identity, belonging and citizenship in the twenty-first century.

Chapter 8 — Digital places: Globalising identity and citizenship:
http://turangawaewae.massey.ac.nz/chapter8.html

Recommended reading

Castells, M. (2015). *Networks of outrage and hope: Social movements in the internet age*. London, England: John Wiley & Sons.

Gehl, R. (2014). *Reverse engineering social media: Software, culture, and political economy in new media capitalism*. Philadelphia, PA: Temple University Press.

Kitchin, R., & Dodge, M. (2011). *Code/Space: Software and everyday life*. Cambridge, MA: MIT Press.

Van Dijck, J. (2013). *The culture of connectivity: A critical history of social media*. Oxford, England: Oxford University Press.

References

Amin, A. (2011). *Post-Fordism: A reader*. London, England: John Wiley & Sons.

Barabási, A.-L., & Albert, R. (1999). Emergence of scaling in random networks. *Science, 286*, 509–512.

Clark, T. C., Fleming, T., Bullen, P., Denny, S., Crengle, S., Dyson, B., Fortune, S., Lucassen, M., Peiris-John, R., Robinson, E., Rossen, F., Sheridan, J., Teevale, T., & Utter, J. (2013). *Youth '12 overview: The health and wellbeing of New Zealand secondary school students in 2012*. Auckland, New Zealand: University of Auckland. Retrieved from https://www.fmhs.auckland.ac.nz/assets/fmhs/faculty/ahrg/docs/2012prevalence-tables-report.pdf

Coghlan, B., Brennan, R. J., Ngoy, P., Dofara, D., Otto, B., Clements, M., & Stewart, T. (2007). Mortality in the Democratic Republic of Congo: A nationwide survey. *The Lancet, 367*(9504), 44–51.

Culkin, J. M. (1967, March 18). A schoolman's guide to Marshall McLuhan. *The Saturday Review, 51*–53, 70–72.

de Certeau, M. (1984). *The practice of everyday life*. Berkeley and Los Angeles, CA: University of California Press.

Dean, J. (2009). *Democracy and other neoliberal fantasies: Communicative capitalism and left politics*. Durham and London, England: Duke University Press.

Habermas, J. (1991). *The structural transformation of the public sphere: An inquiry into a category of bourgeois society*. Cambridge, MA: MIT Press.

Hardt, M., & Negri, A. (2005). *Multitude: War and democracy in the age of empire*. London, England: Penguin.

Holiday, R. (2012). *Trust me, I'm lying: Confessions of a media manipulator*. London, England: Penguin.

Jenkins, H. (2006). *Convergence culture: Where old and new media collide*. New York, NY: New York University Press.

Kellner, D. (1999). Globalisation from below? Toward a radical democratic technopolitics. *Angelaki: Journal of the Theoretical Humanities, 4*(2), 101–113.

Morozov, E. (2012). *The net delusion: The dark side of internet freedom.* London, England: Penguin.

Nest. (2011). *Coltan.* Cambridge, England: Polity Press.

Ovide, S., & Molla, R. (2016, August 2). Technology conquers stock market. *Bloomberg,* Retrieved from https://www.bloomberg.com/gadfly/articles/2016-08-02/tech-giants-form-fab-five-to-dominate-stock-valuation-chart

Pariser, E. (2011). *The filter bubble: What the internet is hiding from you.* London, England: Penguin.

Shirky, C. (2011). Political power of social media-technology, the public sphere, and political change. *Foreign Affairs, 90,* 28–41.

Statistics New Zealand. (2013). *Household use of information and communication technology 2012.* Retrieved from http://www.stats.govt.nz/~/media/Statistics/Browse%20for%20stats/HouseholdUseofICT/HOTP2012/huict-2012-tables.xls

Statistics New Zealand. (2015a). *Internet service provider survey 2015.* Retrieved from http://stats.govt.nz/~/media/Statistics/browse-categories/industry-sectors/information-technology-communications/ISP-survey/isp15-alltables.xlsx

Statistics New Zealand. (2015b). *National population estimates: 30 June 2015.* Retrieved from http://www.stats.govt.nz/browse_for_stats/population/estimates_and_projections/NationalPopulationEstimates_HOTPAt30Jun15.aspx

Taffel, S. (2016). Invisible bodies and forgotten spaces: Materiality, toxicity, and labour in digital ecologies. In H. Randell-Moon & R. Tippet (Eds.), *Security, race, biopower: Essays on technology and corporeality* (pp. 121–141). London, England: Palgrave Macmillan.

PART FOUR: STORIES OF AOTEAROA NEW ZEALAND

Stories:
Introduction

Ella Kahu

Welcome to the last section of the book, the key purpose of which is to critically engage with three major national narratives that make particular assertions about national identity in Aotearoa New Zealand, and examine the ways in which we New Zealanders represent ourselves both to each other and to the wider world.

About Part 4

In Part 1, we explored who makes up our nation, in Part 2 we looked at how those diverse peoples use their voices to participate and have a say in our communities, and then in Part 3 we explored how the places in which we interact with others shape our identities. Now we take a step back and look at how those identities, voices and places are shaped in part by the wider national narratives we tell ourselves (and others) about what it means to be a New Zealander.

Our national identity is more than just our history: 'The facts of history are the bare bones of nationhood; it is in the fleshing out of facts into narratives of meaning that a people are forged' (Liu, McCreanor, McIntosh, & Teaiwa, 2005, p. 13). As British sociologist Duncan Bell (2003) says, those narratives 'tell a particular type of story about the nation and its importance, a story that resonates emotively with people, that glorifies the nation, that is easily transmitted and absorbed' (p. 67). National narratives are important and powerful: they shape our social norms and our view of our world, they include or exclude certain groups, and perhaps most importantly, they impact on who feels they belong in this place and who feels they do not. National stories often grow from a kernel of truth, but, as the following chapters illustrate, that kernel is surrounded by layers of fiction.

Here in Part 4 we explicitly address three of our national narratives (or stories), and the ways in which individuals both reproduce (for example, through language, rituals and behaviour), and have their identities shaped by, these stories. The conceptual template underpinning these chapters is as follows:

1. We look at the nature and origins of each narrative. What is the story, and what messages does each convey? Here we are interested in teasing out the historical, political, economic and social contexts from which our chosen narratives have emerged.
2. We ask: What are the purposes of the narratives? To what ends are they deployed?
3. We explore how these grand, sweeping national stories are propagated and maintained. How are they communicated and reinforced? What have been some of the past and present struggles over the claims to 'truth' and the degrees of accuracy contained within these narratives?
4. For each of the three national stories, we examine the material, social, political and economic consequences for people and for our shared national identity.
5. Finally, we compare the narrative with empirical evidence and circumstance, and explore alternative stories that are marginalised or masked by the dominant narrative. We will pose such questions as: Is the story 'real' for everyone? What's been left out of the national story?

Overview of chapters

So what are the stories that we tell about our nation? About this place? Any nation has multiple narratives, and choosing three was not easy. There are other stories that are just as strong and that have equally important impacts on our national identity: 'New Zealand is a great place to raise kids' or 'We are all one people' are two such examples. We are confident, however, that the three narratives we have selected — New Zealand is an equal society, New Zealand is clean and green, and Anzac as our nation's creation story — will resonate in different ways with many New Zealanders.

In Chapter 9, David Littlewood tackles the story that egalitarianism is a central facet of New Zealand life. He traces the history of this view from the promises made to early British settlers, through the Liberal changes in the late 1800s and early 1900s, to the dramatic neoliberal restructuring of the mid- to late 1980s. He highlights that the consequences of our supposed egalitarianism differ for different identity groups, and that, in terms of outcomes, Māori and women continue to have less claim to equality. Critically, David distinguishes between our attitudes towards equality of opportunity and equality of outcome, and argues that we prioritise the first while not fully understanding that opportunity and outcome are inextricably linked in a generational cycle.

Next, Juliana Mansvelt, in Chapter 10, looks at a story that is, among other things, the backbone of marketing campaigns aimed at selling New Zealand to the world: 100% Pure. Like egalitarianism, our clean green image stems initially from early British settlers contrasting New Zealand to their homeland. Juliana highlights the multiple purposes of this narrative — as a source of national pride, and as an economic tool that supports both tourism and our agricultural export industry. She then looks closely at the evidence for the truth of the narrative: is New Zealand as clean and green as we like to think? Her conclusions remind us that national identity narratives are not always strongly grounded in fact.

Finally, we end this section on the shores of Gallipoli where, according to some, our national identity was first founded. In Chapter 11, Carl Bradley and Rhys Ball explore the Anzac narrative. They look at New Zealand's military history, and how that history has been shaped by other aspects of our national identity, and what the Anzac story tells us about New Zealand. As well, they look at what is missing from the story, and, paralleling the exclusions evident in the story of egalitarianism, they highlight that this story is dominated by masculine, monocultural views and experiences. As we commemorate the centenary of the First World War, the Anzac story shows signs of widening to give greater voice to the experiences of those who have been silenced, including pacifists and conscientious objectors. Carl and Rhys's chapter reminds us, too, that there is still further to go.

Conclusion

Tūrangawaewae is intended to encourage you to think critically about the assumptions we all carry regarding identity and belonging in Aotearoa New Zealand. Our main focus in this final section is to explicitly develop your understanding of how non-material factors, such as ideas and discourses, help shape the world. In earlier sections of the book we tended to look at the material dimensions of identity, such as demography, place, historical events and so forth. In this section, we look at the profound influence that words can have when they are strung together into compelling stories.

There is a second and quite subtle purpose to this section. By studying how narrative (or storytelling) functions, we will directly address how we made sense of and attributed meaning to the content we covered in the earlier sections on faces, voices and places. That is, as you read through these final chapters, we encourage you to think critically about how those topics were framed through particular choices of words, and about the contestability and consequences of such framing.

This final section moves our lens wider, and looks not just at individual identity but also at national identity. The three narratives we analyse provide examples of the ways in which the particular stories we tell about ourselves shape our collective sense of self and place. It is often taken as given that to be a New Zealander means to live in a nation that treats people fairly, that has a pristine environment, and that has a proud history on the world military stage. Many of us wear these stories almost as badges of pride, particularly when we are overseas or talking about this place to others; they can literally define what it means to be a New Zealander. But these stories mask both the lived experiences of some groups in our society, and other narratives we might tell about ourselves. And what does *that* say about our national identity?

References

Bell, D. S. (2003). Mythscapes: Memory, mythology, and national identity. *The British Journal of Sociology, 54*(1), 63–81. doi:10.1080/0007131032000045905

Liu, J. H., McCreanor, T., McIntosh, T., & Teaiwa, T. (2005). Introduction: Constructing New Zealand identities. In J. H. Liu, T. McCreanor, T. McIntosh, & T. Teaiwa (Eds.), *New Zealand identities: Departures and destinations* (pp. 11–20). Wellington, New Zealand: Victoria University Press.

CHAPTER NINE:

We're all equal here, mate

Egalitarianism in Aotearoa New Zealand

David Littlewood

Introduction

In his foreword to a 2016 centenary history of the Labour Party, party leader Andrew Little asserts that the defining feature of the New Zealand Labour Party has always been its efforts to 'promote greater equality of opportunity' (p. 9). Whether true or not, the fact that Little chose to highlight this particular ideal above all others is highly significant. It demonstrates the enduring resonance of one of the most influential narratives in New Zealand's post-1840 history: that this is an egalitarian country, where everyone is treated equally. However, formal definitions of 'egalitarian' or 'egalitarianism' refer not just to the opportunities people have in life, but also to the outcomes they experience as a result — especially their wealth, income and power within society. As Little's choice of words suggests, and as the following discussion will demonstrate, New Zealanders have consistently attached more importance to equality of opportunity than they have to equality of outcome.

This chapter examines the origins, evolution and accuracy of the notion that 'we're all equal here'. It begins by investigating when and why the concept first developed, before outlining three periods that enshrined egalitarianism as a central feature of

New Zealand's national identity. The consequences of the narrative — both positive and negative — are then discussed for different social and ethnic groups. Finally, this chapter looks at how the narrative has been qualified and undermined, to the point where it now bears only a passing resemblance to many people's lived experiences.

A foundational narrative

The portrayal of New Zealand as a fundamentally egalitarian society began during the early stages of European settlement. After the signing of the Treaty of Waitangi (te Tiriti o Waitangi) in 1840, the new colony's administrators wanted to attract as many British immigrants as possible to populate and develop the land. Yet their efforts ran up against a major obstacle. Victorian Britain was one of the richest and most advanced nations in the world, whereas New Zealand was a long and expensive sea voyage away, had very little modern infrastructure, and was reportedly inhabited by a hostile, even cannibalistic, indigenous population. It quickly became apparent that Britons would only relocate in large numbers if doing so were made a more attractive proposition.

Over the following decades, New Zealand's colonial administrators arranged for a vast quantity of propaganda to be targeted at potential immigrants. These articles, pamphlets and posters used a mixture of omission, exaggeration and outright fabrication to depict New Zealand as a paradise, the proverbial 'land of milk and honey', which had retained all of the best features of British society, while also avoiding its problems. And while even the most deceitful publications avoided suggesting that the colony possessed an absolute equality of income, it was consistently marketed as being free from the extremes of wealth and poverty, and from the rigid class divisions, that had come to afflict the Old Country. By moving to New Zealand, the literature declared, individuals from all backgrounds would be guaranteed a fair chance at 'getting on' in life. If they worked hard and acted responsibly, then they would be able to obtain a better standard of living and achieve social advancement. For many of New Zealand's European immigrants, therefore, equality of opportunity and not-too-great an inequality of outcome were both expectations and promises (Belich, 1996).

See the Te Ara Encyclopedia section on 'British Immigration and the New Zealand Company', which includes images of posters and adverts: www.teara.govt.nz/en/history-of-immigration/page-3

Selling paradise

The New Zealand Company was a commercial venture set up to colonise New Zealand, thereby helping relieve the burden of overcrowding in nineteenth-century industrial-era Britain. Investors were promised 100 acres of farmland, but they needed labourers to work the land. An advertising campaign sold New Zealand as 'a Britain of the South', free from class tension and with a good climate (the inconvenient fact that the land was already possessed by Māori or covered in bush was not mentioned). Free passage was offered to people with specific skills, such as mechanics and agricultural labourers, and the Company used idyllic paintings, like this one of Wellington Harbour by Charles Heaphy, to attract the new colonists.

An enduring narrative

The long-term maintenance of this narrative can largely be attributed to the policies and ideals that arose during three significant periods. By the beginning of the 1890s, many New Zealanders believed that the promise of an egalitarian society was not being fulfilled. A small percentage of the colony's population had acquired a sizeable proportion of its agricultural land, the 1880s had witnessed a sustained economic depression, and the number of industrial disputes over working conditions and wages had steadily increased.

The Liberal Government, first elected in 1890, sought to mitigate these issues by enhancing the opportunities for ordinary people to improve their circumstances. This involved government interventions in the market, and the placing of restrictions on what property owners could do with their possessions. By the time the Liberals finally lost power in 1912, they had broken up and redistributed several large land holdings; introduced a graduated income tax; provided low-interest loans to help settlers purchase their own plots of land; set up a state-administered old age pension; and established a compulsory conciliation and arbitration mechanism for resolving disagreements between employers and trade unions. The most famous of the Liberals' measures was passed in 1893, when, as Richard discussed during Chapter 3, New Zealand became the first country in the world to grant women the universal right to vote in parliamentary elections. This extensive programme of reforms helped to restore public faith in the egalitarian ideal, and became a source of considerable national pride. New Zealand again began to market itself as a 'workingman's paradise', and, as historian James Belich notes (2001), it also adopted the mantle of the 'world's social laboratory'.

Egalitarianism became further cemented in the national psyche during the Boer War (1899–1902) and the First World War (1914–1918). These conflicts were the first time that large bodies of New Zealanders travelled overseas, and the first time that they were able to compare themselves directly with their British counterparts. Many were left feeling appalled, but also vindicated, by what they found. New Zealanders scorned the unthinking deference to authority displayed by some lower-class British soldiers, and particularly loathed the pompous speech, manners and attitudes of the upper-class British officers. Letters home frequently asserted that the Anzacs' 'superior' military performance was a result of their greater initiative and flexibility; qualities that were said to have been facilitated by the more informal and equal relationships that existed within their units. Such accounts illustrate the strong links between two of New Zealand's national stories — egalitarianism and the Anzac narrative. This will be looked at further in Chapter 11, where Carl and Rhys explore the idea that New Zealand forged its identity as an independent nation on the beaches of Gallipoli during 1915.

The strongest reinforcement of the egalitarian narrative occurred soon after one of its most serious challenges. During the late 1920s and early 1930s, New Zealand society endured the widespread trauma of the Great Depression. A contraction in international trade and steep falls in export prices caused many businesses to downsize or collapse, which in turn pushed tens of thousands of people into unemployment and poverty. As successive governments proved unable to halt this deterioration through austerity and retrenchment measures, it seemed that the promise of egalitarianism had been dealt a fatal blow. However, New Zealand's political landscape then underwent a seismic shift.

Motivated by its socialist ideologies, the First Labour Government came to power in 1935 determined to manage the economy in a way that would allow healthy people to find work at wages that provided them with a 'decent' standard of living. In other words, families would no longer need to be content with simply 'getting by'. The central plank of this agenda was achieving 'full employment', to which end the government took control of New Zealand's monetary policies and introduced guaranteed prices and import restrictions to protect domestic industries. Further legislation raised death duties and income tax rates, while strengthening the negotiating powers of trade unions and providing for a reasonable adult male pay-rate and an eight-hour working day. A system of state-provided housing, free healthcare, free education and means-tested benefits was also made available to all citizens as of right. On reviewing this raft of reforms and the attitudes they had fostered, American political scientist Leslie Lipson suggested that if the New Zealanders were to erect their own version of the Statue of Liberty on the Waitematā Harbour in Auckland, it would surely be named the 'Statue of Equality'.

The egalitarian narrative has been an important part of New Zealand's self-identity ever since. Labour eventually lost power in 1949, and enjoyed only two more terms in office over the next 35 years. Nonetheless, the intervening National governments accepted the major economic and social initiatives that had been introduced — particularly 'full employment' and the state provision of welfare services — meaning that they remained the basis of official policy up until 1984. Even after the profound changes that were initiated during that year (detailed later in this chapter), notions of equality have continued to find regular expression in New Zealand's politics, media and language. The National Party's 1990 election campaign banner signalled its intention to uphold 'A Decent Society', while the claim that Pākehā and Māori enjoy 'the best race relations in the world' still retains considerable populist appeal.

Out of work and angry

The Great Depression had a devastating impact
on thousands of New Zealanders, and many
communities faced a desperate struggle to feed
and clothe their families. In this photo, taken
in 1932, Jim Roberts — secretary of the New
Zealand Waterside Workers' Union (wearing a
bow tie) — is surrounded by unemployed men at
a demonstration at Parliament.

New Zealanders tend to portray themselves as being inherently sceptical of authority figures, as disliking conspicuous displays of wealth, and as being scornful of anybody who 'talks themselves up' too much — the negative reaction to which is often referred to as 'tall poppy syndrome'. The country's most respected national figure is not a politician nor a member of high society, but the late Sir Edmund Hillary ('Sir Ed'), an 'ordinary' and very humble man who always propounded egalitarian values. Reflecting on his maiden ascent of Mount Everest, and the considerable fame that came after it, Hillary (2000) wrote that 'the media have classified me as a hero, but I have always recognised myself as being a person of modest abilities. My achievements have resulted from a goodly share of imagination and plenty of energy' (p. 11).

The narrative in action

The consequences of this egalitarian narrative have been double-edged. On the one hand, New Zealand possesses a democratic institutional structure, which is underpinned by equal voting rights and by a Mixed Member Proportional electoral system that ensures that most people's votes have at least some impact on the overall result. As Richard mentioned in Chapter 3, considerable progress has been made regarding equality of rights in this area.

New Zealand is also viewed as a world leader when it comes to passing legislation that protects human rights and promotes equal opportunities. The New Zealand Bill of Rights Act was placed on the statute books in 1990, and outlines the fundamental rights and freedoms that should be enjoyed by every person who comes under New Zealand law. Discrimination on a wide variety of grounds, including sex, age, race, ethnicity, religion and sexual orientation, was formally outlawed by the Human Rights Act three years later. Finally, as Ella noted in Chapter 4, in 2013 New Zealand became just the fifteenth country to legalise same-sex marriage through the Marriage (Definition of Marriage) Amendment Act. It was largely on the basis of such progressive legislation that a recent United Nations Human Rights Council (2009) review described New Zealand (with some crucial exceptions) as being a 'fair and equal' society.

Nevertheless, the belief that egalitarianism is inherent to New Zealand, and must not be compromised, has also fostered more problematic trends. Empirical research consistently identifies a wide gap between Māori and Pākehā living standards, a situation that can be traced back to the loss of Māori land and resources during European colonisation. Many New Zealanders would probably agree that something should be done to address this disparity, but their interpretation of the egalitarian narrative frequently leads them to reject the most promising option. While equality of opportunity is seen as an inviolable cornerstone of New Zealand's 'fair society', equality of outcome is accorded relatively little weight. As a result, New Zealanders tend to regard equity measures — giving certain groups of people different levels of access to jobs, services, funding, etc. — with considerable hostility, even if they are designed to ameliorate a blatant inequality of outcome.

Attacks on so-called 'Māori privilege' have focused on a number of areas: the continued existence of the dedicated Māori electorates (colloquially referred to as the 'Māori seats'), which — as Richard explained in Chapter 3 — were first established in 1867; the creation of, and settlements reached by, the Waitangi Tribunal; the recent legislation regarding ownership of the foreshore and seabed; and the awarding of scholarships that are specifically intended for Māori students.

The most famous denouncement occurred in 2004 when the then National Party leader Don Brash used a speech at the Orewa Rotary Club to lambast both the Treaty of Waitangi settlement process and the provision of government funding based on ethnicity. Brash (2004) explicitly appealed to the concept of equal opportunities by insisting that there should be 'one rule for all' and that 'the Treaty of Waitangi should not be used as the basis for giving greater civil, political or democratic rights to *any* particular ethnic group'. 'Māori privilege' remains a highly emotive topic in 2016, as demonstrated by the uproar following TVNZ's KiwiMeter survey, which asked respondents whether 'Māori should receive any special treatment', and by the controversy surrounding then Mayor Andrew Judd's efforts to establish a Māori ward on the New Plymouth City Council.

 See Peter Meihana's *Dominion Post* article about 'Māori privilege': www.stuff.co.nz/dominion-post/comment/78559148/There-is-nothing-new-about-Maori-privilege

The narrative qualified

Some commentators assert that the whole notion of an egalitarian New Zealand has always been more of a myth than a lived experience. One of the leading figures in early European colonisation, New Zealand Company director Edward Gibbon Wakefield, was explicit in his desire for the new society to be based around traditional rural classes, with a land-owning aristocracy supported by small farmers and labourers. A rigid hierarchy certainly existed on the ships that brought out the first European immigrants, which had cabins at the top for the richer passengers who had paid their own way, and steerage below for the working people who had received assisted passage. If the social structure that developed in colonial New Zealand was looser than both of these models, and certainly looser than that in Victorian Britain, there were still significant income disparities and an identifiable commercial and agricultural élite (Belich, 1996). Social and economic cleavages were also reflected in the physical distribution of the housing of different occupations. In early Auckland those divisions were reflected in names such as Mechanics Bay (home to artisans), Commercial Bay (which was originally called Store Bay, where those in commerce lived), Officials Bay (inhabited by those who governed the new settlement), and Freemans Bay (home to sawyers).

Even the reforms implemented during the 'golden eras' of egalitarianism often led to better outcomes for particular groups. As is evident throughout this text, the rights and benefits of citizenship are often dependent on the threads of a person's identity. While the Liberal Government strove to enhance opportunities for New Zealand's Pākehā population, it simultaneously acquired an additional 3.2 million acres of Māori land, often via underhand or coercive methods. When large numbers of Māori subsequently moved to urban areas after the Second World War, poverty and discrimination forced them into poor-quality accommodation, and into poorly paid work. Likewise, the First Labour Government's goals of 'full employment' and reasonable wages must be set against the fact that many women were still struggling to find jobs during the early 1950s, and invariably received much lower pay if they did so (Nolan, 2007).

However, these caveats should not be allowed to obscure the overall picture. From the 1950s to the 1980s, the degree of income inequality in New Zealand declined, for Māori and women as well as for Pākehā and men, at a rate that exceeded the global average. Indeed, the share of pre-tax income received by the country's top 1 per cent of earners reached an all-time low during 1984 (Rashbrooke, 2013). So, while New Zealand has never been a completely egalitarian society, it did possess a *greater* degree of equality than most other developed countries until just a few decades ago.

The narrative undermined

By the early 1980s, the economic and social structures put in place by the First Labour Government were coming under significant strain. The oil shocks of the

1970s had created problems for many countries, but proved particularly damaging to New Zealand, where they coincided with a reduction in agricultural exports to Britain. As national revenue fell and inflation surged, successive governments remained committed to subsidising domestic industries and to funding increasingly expensive social welfare programmes. In consequence, the country's debt ballooned to an unprecedented size and its reserves of foreign currency reached dangerously low levels.

These issues helped to fuel a rising discontent within certain sections of society. Many bankers, professionals and large business owners had grown tired of New Zealand's web of regulations, and began to cast envious glances at what was happening in the United Kingdom and the United States, where the Thatcher Government and the Reagan Administration, respectively, were implementing a 'neoliberal' agenda. This philosophy called for government expenditure and interference in the market to be significantly reduced, in favour of free trade and investment, low taxation on income, and the privatisation of state enterprises and government functions.

The crucial tipping point for New Zealand came in 1984, when the Fourth Labour Government assumed power during a major financial crisis, and used the ensuing turmoil to begin dismantling the central controls that had bound the country's economy for so long. Driven by the neoliberal ideologies of both the Treasury and the Minister of Finance, Roger Douglas, the subsequent six years of 'Rogernomics' saw the focus of government policy switch from providing 'full employment' to driving down inflation. Between 1984 and 1987, financial markets were deregulated, price subsidies were removed, many government activities were corporatised, and income tax rates on high earners were cut in favour of a universal Goods and Services Tax (GST; initially set at 10 per cent, but soon increased to 12.5 per cent).

This was followed from 1987 to 1990 by a reduction in import tariffs, the transfer of responsibility for monetary policy to the Reserve Bank, and the sale of a large number of state-owned assets, including Telecom, Postbank and Air New Zealand. However, the Labour Party's strong links to the trade union movement, and its traditional position as champion of the working class, meant that the Fourth Labour Government avoided making any significant changes to employment or social policy.

The succeeding National Government, under Jim Bolger, exercised no such restraint. In December 1990, Finance Minister Ruth Richardson unveiled a mini-budget that slashed unemployment, sickness and welfare benefits by at least 10 per cent across the board, and completely abolished the universal family benefit. These cuts were accompanied by a pronounced shift in official rhetoric. Benefits were no longer described as a safety net that should be available to all as of right, but as a drain on the country's finances that encouraged dependency and prevented the realisation of individual responsibility. This is a prime example of the intersections between legislation and language, and also demonstrates the power of discourse to impact on citizenship and identity, as discussed in the opening chapter and depicted in the illustration of the core concepts of tūrangawaewae. The remainder of National's 1990–1993 term witnessed a further tranche of reforms — collectively dubbed 'Ruthanasia' by their critics. 'User-pays' mechanisms were introduced for healthcare and education, while an end to collective bargaining and the adoption of individual employment contracts dramatically reduced the negotiating power of trade unions.

In just nine years, the whole structure of New Zealand's economy and society had been altered. Some of the consequences can certainly be viewed as beneficial. With foreign companies and investors rushing to take advantage of the new financial freedoms, New Zealand experienced a surge in immigration, particularly from Asia, which helped to stimulate multiculturalism and ethnic diversity. The relaxing of central controls also increased the availability of consumer goods, and provided people with much greater choices in food, entertainment and services. A number of New Zealand exports, particularly fine wines, managed to carve out a niche in the international market, while the country simultaneously began to promote itself as a tourist destination — complete with adventure sports, majestic scenery and a 'clean, green' environment (a narrative that Juliana examines more closely in the next chapter).

Yet the impact of these reforms on equalities of outcome was nothing less than catastrophic. According to journalist and researcher Max Rashbrooke (2013), 'In the two decades framing these changes, the gap between those at the top and bottom of the income ladder in New Zealand opened up more rapidly than in any other comparable society' (p. 27). Bankers, senior managers and property developers tended to do very well, thanks to the growth in the financial and speculative sectors of the economy and to the reductions in the higher rates of income tax. On the other hand, many middle-class, and particularly lower-class, people encountered tremendous difficulties. The crippling of the trade unions allowed employers to drive down wages and compel longer working hours, while the quest for 'efficiency' and the removal of guaranteed prices caused many businesses to either close down or relocate their operations overseas. Unemployment soared from 4 per cent in 1984 to 11 per cent by the early 1990s and, with benefits slashed and goods and services now subject to GST, increasing numbers of families were unable to make ends meet. It was not long before food banks reappeared in New Zealand for the first time since the Great Depression.

Substantial damage was also done to the country's social fabric. As the former state trading enterprises — particularly forestry, mining and the railways — were corporatised, restructured and, in many cases, sold to private companies, the support and voluntary structures that had grown up around them withered away. Likewise, many family-owned or locally run businesses proved unable to cope with the new era of competition, and were forced to close down after generations of supplying irreplaceable jobs and networks within their provincial communities.

 See Marcia Russell's documentary *Revolution*, which can be viewed in bite-sized chunks on the NZ On Screen website: www.nzonscreen.com/title/revolution-1996/series

The narrative today

Between 1984 and 1993, the advocates of neoliberalism maintained that the 'pain' of transitioning to a free-market society would prove worthwhile, as any short-term rise in inequality would soon be more than offset by a 'trickle-down' of prosperity. Such forecasts have proven to be emphatically wide of the mark. The evidence suggests that, after inequalities of outcome spiralled upwards during the 'Rogernomics' and 'Ruthanasia' eras, there have been *no* significant shifts over the following two decades. In other words, income and wealth distributions had become massively uneven by 1993, and remain just as uneven today (Easton, 2013).

The statistics arising from these developments are staggering. In 2011, the top-earning 1 per cent of adults (around 29,000 people) owned 16 per cent of New Zealand's total wealth, whereas the bottom half of adults (around 1.5 million people) owned just over 5 per cent. That same year, half the population earned a pre-tax income of less than $24,000, whereas the top 10 per cent earned at least $72,000, the top 1 per cent earned at least $170,000 and the top 0.4 per cent (around 13,000 people) earned over $250,000 each. Around three-quarters of a million New Zealanders currently sit below the poverty line — defined as living in a household that earns less than 60 per cent of the median disposable income — and this country has some of the worst rates of child poverty and preventable disease in the developed world (Rashbrooke, 2013). Overall, New Zealand has gone from being the fourteenth most equal of 34 economically developed countries in 1985, to the twenty-fifth most equal today (Easton, 2013).

Within these general figures are a number of specific inequalities. Although the gaps have decreased over the past two decades, women still earn on average around

Struggling in the land of milk and honey

A queue forms outside the City Mission in
Hobson Street, Auckland. Many families are
now reliant on access to food banks to feed
their children, and demand is especially strong
at Christmas. Many charitable organisations
run food-bank systems, and across them all,
throughout New Zealand, the number of food
parcels being handed out is growing every year.

12 per cent less than men, still constitute only one-third of New Zealand's MPs, and still remain under-represented on company boards and in senior managerial roles (Statistics New Zealand, 2016). Furthermore, booming property prices have seen the rate of home ownership decline from three-quarters of all adults in 1993 to just on 50 per cent today (although that figure climbs to nearly 65 per cent if homes held in family trusts are added), with numerous studies predicting a continued reduction over the next few years. This trend has had a disproportionate impact on younger people, increasing the numbers who are facing the prospect that the whole of their adult lives will be spent in rented accommodation (Eaqub & Eaqub, 2015).

However, New Zealand's greatest points of inequality are along racial lines. Its Māori and Pasifika populations sit at the bottom of nearly every social indicator: from income to imprisonment, from education to employment, and from health to housing. Indeed, the 750,000 New Zealanders who are living in poverty comprise around one out of every 10 Pākehā households, but around one out of every five Māori and Pasifika households (Rashbrooke, 2013).

The narrative going forward

There is little reason to think that these gaps will narrow under current conditions. This is partly the result of legislation introduced between 1984 and 1993, the substance of which remains unchanged. People on high incomes pay far less in tax than their counterparts in other economically developed countries, and the New Zealand system is nearly unique in making little or no deductions from wealth, capital gains, inheritances or gifts. At the opposite end of the spectrum, benefits are set at a very low level. The standard unemployment allowance for a single person replaces just a third of the average wage; New Zealand ranks thirty-second out of 34 developed countries in terms of generosity of unemployment benefits (Rashbrooke, 2015).

A more deep-seated obstacle to reducing inequalities is the attitude adopted by many New Zealanders. On the one hand, opinion surveys consistently identify support for egalitarian principles and a belief that the distribution of wealth and income has become too uneven. On the other hand, these same surveys indicate that a majority of people are against raising benefit payments and against increasing taxes on the rich. This contradiction seemingly derives from the same tendency that governs responses towards 'Māori privilege': that of prioritising equality of opportunity over equality of outcome. Discontent has grown up around spiralling house prices and the extent of child poverty — both of which can clearly be regarded as matters of opportunity. In contrast, benefits and tax levels can more easily be perceived as outcomes, and have generated far less public unrest. When discussions do take place around these latter questions, they are often couched in very negative language: individuals end up on benefits due to laziness and a failure to make the most of their opportunities, whereas wealthy people are reaping the benefits of hard work and careful planning.

 See this Wireless article by Max Rashbrooke on public attitudes towards egalitarianism: thewireless.co.nz/themes/value/egali-what-getting-a-fair-go-in-new-zealand

However, attitudes like this are based on an artificial distinction. Opportunities and outcomes are not two separate things, but are instead linked together in a cyclical relationship. For example, children from poorer families tend to go to schools located in more socio-economically deprived areas than those from wealthier families, and are likely to experience worse nutrition, less domestic stability and greater health problems during their formative years. This gives them a reduced chance of succeeding within the education system, which in turn means they are less likely to obtain a well-paid job. These poorer adults then find it harder to provide opportunities for their own children, and so the cycle begins again. Social mobility can allow such patterns to be broken, but it occurs to only a very limited extent. The available figures for New Zealand show that 45 per cent of people who live in poverty are still there at least seven years later (Rashbrooke, 2013).

 See The Pencilsword's story about privilege by Toby Morris: http://thewireless.co.nz/articles/the-pencilsword-on-a-plate

Another consideration is that inequality causes problems for the whole of society, not just for those who earn the lowest incomes. In their influential publication *The Spirit Level*, epidemiologists Richard Wilkinson and Kate Pickett (2010) use a range of indices to compare more and less equal societies. They find that a higher level of inequality hinders the performance of national economies by reducing the overall spending power of the workforce, narrowing the spectrum of people who can rise to positions of importance, and compromising financial stability. Moreover, inequality damages social cohesion by widening the real and perceived gaps between different groups. Finally, as we saw in Richard's discussion in Chapter 3 of why people do not vote, inequality reduces engagement with democratic processes and concentrates power and influence in the hands of a small proportion of the population.

Conclusion

Two conclusions emerge from this chapter. The first is that national narratives are hugely important for developing, or inhibiting, a sense of identity and belonging. Egalitarianism has been at the heart of this country's self-image for nearly 200 years, and continues to influence notions of what it means to live in New Zealand. At a more tangible level, the idea that people are, or should be, 'all equal here' has driven some of the most profound social and economic changes in New Zealand's history, but has also been employed as a means to justify the status quo. Ultimately, the stories people tell about themselves play as great a role in moulding individual and collective understandings of citizenship as each of the other themes discussed in this book. They all come together to determine the rights and responsibilities people have, and the types of places people call 'home'.

The second conclusion is that, despite its enduring influence, the conception of New Zealand as an egalitarian society now bears only a passing resemblance to reality. This country does display a general respect for human rights, and has a great deal of progressive legislation on the statute books. However, its income levels are highly stratified, its Māori and Pasifika populations are disadvantaged in nearly every way, tens of thousands of its children are growing up in poverty, and more and more of its young people are facing the likelihood of never owning their own homes. One can only imagine what the original European immigrants who came here to live in an 'egalitarian paradise' would make of it.

 Chapter 9 — We're all equal here, mate: Egalitarianism in Aotearoa New Zealand: http://turangawaewae.massey.ac.nz/chapter9.html

Recommended reading

Dean, A. (2015). *Ruth, Roger and me: Debts and legacies*. Wellington, New Zealand: Bridget Williams Books.

Rashbrooke, M. (Ed.) (2013). *Inequality: A New Zealand crisis*. Wellington, New Zealand: Bridget Williams Books.

Skilling, P. (2013). Egalitarian myths in New Zealand: A review of public opinion data on inequality and redistribution. *New Zealand Sociology, 28*(2), 16–43.

Wilkinson, R., & Pickett, K. (2010). *The spirit level: Why equality is better for everyone*. London, England: Penguin.

References

Belich, J. (1996). *Making peoples: A history of the New Zealanders from Polynesian settlement to the end of the nineteenth century*. Auckland, New Zealand: Allen Lane.

Belich, J. (2001). *Paradise reforged: A history of the New Zealanders from the 1880s to the year 2000*. Auckland, New Zealand: Allen Lane.

Brash, D. (2004, January 27). *Orewa Speech — nationhood* [address to the Orewa Rotary Club, Auckland]. Retrieved from http://www.donbrash.com/national-party/orewa-2004-nationhood/

Eaqub, S., & Eaqub, S. (2015). *Generation rent: Rethinking New Zealand's priorities*. Wellington, New Zealand: Bridget Williams Books.

Easton, B. (2013). Economic inequality in New Zealand: A user's guide. *New Zealand Sociology, 28*(3), 19–66.

Hillary, E. (2000). *View from the summit*. London, England: Corgi.

Little, A. (2016). Foreword. In P. Franks & J. McAloon (Eds.), *Labour: The New Zealand Labour Party, 1916–2016* (pp. 9–10). Wellington, New Zealand: Victoria University Press.

Nolan, M. (2007). The reality and myth of New Zealand egalitarianism: Explaining the pattern of labour historiography at the edge of empires. *Labour History Review, 72*(2), 113–134.

Rashbrooke, M. (2013). Inequality and New Zealand. In M. Rashbrooke (Ed.), *Inequality: A New Zealand crisis* (pp. 20–34). Wellington, New Zealand: Bridget Williams Books.

Rashbrooke, M. (2015). *Wealth and New Zealand*. Wellington, New Zealand: Bridget Williams Books.

Statistics New Zealand. (2016). *Measuring the gender pay gap*. Retrieved from http://www.stats.govt.nz/browse_for_stats/income-and-work/Income/gender-pay-gap.aspx

United Nations Human Rights Council. (2009, May 7). *Report of the working group on the Universal Periodic Review: New Zealand*. Retrieved from www.justice.govt.nz/policy/constitutional-law-and-human-rights/human-rights/international-human-rights-instruments/universal-periodic-review/upr-documents-relating-to-new-zealand-1/first-report-2009/NZ_UPR_Report_of_Working_Group_incl_Recs_June2009.pdf

Wilkinson, R., & Pickett, K. (2010). *The spirit level: Why equality is better for everyone*. London, England: Penguin.

100% Pure
Clean, green and proud of it!

Juliana Mansvelt

Introduction

Perhaps one of the most pervasive and powerful narratives surrounding Aotearoa New Zealand is based on the representations that have become attached to place and environment: the narrative of being 'clean, green' and (in recent years) '100% Pure New Zealand'. This story is powerful because it has a role in shaping individual and collective identities that surround being and belonging in place, because it influences the ways in which New Zealanders understand what constitutes 'natural' environments, and because it has become a part of how New Zealand as a nation state represents itself to the world.

The relationships that individuals have with the natural environment may be intense and emotional. Understandings of environments as 'non-human surroundings' (Simmons, 1993, as cited in Clayton & Opotow, 2003, p. 6) are always socially constructed. For example, perspectives on what constitutes a natural environment are likely to differ between individuals and groups who dwell in different place and time contexts. Accordingly, some individuals may have deep-seated but unexamined values and beliefs concerning the environment, while others may hold strong preferences and positions about the environment and environmental change (Clayton & Opotow, 2003). These differing values, beliefs and understandings of environment can result in enduring attachments to place, and may act as a basis for individual and collective identification. The different voices, stories and place meanings that circulate about the nature of Aotearoa New Zealand's natural environment can consequently influence encounters between people, resulting in outcomes which may range from strong collective affinities to place, to land-use conflicts.

How one such story about Aotearoa New Zealand's natural environment came not only to stand for the nature of place in New Zealand, but also to be a part of citizens' understanding of national identity and the construction of Aotearoa New Zealand's place in the world is the focus of this chapter. Moving from its colonial origins, I explore how the clean, green and pure story was created and propagated through a range of agents and organisations, from early scientists and writers to tourism and business firms. The purpose of the narrative is discussed, and the effects of this narrative for individual and collective identifications explored. Finally, the chapter moves to look at an alternative story of Aotearoa New Zealand's environment, reflecting on the consequences of critiquing the clean, green and pure narrative, and the challenges for maintaining this story in the context of environmental degradation.

Nature and origins of the narrative

In this book, we have suggested that places can be a means of shaping individual and collective identities. The clean, green narrative has become extremely important in the ways in which a range of individuals and agencies (in tourism, business, media, marketing, and local and national governments) portray New Zealand's national identity to the world, and the responses which arise from this. Although the catchphrase 'Clean, Green and 100% Pure' comes from the promotion and tourism marketing campaigns of the late 1990s, the origins of the clean, green and pure story can be found in New Zealand's colonial heritage.

Nineteenth-century colonial artists, poets and writers produced a vision of nature that strongly emphasised its centrality to the nation (Clark, 2004), with nature frequently presented as spectacular, unspoiled and beautiful (McClure, 2004). Geologists and botanists of the time also disagreed with their European colleagues that New Zealand was immature and degenerate, and instead focused on the rarity, uniqueness and wondrous nature of landforms, flora and fauna (Clark, 2004). With the rapid conversion of lowland ecosystems to farming in the nineteenth and twentieth centuries, tensions between, and histories of, Māori, Pākehā and other new settlers over land use were somewhat obscured in the attribution of 'green' to the newly emerging pastoral landscapes. Over the course of the past two centuries, notions of clean and green have extended beyond pristine natural landscapes to encompass agricultural land uses, with both scenery preservation and human transformations of rural places emphasising a natural affinity to the land and a healthiness of life lived close to nature (Clark, 2004; Pawson, 1997).

During the 1980s, clean and green New Zealand also became associated with New Zealand's anti-nuclear stance (Coyle & Fairweather, 2005; Tucker, 2017), an association which was forged in the context of protests against French nuclear testing in the Pacific, the bombing and sinking of the Greenpeace ship the *Rainbow Warrior* in 1985, and the passing of nuclear-free-zone legislation in 1987.

What purpose does the clean and green narrative serve?

The clean and green narrative has become central to the invention of New Zealand, shaping a sense of national consciousness and national pride; a story that is reproduced by citizens, civil society and the state (Bell, 1996). The narrative incorporates elements of nostalgia (Pawson, 1997), based on frontier culture and images of a healthy life lived close to nature — a story that still has meaning today despite the fact that only 13.8 per cent of New Zealanders dwell in a rural area (Worldbank, 2016).

For more on New Zealand's changing urban population, see: http://www.tradingeconomics.com/new-zealand/urban-population-wb-data.html

Clean and green is also part of New Zealanders' individual and social identification, a construction that can be a source of pride and wellbeing. For many New Zealanders, 'getting away from it all' may mean leaving New Zealand's urban areas to experience the natural environment — sea, mountain and bush. Engaging with and experiencing clean and green environments has long been associated with active and outdoor pursuits (Cloke & Perkins, 1998), such as tramping, hunting, fishing, climbing, mountain biking and kayaking, and these are seen as central to the New Zealand way of life. For Māori, the environment can be a significant part of mana whenua (the mana and identification derived from attachment to the land). Landscapes and environments (and the entities which comprise them — rivers, mountains, lakes, flora and fauna) provide a source

SHEEP DROVING

in
NEW ZEALAND

MARCUS KING

Country of dreams #1

From the 1920s to the 1970s, the artist and illustrator Marcus King created a number of tourism posters for various government departments that were similar in style to this glorious image of a high-country farmer and his heading dog moving a mob of sheep.

of affective attachment to place, and may hold significant social and spiritual meanings for people and groups.

Sitting alongside personal connections to the environment is the emergence of clean, green and pure as a narrative that serves economic purposes. Although representations of clean and green were integral to the romanticised image of New Zealand portrayed in order to attract immigrants and visitors from the 1890s (similar to the story of egalitarianism discussed in the previous chapter), the idea of New Zealand as a utopian environmental paradise was explicitly marketed in the 100% Pure tourist campaign, which was instigated in 1999 by the New Zealand Tourist Board (Yeoman, Palomino-Schalscha & McMahon-Beattie, 2015). The 1999 campaign, developed by M&C Saatchi, heralded a specific imagineering of New Zealand, one which connected with the personal pride New Zealanders might feel in beautiful landscapes and places, but which was intended to attract tourists and increase visitor spending.

For a more recent incarnation of the campaign see the Tourism New Zealand website: http://www.newzealand.com/int/

The campaign uses images of unspoilt natural environments, magnificent vistas and green pastoral landscapes, with visitors both gazing on and actively engaging in these spaces (Cloke & Perkins, 1998), portraying a sense of New Zealand's uniqueness, bounty, an affinity with nature and a relaxed pace (Yeoman et al., 2015). The 100% Pure brand has served Aotearoa New Zealand well, and has come to stand for many aspects of national identity. The brand is elastic in the sense that it has stretched to encompass not only elements of the experience of visiting New Zealand — encapsulated in terms like '100% pure exhilaration' and '100% pure brilliance' — but also has been taken up by a range of firms promoting both themselves and their commodities to the world.

The rhetoric of clean, green and pure has moved well beyond tourism and found its way into a range of other products, and therefore into the relationships that consumers and investors have with New Zealand firms. Clean, green and pure narratives have been aligned with the marketing of agricultural products as environmentally friendly, untainted, safe and fresh (particularly dairy, meat and horticultural produce), a representation which includes the 'pure discovery' of our export-quality New Zealand wines (Cloke & Perkins, 1998; Lewis, 2011). Used alongside the silver FernMark (registered as a trademark in 1991), the 100% Pure brand also portrays the personality of a vibrant country seeking to market itself to the world. Brand, place and lifestyle qualities became fused in the marketing of goods and services, and the way New Zealanders do business; with clean, green and pure underpinning political and economic constructions of Aotearoa New Zealand's identity in a global world. 'The New Zealand way' encapsulates a country that is young, fresh, innovative, comprising quiet achievers seeking contemporary solutions to a range of issues (Insch, 2011).

Brands such as Steinlager Pure, Anchor, 42Below Vodka and The Clean Green Shirt Company have capitalised on these associations. By the mid-2000s the clean, green and 100% Pure narrative was linked to the 'New' New Zealand Thinking campaign designed by New Zealand Trade and Enterprise, which was premised on high technological capability and scientific achievement, including biotechnologies. Clean, green and pure had become a central part of 'Brand New Zealand' (Lewis, 2011).

How is the narrative propagated and maintained?

Clean, green and pure is a narrative that represents a particular and partial story about the relationship between people and places in Aotearoa New Zealand. It has gained almost mythical status as it has been reproduced, accepted, talked about and acted upon by groups and individuals over time. Connections between identity and the environment are reproduced through talk (consider, for example, how and why New Zealanders overseas might choose to talk about New Zealand's environment and landscape in terms of its spectacular scenery). Identity threads connecting people and environments are also reinforced by the practices people engage in. 'Going bush' or taking a trip to the beach, engaging in an environmental campaign, state and local governments' regulations around pollution control — all of these involve practices which may help perpetuate or challenge depictions of Aotearoa New Zealand as clean, green and pure.

Environmental meanings and narratives are also reproduced through stories, waiata, the performing and visual arts, and through popular culture and the media, and can provide a source of pleasure, pride and belonging. Images of mountains, rivers, beaches, and rugged and agricultural landscapes portrayed on television, for example, may encourage citizens to see and understand landscapes and the practices associated with them as clean, green and pristine. Tourism New Zealand continues to draw on clean green and pure, through its slogans and images, to market the country as a destination for overseas tourists through multiple media:

Whangaroa

100% PURE
NEW ZEALAND

TODAY
ALL OF THIS
IS YOURS
TO EXPLORE

EVERY DAY A
DIFFERENT
JOURNEY
IN NORTHLAND

newzealand.com/northland

Country of dreams #2

Happy, fit young people, sparkling water, lush bush . . . one of the
iterations of the 100% Pure New Zealand campaign.

websites, print images, posters, trade shows and magazines. Media and film have also been significant in publicising 'Brand New Zealand' — albeit with tongue firmly in cheek in the case of the highly successful comedy series *Flight of the Conchords,* which aired on HBO in the United States.

 Check out the posters on Murray's office wall in *Flight of the Conchords*: https://www.youtube.com/watch?v=vDjJc_zH6dk

The *Lord of the Rings* and *Hobbit* film trilogies have been significant vehicles through which the clean, green narrative has been promulgated. The creation of maps, tours and sites of Middle-earth has not only provided an extension of the clean, green New Zealand brand for overseas film audiences, it has also enabled opportunities for the further commodification of place, with one tourism poster proclaiming New Zealand as the 'Best supporting country in a Motion Picture'! Many New Zealanders seem to have embraced Aotearoa as the home of Middle-earth (Organ, 2013). The creation of a whole new raft of New Zealand places as Middle-earth tourist destinations was an opportunity not lost on Air New Zealand, which marketed flights to New Zealand, plastered its planes with film images, and produced a safety video drawing on characters from the movies (Jutel, 2004).

It would be easy to assume that global marketing and media campaigns, and the reworking of New Zealand's natural and constructed landscapes as the home of Middle-earth, are simply the framings of organisations and firms keen to sell New Zealand to the world; but these are also intimately connected to the meanings, experiences and practices of individuals. One-third of visitors to New Zealand now have some form of 'hobbit' experience, contributing to the local economies and livelihoods of New Zealanders in the sites and places of Middle-earth. Hobbiton, near Matamata, has seen an increase in annual visitor numbers in the past five years from 33,000 to 468,000, and staff numbers have increased from 17 to 200.

Similarly, the Keep New Zealand Beautiful campaign argues on its website that 'Keep NZ Beautiful Week is not just about the clean-ups. These events build and strengthen community spirit and allow people to demonstrate their pride in where they live' (Keep New Zealand Beautiful, 2016). Thus the practices and narratives of firms and organisations promoting clean, green and pure intersect with individual meanings and experiences of landscape to produce a dominant version of national identity which is reproduced by individuals. The consequences of this clean and green story for New Zealand and its citizens are explored in the section which follows.

Consequences

Clean, green and pure has been taken up as a rhetoric of government and industry bodies such as Fonterra, ENZA and New Zealand Wine. As mentioned previously, the 100% Pure campaign has been strongly aligned to the FernMark, and the promotion of 'Brand New Zealand' by New Zealand Trade and Enterprise (Lewis, 2011). In parliamentary speeches and government reports (e.g. Ministry for the Environment and Statistics New Zealand 2015; Ministry for the Environment, 2013), mention is made of the significance of clean and green to economic revenues. A Ministry for the Environment (2001) report noted that 'if New Zealand were to lose its clean green image it would have an enormous effect on the economy' (p. 4), with an estimated loss of a minimum of $241 million to the dairy sector, and $530–$938 million in terms of tourism.

The maintenance of a clean and green environment is also important to the quality of life of New Zealanders, whose livelihoods, recreational pastimes and emotional attachments may draw from that environment. Public health researchers Elizabeth Butcher and Mary Breheny (2016) note with regard to Māori, for example, that place attachment is vital, and that the 'loss of these connections may have a damaging effect on identity' (p. 50) — much the same point was made by Te Rina, Margaret and Veronica in Chapter 2 of this book. Loss of such connections through uncertainty of access to natural resources, or through degraded natural environments which affect the harvesting or hunting of kai, may be significant. Clean and green and pure narratives which rest on biodiversity and ecological sustainability also sit alongside representations of New Zealand as an innovative, progressive and forward-thinking nation.

Over the past two decades, a focus on New Zealand as an entrepreneurial knowledge economy has seen clean (non-polluting) digital and bio technologies identified as part of Brand New Zealand. As a biotechnology, the application of genetic engineering (GE) techniques to solve issues such as crop failure and animal diseases helps support the narrative of a clean and green New Zealand free of unwanted pests or pesticides (Coyle & Fairweather, 2005). But these techniques also occupy an ambiguous role in relation to the narrative, with GE-free campaigners arguing that genetic modification may put the clean, green 100% Pure branding at risk, leaving New Zealand behind in the organic marketplace and threatening the 'natural' environment (Henderson, 2005).

Clean, green and 100% Pure is thus a story that is reproduced by individuals both resident and living outside of Aotearoa, and by a variety of public and private sector agencies which aim to promote New Zealand places and products for consumption.

Yet, as Morgan and Pritchard (1998) suggest, the imagery reveals as much about the power relations that comprise it as it does about the place and commodities which it promotes. Clean, green and 100% Pure is a shifting social construction which encompasses a diverse range of identity, place and product constructions. Despite its complex and shifting meanings over time, it provides a selective story about New Zealand as a nation, its history, landscape, identity and aspirations. Accordingly, it remains a narrative with limits to its representational claims. We turn now to look at the ways in which the utopian representation of New Zealand as a clean, green paradise is being challenged.

Is New Zealand really clean and green? Cracks in 'paradise'

This chapter has suggested that New Zealand landscapes and orientations to nature have long been socially constructed (Werry, 2011) by a range of public and private sector agencies, creating an inexorable link between environment and the production of New Zealand and its economy in a global arena. The construction of the environment as clean, green and pure is also tied up in the creation of nationhood and belonging (Clark, 2004), influencing how New Zealanders might see the place of their nation in the world, and their own place within Aotearoa New Zealand. Consequently, if the connections between the environment and the rhetoric are vital to individual and collective identity, a sense of tūrangawaewae, and the economic fortunes of the country, it is important to ask: Is the narrative that Aotearoa New Zealand is clean, green and pure a myth?

As sociologist Corinna Tucker (2017) argues, the answer to this question depends on how we look at it. Based on a lower population density and the environment's capacity to cope with current practices, and compared to other nations, she suggests an argument could be made that we are clean and green. However, she also notes that taking per capita consumption of resources and current land-use practices into account means New Zealand's environmental integrity can be questioned. While New Zealand's absolute environmental impact may be low, a study by Bradshaw, Giam and Sodhi (2010) — which accounted for population and resource availability and measured countries' loss of native vegetation, native habitat, the number of endangered species and water quality — showed that, per capita, New Zealand was ranked eighteenth worst country for its environmental impact. Chris Howe, director of the World Wildlife Fund, notes that 'Aotearoa, the land of the long white cloud, is now a land of polluted rivers and lakes, rising greenhouse gas emissions, pressured marine ecosystems and disappearing bird and mammal species' (World Wildlife Fund, 2012).

On many environmental indicators, New Zealand is less than 100% clean, green and pure. The removal of indigenous forests and the destruction of natural environments also makes for sobering reading. Almost one-third of New Zealand's landscape has less than 10 per cent of its indigenous cover remaining, while 46 per cent of New Zealand's land area has less than 20 per cent remaining. Of New Zealand's original wetlands, fully 90 per cent are gone (Ministry for the Environment & Statistics New Zealand, 2015). In addition, nearly 40 per cent of New Zealand's indigenous vascular plant species are at risk or are threatened with extinction.

While air quality has generally improved since 2006, according to the Ministry of the Environment and Statistics New Zealand (2015) carbon dioxide (a greenhouse gas) emissions have actually increased 21 per cent from 326 parts per million (ppm) in December 1972 to 394 ppm in December 2013. Forty-three per cent of monitored lakes in New Zealand are now classed as polluted, with an estimated 18,000–34,000 people annually catching waterborne diseases. Between 1989 and 2013, total nitrogen levels in rivers increased 12 per cent, with 60 per cent of monitored sites showing statistically significant increases in nitrogen. About 49 per cent of monitored river sites have enough nitrogen to trigger nuisance algal growth (Ministry for the Environment & Statistics New Zealand, 2015).

The situation with wildlife in Aotearoa New Zealand also makes grim reading. Introduced pests, such as possums, rats and stoats, are found in over 94 per cent of the country, and other native bird and animal species are threatened, including more than 80 per cent of New Zealand's living bird species and 90 per cent of our lizard species (ibid.). Seventy-two per cent of our indigenous freshwater fish species are classified as at risk or threatened with extinction (ibid.), with the risk of extinction increasing for eight species between 2005 and 2011. Seven of New Zealand's 10 official indicator species for measuring biodiversity status are threatened. The kōkako, for example, has suffered a 90 per cent contraction in its range since the 1970s (ibid.). The diversity of freshwater fish communities has diminished at observational sites since 1970, and the Parliamentary Commissioner for the Environment (2010) concluded that New Zealand's largest freshwater fish, the tuna or longfin eel, was in a steady state of decline.

These are sobering statistics, and many of them are produced by the government's own departments. Yet despite these counter-narratives, it remains difficult to challenge the clean, green and 100% Pure myth, because of its significance as part of national identity and the way in which it has come to be intertwined with the country's economic fortunes. Almost two decades ago, environmentalist

Cath Wallace (1997) argued that we cannot rely on the clean and green mantra to pretend we do not have 'deep-seated and complex environment problems' (p. 29). Although government ministries have acknowledged the potential costs of not living up to the reality of clean and green (Ministry for the Environment, 2001), they have done little to alter the power of the dominant narrative or the persuasive rhetoric surrounding it.

Perhaps the most visible contestation of the narrative thus far has been the writings of Mike Joy, a Massey University freshwater ecologist. Joy (2011, 2014, 2015) has drawn attention to the fragility of claims associated with '100% Pure' in articles noting New Zealand's poor environmental record with regard to increasing water pollution, the negative effects of intensive land use (particularly in relation to dairying) and the decline in biodiversity.

Joy's comments have attracted international attention. He was cited in *The New York Times* as saying 'There are almost two worlds in New Zealand. There is the picture-postcard world, and then there is the reality' (Anderson, 2012), contrasting the landscapes (many of them from New Zealand's pristine national parks) presented to tourists and visitors with the reality of environmental degradation experienced elsewhere. Joy was later quoted in a *New Zealand Herald* article as saying 'We don't deserve 100% Pure. We are nowhere near the best in the world, we are not even in the top half of countries in the world when it comes to being clean and green' (Preston, 2012). He also argued that in 'five decades New Zealand has gone from a world famous clean, green paradise to an ecologically compromised island nation near the bottom of the heap of so-called developed countries' (Joy, 2011).

 Here is a link to one of Mike Joy's presentations. This one was given to the New Zealand Forest and Bird Society in 2014, and has some startling statistics: http://www.forestandbird.org.nz/files/file/Forest%20and%20Bird%20AGM%202011%20cut.pdf

While there was media commentary both in favour of and against Joy's views, the economic significance of an individual publicly contesting the narrative was not lost on businesses and tourism industry representatives, with some suggesting it was irresponsible to refute the myth. Joy was accused of tourism industry sabotage, with the advertising agency FCB's managing director Derek Lyndsay (cited in Preston, 2012) claiming that 'a lot of tourists, particularly the big spenders, came from the US, so having writers for *The New York Times* contradict the campaign's claim could be potentially damaging for tourism'.

Joy's hope was that the publicity around his research on New Zealand's environmental failings would provoke the New Zealand government to act to protect its clean and green image (Preston, 2012). He based his challenge to the narrative on his own research, and also quoted statistics produced by government agencies themselves. However, when then prime minister John Key agreed to appear on a *Hardtalk* BBC interview, he refuted Joy's narrative (Browning, 2011). During the interview, in which Stephen Sackur probed New Zealand's environmental record, the prime minister endeavoured to debunk both Joy's science and his assertions, stating that Joy was simply offering 'his view'. That Key should dismiss a scientist in such a public way demonstrates the considerable amount of national identity value — and political and economic capital — that is at stake in perpetuating representations of clean, green and pure New Zealand to the world.

 You can watch the *Hardtalk* interview with John Key here: https://www.youtube.com/watch?v=c3yFiNk_Ufw

Joy (2011) notes that in recent years there has been a subtle shift in New Zealand Tourism's branding from 100% Pure New Zealand to 100% Pure You — a claim connected to experience which is less easily contradicted by the facts and statistics of New Zealand's environmental degradation. Despite the weight of evidence about the costs of the rhetoric of clean, green and pure not aligning with the reality, Joy sees little evidence of a desire to shore up the narrative through regulation that would require individuals, organisations and firms to act in ways which will prevent environmental degradation.

The groundswell of data emerging from academics, advocacy groups and successive governments' own reports has highlighted the need for environment protections, improved waste minimisation and management practices, and better environmental performance. Debates about mining/prospecting licences, intensive forms of agriculture, 1080 poisoning, genetic modification, climate change action/inaction, greenhouse gas emissions and, most recently, animal cruelty (*The New Zealand Herald*, 2015) further muddy the coherence of clean, green and pure as a metaphor for New Zealand's future economic growth, and as a symbol of its products and the ways in which these are produced (see Coyle & Fairweather, 2005; Henderson, 2005; Joy, 2014; Knight, 2011; Pearce, 2009; Rudzitis & Bird, 2011; Tucker, 2011).

Many of these protesters also draw on the clean, green and pure narrative as a means of giving voice to their concerns about the negative environmental impacts of human activity in Aotearoa New Zealand. Publicity around the effects of contaminated groundwater and increased human and animal health issues (such as cynobacterial growth in rivers, unswimmable lakes and rivers, and the unsafe harvesting of kaimoana) also confront visions of New Zealanders' healthy and active engagement in the outdoors, challenging imaginings of lives lived close to nature.

Scientific data and debates around New Zealand's future environmental sustainability draw attention to the concern about the consequences of the rhetoric of the narrative not meeting the reality, raising the issue of the extent to which clean, green and 100% Pure can continue to have traction as a means of shaping society, economy and place.

Conclusion

A study by Gendall (1993, cited in Coyle & Fairweather, 2005) showed that even 20 years ago less than half of the population surveyed believed that the clean, green concept was a true representation of Aotearoa New Zealand. Despite this, the narrative endures, both as a medium for the economic promotion of New Zealand and its products, and as a foundation for the shaping of national identity. Aside from economic concerns about a potential decline in agricultural and tourist revenues, and the impact on rural and urban communities of any reduction in export incomes, if the reality of Aotearoa New Zealand's environmental record doesn't match the rhetoric, then much more than economic revenue is at stake.

In addition to health and livelihood concerns surrounding environmental degradation, loss of biodiversity, pollution and unsustainable land-use practices, a key source of national identity is troubled. Clean, green and pure has been significant as a basis for emotional and spiritual attachments to place and national pride. Indeed, efforts to protect the environment led by a range of non-governmental organisations have long been a part of Aotearoa's history. However, if the meanings, attributes and experiences of encounters with Aotearoa New Zealand's natural landscapes are changed negatively as a consequence of environmental degradation, then a central foundation for belonging, wellbeing and identity formation for New Zealand citizens is lost. As sociologist Claudia Bell (1996) argues of the clean, green and pure narrative, we can 'sell it to tourists as national identity; and half believe it ourselves' (p. 48). Consequently 'Clean, Green, 100% Pure' as a representation of Aotearoa New Zealand's nationhood and economy may be contested, but it still has currency.

Chapter 10 — 100% Pure: Clean, green and proud of it: http://turangawaewae.massey.ac.nz/chapter10.html

Recommended reading

Anderson, C. (2012, November 16). New Zealand's green tourism push clashes with realities. *The New York Times.* Retrieved from http://www.nytimes.com/2012/11/17/business/global/new-zealands-green-tourism-push-clashes-with-realities.html

Joy, M. (2015). *Polluted inheritance: New Zealand's freshwater crisis.* Wellington, New Zealand: Bridget Williams Books.

Tucker, C. (2017). Clean, green Aotearoa New Zealand? In A. Bell, V. Elizabeth, T. McIntosh, & M. Wynyard (Eds.), *A land of milk and honey? Making sense of Aotearoa New Zealand.* Auckland, New Zealand: Auckland University Press.

References

Anderson, C. (2012, November 16). New Zealand's green tourism push clashes with realities. *The New York Times.* Retrieved from http://www.nytimes.com/2012/11/17/business/global/new-zealands-green-tourism-push-clashes-with-realities.html

Bell, C. (1996). *Inventing New Zealand: Everyday myths of Pakeha identity.* Auckland, New Zealand: Penguin.

Bradshaw, C. J. A., Giam, X., & Sodhi, N. S. (2010). Evaluating the relative environmental impact of countries. *PLoS ONE, 5*(5). e10440. doi: 10.1371/journal.pone.0010440

Browning, C. (2011, June 28). Mike Joy answers the PM, with hard facts. *Pundit.* Retrieved from http://pundit.co.nz/print/1915

Butcher, E., & Breheny, M. (2016). Dependence on place: A source of autonomy in later life for older Māori. *Journal of Aging Studies, 37,* 48–58. doi: 10.1016/j.jaging.2016.02.004

Clark, N. (2004). Cultural studies for shaky islands. In C. Bell & S. Matthewman (Eds.), *Cultural studies in Aotearoa New Zealand. Identity, space and place* (pp. 3–18). Melbourne, Australia: Oxford University Press.

Clayton, S., & Opotow, S. (2003). Introduction: Identity and the natural environment. In S. Opotow & S. D. Clayton (Eds.), *Identity and the natural environment: The psychological significance of nature* (pp. 1–24). Cambridge, MA: MIT Press.

Cloke, P., & Perkins, H. C. (1998). 'Cracking the canyon with the awesome foursome': Representations of adventure tourism in New Zealand. *Environment and Planning D: Society and Space, 16*(2), 185–218.

Coyle, F., & Fairweather, J. (2005). Challenging a place myth: New Zealand's clean green image meets the biotechnology revolution. *Area, 37*(2), 148–158. doi: 10.1111/j.1475-4762.2005.00617.x

Henderson, A. (2005). Activism in 'Paradise': Identity management in a public relations campaign against genetic engineering. *Journal of Public Relations Research, 17*(2), 117–137. doi: 10.1207/s1532754xjprr1702_4

Insch, A. (2011). Leveraging nation branding for export promotion — 100% sustainable? In R. Fletcher & H. Crawford (Eds.), *International marketing: An Asia-Pacific perspective* (5th ed., pp. 616–619). Frenchs Forest, Australia: Pearson.

Joy, M. (2011, April 25). Mike Joy: The dying myth of a clean, green Aotearoa. *The New Zealand Herald.* Retrieved from http://www.nzherald.co.nz/business/news/article.cfm?c_id=3&objectid=10721337

Joy, M. (2014). Cool, clear water. In D. Cooke, C. Hill, P. Baskett, & R. Irwin (Eds.), *Beyond the free market: Rebuilding a just society in New Zealand* (pp. 102–107). Wellington, New Zealand: Dunmore Press.

Joy, M. (2015). *Polluted inheritance: New Zealand's freshwater crisis.* Wellington, New Zealand: Bridget Williams Books.

Jutel, T. (2004). *Lord of the Rings:* Landscape, transformation, and the geography of the virtual. In C. Bell & S. Matthewman (Eds.), *Cultural studies in Aotearoa New Zealand: Identity, space and place* (pp. 54–65). Melbourne, Australia: Oxford University Press.

Keep New Zealand Beautiful. (2016). *KNZB clean up week.* Retrieved from: http://www.knzb.org.nz/cleanupweek

Knight, J. G. (2011). *New Zealand's 'clean green' image: Will GM plants damage it?* Dunedin, New Zealand: University of Otago.

Lewis, N. (2011). Packaging political projects in geographical imaginaries: The rise of nation branding. In A. Pike (Ed.), *Brands and branding geographies* (pp. 264–288). Cheltenham, England: Edward Elgar.

McClure, M. (2004). *The wonder country: Making New Zealand tourism.* Auckland, New Zealand: Auckland University Press.

Ministry for the Environment. (2001). *Our clean green image: What's it worth?* Retrieved from https://www.mfe.govt.nz/sites/default/files/clean-green-aug01-final.pdf

Ministry for the Environment. (2013). *Freshwater reform 2013 and beyond.* Retrieved from http://www.mfe.govt.nz/publications/fresh-water/freshwater-reform-2013-and-beyond

Ministry for the Environment & Statistics New Zealand. (2015, October). *Environment Aotearoa 2015.* Retrieved from http://www.mfe.govt.nz/publications/environmental-reporting/environment-aotearoa-2015

Morgan, N., & Pritchard, A. (1998). *Tourism promotion and power: Creating images, creating identities:* New York, NY: John Wiley & Sons.

Organ, M. (2013). 'Please Mr Frodo, is this New Zealand? Or Australia?' . . . 'No Sam, it's Middle-earth.' *Metro, 177,* 56–61.

Parliamentary Commissioner for the Environment. (2010, April 1). *How clean is New Zealand? Measuring and reporting on the health of our environment.* Retrieved from http://www.pce.parliament.nz/publications/how-clean-is-new-zealand-measuring-and-reporting-on-the-health-of-our-environment

Pawson, E. (1997). Branding strategies and languages of consumption. *New Zealand Geographer, 53*(2), 16–21. doi: 10.1111/j.1745-7939.1997.tb00494.x

Pearce, F. (2009, November 12). New Zealand was a friend to Middle Earth, but it's no friend of the earth. *The Guardian.* Retrieved from http://www.theguardian.com/environment/cif-green/2009/nov/12/new-zealand-greenwash

Preston, N. (2012, November 19). Clean, green image of NZ 'fantastical'. *The New Zealand Herald.* Retrieved from http://www.nzherald.co.nz/entertainment/news/article.cfm?c_id=1501119&objectid=10848410

Rudzitis, G., & Bird, K. (2011). The myth and reality of sustainable New Zealand: Mining in a pristine land. *Environment. Science and Policy for Sustainable Development.* Retrieved from http://www.environmentmagazine.org/Archives/Back%20Issues/2011/November-December%202011/Myths-full.html

The New Zealand Herald. (2015, November 30). Calves 'beaten to death' — shocking video exposes dairy industry cruelty. *The New Zealand Herald.* Retrieved from http://www.nzherald.co.nz/nz/news/article.cfm?c_id=1&objectid=11553152

Tucker, C. (2011). The social construction of clean and green in the genetic engineering resistance movement of New Zealand. *New Zealand Sociology, 26*(11), 110–121.

Tucker, C. (2017). Clean, green Aotearoa New Zealand? In A. Bell, V. Elizabeth, T. McIntosh, & M. Wynyard (Eds.), *A land of milk and honey? Making sense of Aotearoa New Zealand.* Auckland, New Zealand: Auckland University Press.

Wallace, C. (1997). The 'clean green' delusion: Behind the myths. *New Zealand Studies,* March, 22–29.

Werry, M. (2011). *The tourist state: Performing leisure, liberalism, and race in New Zealand.* Minneapolis, MN: University of Minnesota Press.

World Wildlife Fund. (2012, May 27). *Paradise lost. New report shows 20 years of environmental action threatens NZ's natural heritage.* Retrieved from http://www.wwf.org.nz/?8941/Paradise-lost-New-report-shows-20-years-of-environmental-inaction-threatens

Worldbank. (2016). *Urban population in New Zealand.* Retrieved from http://www.tradingeconomics.com/new-zealand/urban-population-wb-data.html

Yeoman, I., Palomino-Schalscha, M., & McMahon-Beattie, U. (2015). Keeping it pure: Could New Zealand be an eco paradise? *Journal of Tourism Futures, 1*(1), 19–35. doi: 10.1108/JTF-12-2014-0017

CHAPTER ELEVEN:

Anzac
A nation's creation story

Carl Bradley and Rhys Ball

Introduction

Anzac has become arguably this nation's defining story. The nature of the narrative based on Aotearoa New Zealand's experience in the First World War is that we punched above our weight; that we stood by our friends and held our ground against overwhelming odds; that we were the victims of abject failures of (British) leadership; that we died for the flag and protected our way of life; and that it was on the shores of Gallipoli that New Zealand's identity as an independent nation was born. What does this narrative say about what it means to be a New Zealander, a citizen of this land? Is the story we feel we know an accurate one, and do we need to question this Anzac narrative as a true reflection of being a citizen in the national and international sense?

There has been a steady increase in the numbers of people observing the dawn services on Anzac Day, with the gap between generations bridged as grandparents open up to the questioning of their grandchildren, something they would not do with their own children. The increased attendance of young (and not-so-young) Kiwis at dawn services at Gallipoli has become a rite of passage during the OE (overseas experience) pilgrimage, a fact that the media and politicians have latched onto. 'Anzac' has also become a fully accepted term when describing sports events between Australia and New Zealand. The last Rugby World Cup was called an Anzac final, and our two countries have an annual Anzac test as part of the international rugby league calendar. Recognising the military origins that Anzac represents, the Anzac Bridge in

Sydney is a constant reminder of that relationship, with both countries' flags flying over statues of Australian and New Zealand Army Corps (ANZAC) soldiers.

What does the Anzac story say about the New Zealand national identity? When we speak about Anzac — the Anzac tradition, Anzac Day, the Anzac spirit and the Anzac myth — we have a variety of views, notions, beliefs and understandings about its history and origins. The Anzac commemorations and associated narrative extend well beyond the beaches of Gallipoli and into New Zealand's wider role on the world military stage. How we understand the Anzac story, the narrative, is very much placed within the context of what we think has been the impact on New Zealand society of its soldiers' deeds in all the conflicts that it has been involved in. The Anzac legend begins in 1915, over 100 years ago now, and for at least half of that time — say for the first half of the twentieth century — the collective Kiwi military experience was viewed as a unifying one. But is the Anzac story appropriate for some of the assertions attached to it, and does it tell the whole story of New Zealanders' war experiences?

This chapter will look at the nature and origins of the Anzac narrative, and how this grew out of the experiences of war, using two major twentieth-century conflicts in New Zealand's history: Gallipoli and Vietnam. From the Turkish coast of Gallipoli to the jungles of South Vietnam, we shall explore how this narrative has evolved in the eyes of those who have directly participated, as well as those of us who have seen, and see, our varying contributions to the efforts of international peace and prosperity both now and into the future. We will then look at whose stories are not included in the Anzac narrative. What are some of the voices that have been historically absent but are now coming to the fore?

Gallipoli

The Gallipoli landings form the foundation of the Anzac narrative for this country and Australia, and are a measure against which all subsequent military contributions have been compared. But if we examine the statistics as well as the overall strategic impact and assessment, then we begin to consider our contribution more dispassionately and less as triumph in adversity, gallant action against overwhelming odds, or honourable conduct and superhuman deeds. It is prudent to now look at some of those contributions with a mind to assess how they have shaped the Anzac narrative.

When New Zealand first went to war in 1914, the New Zealand Expeditionary Force (NZEF) was not large enough to form a complete military division along similar dimensions of the British Army. Therefore, an agreement between governments saw the NZEF join with the Australian Imperial Forces (AIF) to form a joint division. By the time they got to Egypt at the end of the year, they had become the Australian and New Zealand Army Corps (Pugsley & Ferrall, 2015).

War historian Ian McGibbon (1991) has written that New Zealanders at home 'thrilled to the news that their country's forces were in action with the enemy, a sense of exhilaration that was tempered only by the long casualty lists which soon began to appear in the newspapers' (p. 1). By the end of the campaign on Gallipoli, the price was truly staggering. Gallipoli cost New Zealand forces 7991 casualties, including 2779 dead, which amounted to a 53 per cent casualty rate of the 16,000–18,000 New Zealanders who took part in the campaign (Ministry for Culture and Heritage, 2016). The Australian losses — it is understood that between 50,000 and 60,000 Australians fought in the campaign — numbered 28,150, and this included 8709 dead with a casualty rate of between 47 and 56 per cent (Pugsley & Ferrall, 2015, p. 21). It was by all accounts, from the military operational and strategic perspective to the human cost, a disaster.

For more on the Gallipoli campaign, visit: https://nzhistory.govt.nz/war/the-gallipoli-campaign/introduction

McGibbon tells us that, before Gallipoli, New Zealand's attitude to security had evolved in the 75 years since the establishment of the colony with a very clear recognition of its lack of viable defence options. By 1914, most New Zealanders believed that war in Europe could spell defeat for the British Empire, and was therefore a threat to this country. In these terms, supporting the Empire was a logical approach, a means to an end. By the end of the war, this had all changed. The cost to this country was clearly out of proportion to any other contributing member of the British Empire during the Great War. This was not lost on New Zealand, and the impact would have lasting societal, cultural and military ramifications for the rest of the century. However, for all that it was a disaster, the Anzac experience has been described as the start of a true New Zealand identity, what history scholar James Bennett (2003) calls an 'un-English' identity. A New Zealand officer, Lieutenant William Deans of the Canterbury Mounted Rifles, reflected:

> Gallipoli was a proper disaster. Nothing else but a disaster. It was caused through bad management and bad generalship . . . But if Gallipoli had gone

FAIRFAX MEDIA NZ.

Honouring the fallen

An Anzac Day dawn service at Hamilton
Memorial Park.

right, it would've been worth it. I think it was worth it in the way that it proved the worth of New Zealand and Australian soldiers. I sort of feel that after Gallipoli we were New Zealanders, before that we were colonials. (Pugsley & Ferrall, 2015, p. 297)

The view that war is an important part of the historical development of our national identity is not limited to the Gallipoli campaign. New Zealand military scholar John McLeod (1986) has noted that New Zealand's contribution to the two world wars contributed greatly to 'stirring our national consciousness and promoting the development of a national identity' (p. 190). This statement says something about how we see ourselves, but it also suggests something about our attitude to war and conflict.

New Zealand attitudes to war and conflict

Each country will endeavour to create a unique image of it's military forces, its fighters, through which it aims to personalise and strengthen its national identity. What does it mean to be a New Zealand serviceman or servicewoman? How do they fight, how do they conduct themselves, and are they shaped and moulded by the country that they have come from? An important part of this are the heroes. Heroes tell a story of individual bravery that then shapes our view of ourselves as a brave nation of fighters. Heroism is important, and we see the evolution of this through the years. How many of us recognise the three New Zealanders in the photographs below? How does New Zealand see the three men below, how might they have seen themselves, and does this combination tell us anything about our identity?

REF: PACOLL-6001-05, ATL

REF: DA-06918, ATL

The first, Cyril Bassett, was a signalman, and the only New Zealander to win a Victoria Cross at Gallipoli. It was a point that, according to military historians Glyn Harper and Colin Richardson (2006), irritated him in later life: 'When I got the medal I was disappointed to find I was the only New Zealander to get one at Gallipoli, because hundreds of Victoria Crosses should have been awarded there . . . All my mates ever got were wooden crosses' (pp. 87–88). The second, Charles Upham, is the only combat soldier to be awarded the Victoria Cross award twice. He was a man of few words, and felt decidedly uncomfortable about receiving this ultimate gallantry award on two occasions. Harper and Richardson (2006) write that Upham was 'embarrassed at receiving the [first] Victoria Cross and felt that he had only been part of a much larger team effort' (p. 170). As his biographer Kenneth Sandford (1962) observed, Upham, a man noted for his extreme modesty, 'never really [overcame] that first feeling of embarrassed defensiveness. It remained with him throughout the years' (p. 107).

The final recipient depicted is Willie Apiata. In 2006, Harper and Richardson wrote that it had been 'more than 60 years since a New Zealander' had been awarded the Victoria Cross, and questioned the value of having such a gallantry award on the books 'if no one in the country [was] good enough to win' (p. 229). The following year, Willie Apiata received his Victoria Cross decoration for gallantry, although the action had taken place in Afghanistan three years earlier. The prime minister at the time, Helen Clark, said Apiata had displayed stunning courage, but when pressed by the media shortly after the announcement, the soldier showed similar characteristics of humility, stressing the importance of camaraderie and mateship that Bassett and Upham had embodied much earlier.

These three heroes, and their responses to their awards, highlight an important incongruity in New Zealand's national identity. While bravery and sacrifice are part of that identity, as depicted in the Anzac narrative, so is humility and the belief that an individual should not be singled out for praise — the 'tall poppy syndrome' as it is colloquially known. McLeod (1986) highlights, too, the importance of having a more realistic view of soldiers at war:

> We are not natural soldiers and we are not immune to all the failings of men at war. At times our men were as good, if not better, than allies and enemies alike; at other times, they were just as bad or even worse. We have much to gain by understanding this reality of our men at war . . . I think if the lessons are going to be of any benefit to future generations, they must first realise that ex-servicemen and women were a cross section of ordinary New Zealanders and were not either: (a) heroes or (b) warmongers. (p. 191)

Every year on 25 April, thousands of people gather at local war memorials in every district and community throughout New Zealand and Australia. Overseas, expatriates do the same. On the Gallipoli Peninsula of Turkey, thousands of Australians and New Zealanders converge on Anzac Cove, almost as many as on the day itself back in 1915. All this for a battle that is small and insignificant in world terms, and a disaster in military terms, but important to us because it depicts a national image that confirmed public expectations (Pugsley, 2004). It defined our identity as separate from Britain, and also as separate from Australia. As Pugsley (2004) says, the Australian and New Zealand experience during the First World War 'confirmed that we are two different countries with very different approaches to how we see the world and how we assess matters of individual national interest' (p. 308).

New Zealand's experiences in the Second World War provided a degree of respect and pride after the First World War. The returned servicemen and servicewomen of the Second World War mainly served in the 2nd and 3rd Divisions, which were autonomous New Zealand units answerable to the government back home. While not Anzacs in the truest sense, these servicemen and -women gave impetus to the Anzac tradition and to the guardianship of this Anzac ideal by the Returned and Services Association (RSA). In contrast, the conflict in South Vietnam, and New Zealand's commitment (as an Anzac unit) to that war, would test the very ideals of New Zealand veterans and the notions of Anzac.

Vietnam

Historically, thinking about national security in New Zealand has been less influenced by the historical and formative experiences of the state, and more by the philosophical, political, cultural and cognitive characteristics of its current decision-makers and their experiences and development. The Second World War's end in 1945 brought no comforting guarantee of security, but a consciousness that our national defence was bound up in Western alliances. Up until the mid-1950s, New Zealand defence thinking took place in terms of total mobilisation in the event of global war — much as it had done on the previous two occasions. After Korea and the Malayan Emergency campaigns, and in line with communist containment, the country concentrated its contributions to events largely in the context of relations with its most important allies.

The threat from a communist expansion spurred the re-examination of New Zealand's defence policy, structure and preparations for war. As the United States and its anti-communist allies escalated military involvement in South East Asia, New Zealand came under increasing pressure to provide combat assistance to the United States (and Australia) in a then little-known country: Vietnam.

As with the First World War, in the early stages of the conflict the decision to send combat forces to Vietnam appeared to enjoy reasonably high levels of public support. However, New Zealand's military involvement in Vietnam was later overshadowed by the wide-ranging debate about the conflict, which erupted at home (and internationally) following the rise of an organised anti-war movement. As Ella discusses in Chapter 4, the 1960s and 1970s were a time of significant social change, and anti-war protests were an important part of that. Despite having no decisive impact on official policy-making — the political-military culture if you like — the anti-war movement attracted increasing support, especially during the closing stages of the war. The Vietnam War ultimately brought with it a polarisation of opinion and a questioning of the government's Australia, New Zealand and United States of America (ANZUS) alliance commitments and policies, particularly by young people in higher education. The Vietnam War had a lasting impact on how New Zealanders thought about war, defence and security issues, and many of the protesters later entered politics and emerged as key ministers, and prime ministers in some cases.

 The website vietnamwar.govt.nz was created as part of the Vietnam War Oral History Project and brings together interviews, photos and essays on New Zealanders' experiences in the war

So where do the New Zealand soldiers who fought in Vietnam as an Anzac unit fit into the Anzac story? Does the image of the Anzac soldier in Vietnam stir similar feelings of bravery and heroism as the image of the Anzac soldier who fought at Gallipoli? The treatment of soldiers after they completed their deployment in Vietnam is an interesting and sad part of New Zealand's military history. Psychologist Veronica Hopner (2014) analysed oral histories of returning New Zealand servicemen, and social rejection was discussed by just one First World War veteran and no Second World War veterans.

In contrast, rejection featured heavily in the Vietnam veterans' stories. McGibbon (2010, p. 525) describes expressions of community hostility as being confined to 'activist anti-war protesters, who represented only a small minority of those opposed to New Zealand's involvement in Vietnam', but many veteran testimonies would dispute these views. They came home to an environment that

Angry years

Demonstrators are removed from a parade
welcoming home soldiers from Vietnam in
Auckland, 1971.

was 'unsupportive, unwelcoming and on occasion openly hostile' (Hopner, 2014, p. 148), which was a shock, given that for many patriotic pride had motivated them to serve. This was a wound that struck deep for some, and it raises questions of how inclusive the Anzac story of patriotism and pride actually is.

One example that highlights such rejection was offered by a Vietnam veteran who had been asked to speak to a Scout group one Anzac Day:

> I was quite happy to because remember I was a member of an ANZAC unit on active service in Vietnam, which was the most stupid thing I could possibly have said, because man alive, all hell broke loose. 'Oh you are a baby killer, one of those mercenaries' and they were going to take their kids out of Scouts not to have them anywhere near a mongrel like me so I quit right there on the spot . . . and that was very, very hurtful . . . they were the sort of things that struck you everywhere. (Hopner, 2014, p. 153)

National identity and citizenship should guarantee inclusion (Biles & Spoonley, 2007). For some Vietnam veterans this was not the case, and their exclusion by society was seen as punishment for a war that was unpopular and ultimately a defeat (Challinor & Lancaster, 2000). These Anzac soldiers did not enjoy the respect granted to the generations of soldiers who had fought overseas before them. For instance, there is anecdotal evidence that local RSAs refused to accept membership from Vietnam veterans on the grounds that the Vietnam War was not like the First World War and the Second World War (*Otago Daily Times*, 2008).

Questioning the Anzac narrative: inclusion and exclusion

The Anzac narrative has been the focus of academic critique, and there is a suggestion that this narrative is dominated by a demographic that is male and monocultural (Hoverd, 2015; Greener & Powles, 2015). The construction of a particular masculine New Zealand identity, and the accent on imperial unity, served clear political objectives in the early twentieth century (Bennett, 2003). Today, Anzac commemorations are dominated by the RSA, and reflect this dominant demographic which prioritises Pākehā, and sometimes Māori, over other groups. For instance, Chinese people were restricted from serving because of issues of citizenship. Nonetheless, between 50 and 150 Chinese fought for New Zealand at Gallipoli and on the Western Front, yet their stories, until recently, have been excluded from the Anzac narrative (Stone, 2014). Similarly, despite 458 men from the Pacific serving during the First World War, their story has been mainly ignored in the New Zealand narrative (Walker, 2012). With the one hundredth anniversary of the First World War and New Zealand's involvement in that conflict, there is an opportunity to address some of the forgotten Anzacs. However, there is still a risk of simply rewriting or reinforcing the dominant narrative of Anzac, and celebrating questionable aspects of New Zealand's history.

Hoverd (2015), in reflecting on the Anzac narrative, states that there is a need 'to ask New Zealand to think reflectively about the consequences of how we memorialise our conflict' and 'to think about an Anzac discourse that is inclusionary rather than exclusionary' (p. 2). There is concern, for instance, that the Gallipoli–Turkey discourse, which underscores the Anzac narrative, has implications for any future relationship with Turkey and other Muslim countries. The Anzac narrative also reinvents a First World War-era New Zealand, a society where the legal dimensions of the Treaty of Waitangi were absent, for example.

As we have seen, the birth of the Anzac narrative was formed from a military designation of soldiers from New Zealand and Australia who served in a joint corps during the First World War. It appears that some colonial narratives of their fighting troops were based on a bush/frontier origin. The New Zealand version, the 'gentlemen of the bush', was a myth that had gained widespread currency before the war, demarcating a distinctive New Zealand colonial identity; one that constructed itself in part through notions of Englishness, a key boundary-marker (Bennett, 2003, p. 53).

However, no analysis of the New Zealand Anzac identity would be complete without acknowledgement of the unquestioning influence, role and impact of Māori in the New Zealand history of conflict. While Māori participation is these days an important part of the Anzac commemorations, their actual early war experiences are not a simple story of inclusion. Bennett (2003) tells us that key Māori saw a willingness to fight for 'King and Country' as leverage that would not only reduce discrimination by Pākehā, but more significantly also allow them to 'claim the status of equality for Māoridom in New Zealand society' (p. 32).

The response of Māori to the call of the imperial bugle in the First World War was far from united, however. This reflected the dual traditions of reform and protest in Māori political organisation, which had crystallised in the years from 1890 to 1910. A significant source of opposition to conscription of Māori in the war came from the Waikato, who had been one of the principal victims of sweeping land confiscation in the 1860s (Bennett, 2001, p. 43).

Little changed upon their return. Despite having fought as equals, most Māori returned servicemen were denied war pensions and rehabilitation assistance (ibid.). Historian Claudia Orange (2000) suggests that Māori contributions in the Second World War would once again offer the 'price' for citizenship, and while significant moves were made to eradicate blatant paternalism and inequalities — the word 'Māori' replaced 'Native' in official usage; drinking laws were 'equalised' and 'inequalities in the allocation of social security benefits were gradually eliminated' — fuller attempts to put in place adequate policies and practices in the Māori affairs area left a legacy of problems in the post-war years that would constrain equal and genuine inclusion (ibid., pp. 248–249).

Another group that has, until recently, been ignored within the Anzac narrative are the conscientious objectors. Shoebridge (2016) explains that:

> Conscripted men who refused military service were known as 'conscientious objectors', because their refusal to serve was based on their personal beliefs (or consciences). About 600 men declared conscientious objections, of whom around 286 were ultimately imprisoned in New Zealand as an example to other would-be objectors (others accepted non-combatant service or were exempt). Fourteen imprisoned objectors were forcibly despatched overseas in July 1917, with some ultimately transported to the Western Front and subjected to military punishments and incarceration. The broad question of dissent — and the specific experiences of 'the 14' — remain among the most controversial legacies of New Zealand's First World War. (p. 2)

Some of the conscientious objectors remained uncompromising in their refusal to fight at the front serving in non-combatant roles (Grant, 1986). Only two, Archibald Baxter and Mark Briggs, refused to give in to the military's efforts, often harsh and brutal, to make them serve in non-combatant roles (ibid.). Baxter, a committed socialist pacifist (and father of the New Zealand poet James K. Baxter), was unsuccessful in being classified as a conscientious objector and was sent to the Western Front, before being sent home after being dubiously diagnosed as insane (McGibbon & Goldstone, 2000). In 1939, his compelling account of his war-time treatment, *We Will Not Cease*, was published in the UK. A New Zealand edition was published in 1968.

The last New Zealander imprisoned for their conscientious objection was released in 1920 (once the last of the soldiers returned home). Those who had served time in prison as defaulters lost the right to vote for 10 years and were barred from working for the government or local bodies (Shoebridge, 2016). This loss of voting rights and employment exclusion certainly constitutes a breach of fundamental citizenship rights.

The stories of the conscientious objectors and the voices of pacifists are now starting to be heard. In the United Kingdom, there is a movement to recognise peace through the wearing of a white poppy (as opposed to a red one) to remember the victims of war on their Armistice Day (11 November). In Wellington, as discussed by Trudie in Chapter 5, during the Anzac 100-year commemorations in 2016, protesters erected three statues of Archibald Baxter in the field punishment No. 1 position, a cruel punishment technique used on Baxter and other conscientious objectors. The protest's goal was to 'end the romanticisation of war and the militarisation of Anzac Day' (Peace Action Wellington, 2016).

The role of women in this narrative similarly raises questions of how the image of Anzac can be a narrative for all New Zealanders. Former Australian prime minister Tony Abbott's reference to the 'splendid sons of Anzac' in discussing the deployment of troops to Iraq at the Pukeahu National War Memorial Park opening in Wellington in 2015 is such an example. In this statement he 'marginalised the good efforts made on both sides of the Tasman to advance the role of women in the military' (Greener & Powles, 2015). While academics recognise the historical exclusivity of the young male Anzac, some also state that this image is in no way reflective of New Zealand's military today. For instance, the Royal New Zealand Air Force (RNZAF) was the first of the services to admit women into combat roles, in 1988, and an amendment to the Human Rights Act was finally passed in 2007 that removed exemptions barring women from combat roles (Hoverd, 2015, p. 3). Further, Greener and Powles (2015) point out that 'Abbott's comments speak to the heart of gender issues, but also hint at a broader issue that we need to begin to address; that is, what "ANZAC" represents and how we want to remember war and conflict'.

The importance of inclusivity, and the concern surrounding exclusion, are both fundamental issues for consideration, given the importance we attach to the Anzac story. The changing sense we make of events that are now a century behind us, especially as we continue to evolve our understanding of identity and belonging, is manifestly sharpened by the way we 'do' Anzac Day today.

Just another holiday?

Our calendar is replete with national holidays that have iconic meaning associated with them; the very reasons why they have become holidays in the first place. Anzac Day, 25 April, is very much an iconic and defining point in history which different citizens today choose to commemorate in numerous and varying ways, some rather different to those practised during the first Anzac Day in 1916. A day of singular sombre reflection and remembrance has now evolved to include this as well as a much broader public and, at times, vocal discussion of war, conflict and identity. Old veterans may spend the day recounting their experiences to each other, others may tell stories about their mates to children, grandchildren or great-grandchildren. Younger military veterans might send around emails to recall stories about 'that one time' that a certain friend did something great or funny or crazy before he was gone. Many current and former servicemen and -women will attend a dawn service, some will visit cemeteries, others will spend some time alone, and still others will enjoy a day off from work. Families of these veterans, and other members of the community, will choose to do similar things, too.

In some sectors, there is a genuine concern that the steady stream of Anzac coverage is sending the wrong message, and raises issues around the language used when commemorating Anzac Day. There are those who feel that Anzac Day and its true meaning has been misinterpreted or exploited, thanks to business and commercial activity being allowed to take place during the second half of the day. Paulin (2015) suggests the tidy symbolism and euphemisms of the way we pay homage to the soldiers of the First World War risks glorifying and sanitising the reality of war, and our focus on the events of 100 years ago blinds us to the realities of war now. The stories we tell of ourselves as a nation can and do change, and Hoverd (2015) believes that Anzac Day is a 'social construction that we need to revise so that our historical remembrance of Anzac commemoration of Gallipoli informs where we, as a nation, have come from but does not drive where we are going'. Anzac Day and its commemorations are no longer just commemorations for First World War veterans; Anzac Day now reflects New Zealand's contributions to all conflicts — before and since. Language and symbolism are important in creating new possible meanings and understandings about the nation of people we aspire to become.

While some things have changed, others perhaps have not. Following the historical mistakes made with returning soldiers, particularly our Vietnam veterans, and the absence of recognition of women and minority groups when looking at the Anzac narrative, Anzac Day 2016 showed signs that the issues of inclusion and exclusion of returned service personnel are not yet consigned to history. New Zealand service personnel have served on a series of United Nations-mandated peacekeeping, and peacemaking, missions since 1973, importantly maintaining our commitment to peace and global security since the end of the Second World War. It was concerning to note that some of these peacekeepers were receiving similar treatment from their local RSA as had their Vietnam counterparts. Aaron Wood, a veteran of service in East Timor, Somalia and Afghanistan, believed that recent veterans have themselves been treated with apathy and indifference by those same veterans who experienced exactly the same thing when they came home from Vietnam (*National Business Review*, 2016). We need to ensure that the narrative that we use to explain our military historical identity also acknowledges our current environment and perhaps that of the future.

Conclusion: Anzac — spirit or myth?

Where do we go from here? The Anzac experience was very much a discovery of self, a confirmation of the fact that both Australia and New Zealand were different, both from England and from each other, in terms of peoples, culture, history, and views of the rest of the world. This is still obvious today, with different attitudes to international relations, military and economic interests and responsibilities, and the attitudes to our multicultural societies and an increasingly interconnected globalised world. Anzac Day, says Pugsley (2004), is a day 'where the national consciousness is one of cost . . . a commemoration of the price New Zealand has paid on its journey to nationhood, and the price that it may be asked to pay again if it commits itself while as unprepared as it was in two world wars' (p. 309).

Australian historian Martin Crotty (2009) tells us that war 'is often difficult and emotive for historians and history teachers to traverse' (p. 14), because in order to understand exactly what went on, and most importantly why, there is a need to unpack the narrative, to strip away the 'veneer of myth' and deal with the harsh realities of conflict. Hamilton (2015) has articulated that the use of the word 'myth' 'recognises that any historical event embraces the actions and suffering of many people who plan it, help realise it, or are affected by it'. Often an examination of the past unearths stark realities not born of our traditional understanding of a campaign or an event, and as a result creates questions that may prove to be uncomfortable for individuals, for families, for organisations and for states. Crotty suggests that, for Anzac, historians have collectively exposed gaps between 'Anzac the mythology and Anzac the reality' (p. 14). When the realities of conflict and war are examined, we see the experiences, we see the death and destruction, the hardship and trauma caused, and perhaps this assists the understanding that such a history is a particularly grim and dark subject for most of us. This may explain why many veterans came home and rarely spoke of their experiences, and why it fell to others to describe it for us in official history, or designed narrative.

Australian cultural historian Graham Seal (2007) states that, 'like all cultural constructs, Anzac is a conflation of history and myth' (p. 136). History gives us the opportunity to examine why and how certain Anzac narratives — be it myth or legend — have come about over time. Critical inquiry enables us to consider where the Anzac legend came from and how it became so cemented in the national psyche. Also, we can examine those who challenge the narrative, and think about why that might be important. As Crotty (2009) puts it:

> It is instructive to consider Anzac as a set of sometimes complementary and sometimes competing discourses — many voices, and many versions of Anzac, some of which are privileged, and others of which are silenced. But we need to remember in our teaching that Anzac is about much more than competing discourses. We need also to recognise that the Anzac legend cannot be so easily divorced from the realities that underlie it and which gave rise to it. Those very real human experiences, those moments of heroism and triumph, tragedy and farce, success and failure, deserve consideration for what they are — meaningful and profound human experiences worthy of recognition in their own right. (p. 15)

We may arrive at an understanding of the Anzac story, and of other conflict stories, by considering them through a full range of viewpoints — from soldiers and politicians to families, groups within our community, and the state as a whole. Crotty (2009) adds that our understanding of war and conflict is incredibly important, 'just too important for us to not get it right' (p. 17), and we have a responsibility, as critical thinkers, to provide this beyond what we might see in newspapers and television, and beyond what we might hear from politicians, or indeed others — including the RSA — with interests in emphasising particular elements of the story at the expense of others.

This chapter began with an invitation to reflect on the nature and meaning of Anzac. Its major aim was to consider the nature and origins of the Anzac narrative, and how it has evolved, using two major twentieth-century conflicts in New Zealand's history: Gallipoli and Vietnam. While the Anzac narrative is largely based on New Zealand's experience in the First World War, it continues to evolve as it takes into account subsequent conflict, and embraces an idea of including those who have been deliberately removed or accidentally left out of the story. It is acknowledged that it was on the shores of Gallipoli that New Zealand's identity as an independent nation was born, but does commemorating Anzac

Day today reflect a growing recognition of all citizens of this land? And does the commemoration accept that the idea of Anzac and its place in our nation's story is as varied as the people who make New Zealand what it is? Can we look at our military history and use this foundation 'myth' to define our wider society beyond the veteran community and those men and women who serve in the New Zealand Defence Force today? The Anzac story is transitioning from a narrative that was used to explain our historical military identity to a far more inclusive and accurate chronicle that not only acknowledges where we have come from in the recent past, but also looks at our current place in the world, and perhaps at what our identity might look like in the future.

 Chapter 11 — Anzac: A nation's creation story: http://turangawaewae.massey.ac.nz/chapter11.html

Recommended reading

Bennett, J. (2003). 'Massey's Sunday School picnic party': 'The other Anzacs' or honorary Australians?. *War and Society, 21*(2), 23–54.

Greener, B. K., & Powles, A. R. (2015, May 5). The 'sons — and daughters — of ANZAC'?. *The Strategist.* Retrieved from http://www.aspistrategist.org.au/the-sons-and-daughters-of-anzac/

Harper, G., & Richardson, C. (2006). *In the face of the enemy: The complete history of the Victoria Cross and New Zealand.* Auckland, New Zealand: HarperCollins.

Littlewood, D. (2017). Personal, local and enduring: Masculine citizenship in First World War Britain. In A. Brown & J. Griffiths (Eds.), *The citizen: Past and present* (pp. 171–195). Auckland, New Zealand: Massey University Press.

Seal, G. (2007). ANZAC: The sacred in the secular. *Journal of Australian Studies 31*(91), 135–144.

References

Baxter, A. (1968). *We will not cease.* Christchurch, New Zealand: Caxton Press. (Original work published 1939).

Bennett, J. (2001). Māori as honorary members of the white tribe. *The Journal of Imperial and Commonwealth History, 29*(3), 33–54.

Bennett, J. (2003). 'Massey's Sunday School picnic party': 'The other Anzacs' or honorary Australians?. *War and Society, 21*(2), 23–54.

Biles, J., & Spoonley, P. (2007). National identity: What it can tell us about inclusion and exclusion. *National Identities, 9*(3), 191–195.

Challinor, D., & Lancaster, E. (2000). *Who'll stop the rain? Agent Orange and the children of New Zealand's Vietnam veterans.* Auckland, New Zealand: HarperCollins.

Crotty, M. A. (2009). Teaching Anzac: Fraught territory, teachable moments and professional responsibility. *Agora, 44*(2), 13–17.

Grant, D. (1986). *Out in the cold: Pacifists and conscientious objectors in New Zealand during World War II.* Auckland, New Zealand: Reed Methuen.

Greener, B. K., & Powles, A. R. (2015, May 5). The 'sons — and daughters — of ANZAC'?. *The Strategist.* Retrieved from http://www.aspistrategist.org.au/the-sons-and-daughters-of-anzac/

Hamilton, A. (2015, May 6). The exploitation of Anzac and other myths. Retrieved from www.eurekastreet.com.au/article.aspx?aeid=43732

Harper, G., & Richardson, C. (2006). *In the face of the enemy: The complete history of the Victoria Cross and New Zealand.* Auckland, New Zealand: HarperCollins.

Hopner, V. (2014). *Home from war* (Unpublished Doctorate thesis). Massey University, Auckland, New Zealand.

Hoverd, W. (2015, April 22). Rethinking Anzac Day: The dangers of an exclusionary discourse. Retrieved from http://www.esocsci.org.nz/rethinking-anzac-day-the-dangers-of-an-exclusionary-discourse/

McGibbon, I. C. (1991). *The path to Gallipoli: Defending New Zealand, 1840–1915.* Wellington, New Zealand: GP Books.

McGibbon, I. C. (2010). *New Zealand's Vietnam War: A history of combat, commitment and controversy.* Auckland, New Zealand: Exisle.

McGibbon, I. C., & Goldstone, P. (Eds.). (2000). *The Oxford companion to New Zealand military history.* Auckland, New Zealand: Oxford University Press.

McLeod, J. (1986). *Myth and reality: The New Zealand soldier in World War II.* Auckland, New Zealand: Heinemann Reed.

Ministry for Culture and Heritage (2016, March 22). *New research dramatically increases the numbers of New Zealand soldiers at Gallipoli.* Retrieved from: http://www.mch.govt.nz/new-research-dramatically-increases-numbers-new-zealand-soldiers-gallipoli

National Business Review. (2016, April 24). Veterans from wars since Vietnam 'treated with indifference'. *NBR, Weekend Review.* Retrieved from http://www.nbr.co.nz/article/veterans-wars-vietnam-treated-indifference-188138-ck?u

Orange, C. (2000). The price of citizenship? The Maori war effort. In J. Crawford (Ed.), *Kia Kaha: New Zealand in the Second World War.* Auckland, New Zealand: Oxford University Press.

Otago Daily Times (2008, December 15). Vietnam veterans remain divided. Retrieved from: https://www.odt.co.nz/news/national/vietnam-veterans-remain-divided

Paulin, A. (2015, April 11). On the brink of WWI overload. Retrieved from http://www.stuff.co.nz/nelson-mail/opinion/67679161/on-the-brink-of-wwi-overload

Peace Action Wellington (2016, April 25). Remembering the conscientious objectors. Retrieved from https://peaceactionwellington.wordpress.com/2016/04/25/remembering-the-conscientious-objectors/

Pugsley, C. (2004). *The ANZAC experience: New Zealand, Australia and Empire in the First World War*. Auckland, New Zealand: Reed Books.

Pugsley, C., & Ferrall, C. (2015). *Remembering Gallipoli: Interviews with New Zealand Gallipoli veterans*. Wellington, New Zealand: Victoria University Press.

Sandford, K. (1962). *Mark of the lion: The story of Capt. Charles Upham, V.C. and Bar*. London, England: Hutchinson.

Seal, G. (2007). ANZAC: The sacred in the secular. *Journal of Australian Studies 31*(91), 135–144.

Shoebridge, T. (2016). Conscientious objection and dissent in the First World War. Retrieved from http://www.nzhistory.net.nz/war/first-world-war/conscientious-objection

Stone, A. (2014, August 16). 100 Kiwi stories: Chinese soldier a hero to mates. *The New Zealand Herald.* Retrieved from: http://www.nzherald.co.nz/nz/news/article.cfm?c_id=1&objectid=11309675

Walker, F. (2012). 'Descendants of a warrior race': The Māori contingent, New Zealand Pioneer Battalion, and martial race myth, 1914–19. *War and Society, 31*(1), 1–21.

CONCLUSION

Identity and belonging in Aotearoa New Zealand

Richard Shaw, Ella Kahu
and Trudie Cain

Introduction

This book has been about what it means to be in and/or of this place, Aotearoa New Zealand, at this particular juncture in history. We haven't ventured a definitive response to the question of what that meaning might be for any given individual — that would have been foolish and presumptuous — but we have sought, to quote from Ella's opening chapter, to provide you with the opportunity 'to probe, prompt and . . . reflect upon aspects of your own sense of self, and of the ways in which we collectively make sense of who we are, that might otherwise continue to enjoy the status of received wisdom'.

In that spirit of reflection and curiosity, in this concluding piece we offer our own thoughts on many of the issues raised in the chapters you have just read, and consider some of the challenges and opportunities posed to our individual and collective sense of identity by the trends, events and developments covered by those who have contributed to this book.

The faces, voices, places and stories of Aotearoa New Zealand

There is a temptation for each generation to assert that the times in which it lives are more momentous, the challenges it faces are of a greater magnitude, and the changes it is going through are more sweeping than those who have come before. As editors, we are aware that by focusing throughout this book largely on things that are changing we risk overlooking the extent to which there is also constancy in Aotearoa New Zealand. If this book is an account of change, it is also one of continuity: migration has always been part of the story of this place; today's protests are motivated by many of the same things (a wish to have one's voice heard, to right a wrong, or to change minds) that compelled people to take to the streets in times past; and much as they have done since the University of New Zealand was created in 1870 (a year after the establishment of Otago University), our universities continue to create and disseminate knowledge.

All the same, at the end of this book the three of us are left with an unavoidable sense that things are *happening* in Aotearoa New Zealand. Establishing whether or not those things — the 'trends, events and developments' referred to immediately above — are of greater (or lesser) significance than those of earlier eras is not the point. What matters is that they are consequential, and therefore need to be made sense of.

Faces

At the risk of stating the obvious, one of the most striking things going on is the extent to which the individual and collective faces of this place are changing. Think back to Trudie's chapter in Part 1, for instance, and you will recall that the proportion of the population aged 65 years or older is climbing steadily. While much of the public debate occasioned by this trend is couched in the language of costs and burdens (it can't have escaped your attention that older people are typically described as one or the other, or both), we think that it is important also to acknowledge that there is much to celebrate in an ageing population. It is worth noting, for example, that the European Commission (2015) estimates that the so-called Silver Economy — the value of public and private sector spending on older people — comprises the third largest economy in the world. Amidst the economic costs, in other words, there also lie opportunities. Moreover, older people contribute their experience and knowledge in paid and voluntary capacities, are important repositories of wisdom, and can provide an historical context for current events that is a valuable complement to the tyranny of the immediate.

There is, of course, a different demographic story unfolding amongst Māori.

In 1856, the decimation of the tangata whenua population was such that Dr Isaac Featherston, a physician and politician, felt moved to observe that Pākehā had a duty to smooth the pillow of a dying race (Buck, 1924). Featherston's observation has not come to pass: instead, Māori have picked up the pillow and hurled it across the room. As explained in Chapter 2, today a third of all Māori are 15 years of age or younger. This poses its own demographic, political and social challenges and opportunities, and it is important that these are not drowned out in the growing public discourse occasioned by an ageing non-Māori population.

Change of a different kind is reflected in the fact that there are now more ethnicities in this country than there are nations in the world (Hayward & Shaw, 2016). It is worth emphasising once again just how quickly things are shifting in this respect: it is estimated, for instance, that the percentage of the population identifying as European or New Zealander will fall from 75 per cent (at the 2013 census) to 66 per cent by 2038 (Statistics New Zealand, 2015).

These sorts of developments have consequences for other aspects of the ways in which things are done in Aotearoa New Zealand. In short, and you have encountered this point repeatedly throughout the book, look closely enough and you will see that our different identity threads, at both the individual and collective levels, are always intricately interwoven: changes in one typically echo in another. Thus, just as ethnicity and age intersect, so do ethnicity and religion.

In Chapter 1, Trudie touched on the fact that much of the recent growth in the Sikh, Hindu and Muslim religions has occurred in Auckland (which was the only region in the country to experience an increase in the number of religious believers during the last census period). You can spot the reason easily enough: Auckland is the destination of much of the inbound migration from different Asian nations, and many of our new migrant and refugee communities bring their religious rituals, practices and beliefs with them. In other words, beyond the obvious pluralisation of our population we are also witnessing the diversification of the practices, rituals and routines through which people go about and make sense of their quotidian lives. And those have or are becoming part of the New Zealand way of life. We use the definite article 'the' in the previous sentence consciously — not to connote a single way of life that is exclusive of others, but to signal one which is spacious and generous enough to encompass different ways of doing things.

Voices

Demographic (and cultural, religious, linguistic, musical, sartorial, culinary and so on) diversification has also altered the sounds, tone and tenor of the voices now heard in the public domain. There was a time in this country when a few voices regularly dominated at the expense of others, but — at the risk of sounding naïve — our view is that that epoch is gradually passing into history. This is not to deny that challenges remain: as Ella pointed out in her chapter on protest, and as David explained in his on inequality, there are voices which — for reasons of exclusion, often on the basis of identity — remain muted or entirely silent. Nonetheless, to some degree at least, the ever-growing inclusion of previously marginalised groups as legitimate members of the national community — most recently through the legalisation of same-sex marriage — is consistent with one particular characterisation of the history of democracy as 'the collapse of one exclusion after another' (Dunn, 2005, p. 136).

We are cautiously optimistic that this collapsing of exclusion will continue, not because the benign march of progress is inevitable, but because people who care about such things will continue to agitate, protest, push and argue for change. But reflecting on Sy's Chapter 8 in particular (which enjoys many connections with the chapters on voice, even though it is ostensibly about places), we would also strike a cautionary note associated with the staggering growth in the number and variety of platforms from which voices can now be expressed (or suppressed). In the context of a book interested in who gets to contribute to public debates (and who does not), and how they do so, this diversification presents both challenges and opportunities. Few of us, surely, would wish to revert to a world lacking the extraordinary opportunities the internet affords us to talk with, listen to, engage with and learn from others.

Yet, in an increasingly cluttered, chaotic and noisy digital environment, there are no guarantees that our particular voice will be heard — much less listened to — by others. The distinction between voicing one's views and being listened to is critical. Expressing voice does not in and of itself lead to dialogue: the former can very well occur in the absence of the latter, such that people talk past each other and are eventually reduced to (or actively choose) shouting into a void. Bluntly, it is difficult to learn from others or to disagree well when the volume has been ratcheted up to 10.

Clearly, this is not restricted to online environments: as Ella explained in Chapter 4, one of the chief reasons people take to the streets in protest is because they feel they are not being listened to. However, the intemperate nature of much of what passes for discourse in online environments does throw into especially sharp relief just how important the capacity to listen to others — especially those with whom we disagree — is to fostering an inclusive, tolerant society. But that, of course, requires encountering those others in the first instance, and the temptation to frequent gated digital communities inhabited by like-minded people can diminish the likelihood of ever encountering these 'Others'.

Perhaps this sounds dystopian (and certainly not everyone hangs out in digital echo chambers). All the same, our sense is that the exercise of voice in digital environments does present a conundrum. Certainly we have many more forums in which we can seek to voice our views and to participate in various communities. But it is also the case that, if we opt to circulate online exclusively with those whose voices we find congenial, we reduce our contact with those with whom we might disagree or who live lives that differ to our own — and are therefore increasingly poorly placed to understand them.

Places

The places in and on which we stand are not immune from the sorts of phenomena covered in the initial sections of the book: they, too, are shifting. We do not necessarily mean that in a literal sense, although the potential for tectonic activity in our islands is such that this, too, is the case, and sometimes with devastating effects. Rather, our sense is that if we were able to take a large step back and literally look into the nation's homes, many of the day-to-day routines and rituals through which people now live their lives would be different to those of the homes of, say, 30 or 40 years ago.

Think of the developments we have touched on or alluded to in this book alone (and they are far from exhaustive): a young and growing Māori population; the advent of sophisticated digital technologies; migration within New Zealand (including from rural to urban centres); the arrival of new migrant and refugee families; and inequalities in the distribution of wealth and income. Now think of the myriad ways in which those and other developments might play out in people's homes, and you get some sense of how rich and varied must be the conventions, norms and rules that shape all of the lives lived in all of our homes.

But for some people, of course, home is not a nurturing or caring environment; it is a place in which damage is done and from which scars are carried. Others do not have homes at all. If variety and richness are part of the story we tell of life at home in Aotearoa New Zealand, then we must also tell of those forced to sleep at night in cars, or live 10 to a room, or who are constantly moving from house to house in search of a home. These stories, too, must be narrated. Aotearoa New Zealand can indeed be a great place in which to raise kids — but that seems unlikely to be the case for some or all of the 305,000 (fully 29 per cent) of our children who live in poverty (Simpson, Duncanson, Oben, Wicken, & Pierson, 2015). In short, alongside the ontological security spoken of in Chapter 6, there exists considerable ontological insecurity.

Insecurity of a different kind besets the nation's universities. They continue to perform the important statutory work of speaking truth to power, but their capacity to do so is under threat. The challenge has in part to do with the mounting cost of securing a university education; it also stems from the increasingly entrenched view that the primary purpose of a university education is to enhance students' employment prospects. Apropos the former, we may already have passed the point at which the price of attending university has become a significant deterrent to some. And while the latter is, in and of itself, no bad thing, if employability becomes the sole basis on which the worth of universities is assessed we risk doing damage to our institutions of higher learning that will be very difficult to repair.

Jointly, both developments have the capacity (if they have not already done so) to significantly alter the nature of the university. We're certainly not suggesting that New Zealand's universities are in imminent danger of abandoning their historic mission to act as critic and conscience of society. However, if Harvard professor Michael Sandel (2012) is correct in arguing that when a price is charged for something then 'market norms will crowd out nonmarket norms' (p. 78), at the very least we should be asking whether or not recent developments are hampering the universities' ability to foster free and independent thought.

Stories

Notwithstanding that they contain kernels of truth, it is no surprise that some of the received wisdoms that may once have applied in this country no longer hold true (or are, at least, coming under stress). Put another way, certain of the narratives we have collectively constructed over the years as a means of explaining ourselves both to each other and the wider world need to be questioned.

In Chapter 9, David demonstrated that — both empirically and rhetorically — the fabric of the broadly egalitarian society constructed across the better part of the twentieth century has been rent by three decades' worth of reform. Much the same point — that material circumstances and the stories told about them are drifting apart — was made by Juliana, Carl and Rhys in the chapters on the environment and the Anzac story.

This general principle is not limited to the narratives that feature in this book. For instance, the increasingly multicultural character of the national population is thought by some to pose a risk to biculturalism. In recent decades a considerable investment has been made in clarifying and setting in place the foundations of a bicultural nation. That project has been greeted with more or less enthusiasm, and is some way from completion. For some, the prospects of completion are challenged by the arrival of people from elsewhere who have not been part of the process thus far. Clearly, migration need not be anathema to biculturalism, but it does generate challenges that need careful political management if the bicultural project is not to slip into irrelevance.

What happens when we are confronted by such discrepancies? When confronted with something — an event, a person, a smell or a sight — that challenges the narrative tools we habitually deploy as sense-making devices, we have two main choices. One is to hold onto the stories with which we are familiar and feel comfortable, even when these are demonstrably at variance with material developments. The other is to not default to these orthodox narratives, but instead to 'use our intelligence freely' (Small, 2013, p. 74) and to adjust the story such that it is consistent with the new or emerging state of affairs.

This does *not* mean we have to repudiate that which is dear to us. The point collectively made by David, Juliana, Carl and Rhys in Part 4 is that we cherish certain narratives in part because they contain truths and embody aspirations of who we would like to be. More than that, they provide us with a sort of existential version of the ontological security discussed in the chapter on home. As British writer Lisa Appignanensi (2011) puts it: 'We are narrative creatures, and the stories we tell friends and ourselves occupy our consciousness for longer than the acts we engage in' (p. 69). Recruited to the purposes of this book, Appignanensi's point is that we recount and reproduce stories of national identity because they provide the co-ordinates through which we locate ourselves in this place; they give us a sense that we belong to a larger community; they help us recognise others like ourselves (which is helpful when you are far from home); and they furnish us with a sense of New Zealand exceptionalism.

For these reasons, it can be intensely unsettling when these foundation stories are called into question. All the same, we know that our grand narratives of national identity are partial and mask other inconvenient truths. For what it may be worth, our own view as editors is that, as circumstances change and new historical interpretations are reached, it is both healthy and necessary to question and revise these narratives. And defensiveness is not the only alternative. Rather, especially when change arrives from the outside (via migration, for instance, and the threats this allegedly poses to 'the New Zealand way of life'), it is possible to remain rooted in our personal understandings of our own cultural context but also to appreciate that 'what is foreign to that culture can . . . still be worthy of thought and respect' (McCumber, 2016). We are, in short, entirely capable of crafting refurbished national stories that are less partial and more inclusive than the ones they supersede.

Conclusion: home and away

The sorts of patterns and trends we have explored in this book beg a question that has been implicit in the chapters you have read, but which we wish now to make explicit. How do we respond, both as individuals and as a wider national community, to these things that are *happening* around us? How do we react — emotionally, personally, politically — to the changes taking place, and which, depending on one's stance, might be construed as either a threat to an existing way of doing things or an opportunity to do those things a little differently (and perhaps a little better)? The three of us would like to end this book with an explicitly normative response to such questions, using New Zealand's reputation as a much-travelled nation as a device for doing so.

That the gap year, or OE (overseas experience), is a rite of passage for young New Zealanders is another of our national truisms. Most of us have first-hand experience of or know someone with tales to tell of how they were received by others in far-off lands. Of how they were made welcome when their face was first encountered. Of how their voice — with its notoriously flattened vowels — was listened to by someone who became a friend. Of how they explored others' places — and perhaps made a home in them for a time. And of how their stories of rugby, beaches and baches were listened to with curiosity by others.

As with all such discourses, the OE or gap-year narrative provides only a partial description of reality, but it exercises considerable sway over our collective imagination nonetheless. Part of its appeal lies in what it says about our better nature: that travel opens our minds and broadens our understanding of the world and those in it. Much the same can also be achieved through the intellectual travel we engage in through reading. Of course, the reverse may equally apply: exposure to new faces, unknown voices, exotic places and unfamiliar stories can reinforce rather than revise one's existing views, beliefs and preferences. For instance, Janine Wiles (2008) has written of the ways in which New Zealanders in London try to recreate a sense of home while overseas by living, socialising and working with other migrant New Zealanders.

The Front Lawn song 'Tomorrow Night' has the immortal lyrics: 'On the [London] Underground she'd ride / talking loud in a Kiwi accent / talking about . . . tomorrow night': https://www.youtube.com/watch?v=zc8-yvHm1io

But at the very least, when we travel we put ourselves in the way of potential encounters with others that can shape how we make sense of what we come across when (or if) we return to Aotearoa New Zealand. Importantly, and as the authors whose work you have read have portrayed, the conditions for developing this sort of reflexive identity via encounters with unfamiliarity also exist here in this place. In the 1980s, the then New Zealand Tourist and Publicity Department ran a highly successful advertising campaign, the punchline of which was — delivered just as our intrepid Kiwi traveller in the ad was about to paddle over the Victoria Falls — 'Don't leave town 'til you've seen the country'. In a sense, this book has offered the opportunity to travel that country, to explore some of its human, physical and historical contours, and — above all — to greet its people, listen to its voices, explore its places and learn its stories.

Watch the New Zealand Tourist and Publicity Department ad here: https://www.youtube.com/watch?v=PVH7uBzQX7I

References

Appignanensi, L. (2011). *All about love: Anatomy of an unruly emotion*. London, England: W. W. Norton.

Buck, P. (Te Rangi Hīroa). (1924). The passing of the Māori. *Transactions and Proceedings of the Royal Society of New Zealand, 55*, 362–375.

Dunn, J. (2005). *Setting the people free: The story of democracy*. London, England: Atlantic Books.

European Commission (2015). *Growing the silver economy in Europe*. Brussels, Belgium: European Commission.

Hayward, J., & Shaw, R. (Eds.) (2016). *Historical and political dictionary of New Zealand*. Lanham, MD: Rowman & Littlefield.

McCumber, J. (2016, October 2). How humanities can help fix the world. *The Chronicle of Higher Education*. Retrieved from http://www.chronicle.com/article/How-Humanities-Can-Help-Fix/237955

Sandel, M. (2012). *What money can't buy: The moral limits of markets*. New York, NY: Farrar, Straus and Giroux.

Simpson, J., Duncanson, M., Oben, G., Wicken, A., & Pierson, M. (2015). *Child poverty monitor technical report*. Dunedin, New Zealand: University of Otago.

Small, H. (2013). *The value of the humanities*. London, England: Oxford University Press.

Statistics New Zealand. (2015). *Ethnic populations projected to grow*. Wellington, New Zealand: Statistics New Zealand. Retrieved from http://www.stats. govt.nz/browse_for_stats/population/estimates_and_projections/ NationalEthnicPopulationProjections_MR2013-38.aspx

Wiles, J. (2008). Sense of home in a transnational social space: New Zealanders in London. *Global Networks, 8*(1), 116–137.

About the contributors

Rhys Ball is a lecturer in Defence and Security Studies at Massey University. His papers examine current New Zealand security risks, and global security risks in general, and the history, roles and functions of intelligence in particular. Rhys is the undergraduate co-ordinator at the Centre for Defence and Security Studies (CDSS), and is based at the Albany campus.

Carl Bradley holds a PhD from the School of Humanities and Social Science (Classics Department), University of Newcastle, Australia. Carl has over 10 years' teaching experience at Massey University, and a background in leadership and management in the private sector. He is now a lecturer in the Centre for Defence and Security Studies (CDSS) at Massey University, with research interests in leadership, warrior societies, Māori warfare and response to military imperialism.

Trudie Cain is a senior lecturer in the School of People, Environment and Planning at Massey University. Her research interests include gendered, sized and migrant identities; qualitative research methodologies and ethics; and the materiality of everyday lives. She is currently involved in a number of collaborative research projects, including an examination of artists as they consider their contribution to national identity; a study of population change across New Zealand; and an exploration of identity construction through material objects.

Ann Dupuis has recently retired from the position of associate professor at Massey University. She has published extensively in a number of areas, including the sociology of housing, housing policy, the meanings of home and home ownership. Her current research interests have focused on issues pertaining to living in multi-generational households, and the insurance implications for owners in the post-earthquake Canterbury environment.

Margaret Forster, Rongomaiwāhine, Ngāti Kahungunu, is a senior lecturer at Te Pūtahi-a-toi, School of Māori Art, Knowledge and Education, and Director BA (Programme) at Massey University. She teaches in the area of Māori knowledge and development, and is engaged in research that explores the politics of indigeneity in resource management.

Ella Kahu is a lecturer in the School of Psychology at Massey University. Her research interests are in social psychology and higher education, and, in particular, how people manage their at times conflicting social roles and identities. She is currently leading a project at the University of the Sunshine Coast in Australia following a group of students through their first year, building on her earlier work on student engagement. She has published widely in higher-education journals, and her PhD thesis was awarded the NZARE Sutton Smith Doctoral Award in 2014.

David Littlewood is a lecturer in History in the School of Humanities at Massey University. He teaches on New Zealand's political and social history, and on topics relating to the world wars. His research focuses on how involvement in the two global conflicts impacted on New Zealand and British society, with particular reference to the implementation of conscription. He has been published in *War in History* and the *New Zealand Journal of History,* and co-edited the book *Experience of a lifetime: People, personalities and leaders in the First World War*, with John Crawford and James Watson.

Juliana Mansvelt is an associate professor in the School of People, Environment and Planning at Massey University. A social geographer, she is interested in the ways people understand and relate to one another in place. Her research interests centre on landscapes and practices of consumption, particularly with regard to the everyday lives of older New Zealanders.

Richard Shaw is a professor of Politics and Director BA (External Connections) at Massey University. With Victoria University's Chris Eichbaum, he is co-author of *Politics and public policy in New Zealand: Institutions, processes and outcomes* (Pearson Education, 2011, 3rd ed.), and co-editor of two volumes on the role of political advisers: *Partisan appointees and public servants: An international analysis of the role of the political adviser* (Edward Elgar, 2010), and *Ministers, minders and mandarins: An international study of relationships at the Executive Summit of Parliamentary Democracies* (Edward Elgar, forthcoming). With Janine Hayward, he is co-editor of the *Historical and political dictionary of New Zealand* (Rowman & Littlefield, 2016). His research on political advisers has been published in leading international journals, including *Governance, Public Administration, Public Management Review* and *Parliamentary Affairs*. He teaches courses in politics and public policy.

Sy Taffel is a lecturer in Media Studies at Massey University. His research interests include political ecologies of digital media, digital media and political activism, the material impacts of media hardware, pervasive/locative media, software studies, digital cultures and social media. He has published work in journals including *Convergence*, *Cultural Politics* and *Culture Machine*, and is the co-editor of *Ecological entanglements in the Anthropocene* with Nicholas Holm. Sy has also worked as a filmmaker and photographer, and has been involved with media activist projects, including Indymedia, Climate Camp and Hacktionlab.

Veronica Tawhai, Ngāti Porou, Ngāti Uepohatu, is a mother of two, community Tiriti o Waitangi educator, and Māori politics and policy lecturer at Te Pūtahi-a-toi, School of Māori Art, Knowledge and Education at Massey University. She is a member of Te Ata Kura Society for Conscientisation, Matike Mai Aotearoa Independent Working Group on Constitutional Transformation, and Aotearoa's Independent Monitoring Mechanism for implementation of the United Nations Declaration on the Rights of Indigenous Peoples. Her doctoral research, supported by a Fulbright-Ngā Pae o te Māramatanga Scholar Award, examines teaching and learning about indigeneity and the implications for citizenship education.

(Krystal) Te Rina Warren, Rangitāne, Raukawa/Maniapoto, Whitikaupeka (Mōkai Pātea), teaches Māori education and pāngarau (mathematics) at Te Pūtahi-a-toi, School of Māori Art, Knowledge and Education at Massey University. Her research is underpinned by philosophies of Māori development and decoloniality, with a particular interest in reaffirming customary practices in contemporary society (including the internet). Te Rina is a member of her iwi rūnanga, several other iwi development groups, and Te Ata Kura Society for Conscientisation. She recently presented evidence on behalf of Ngāti Whitikaupeka to the Waitangi Tribunal on tino rangatiratanga, early economic development and seventeenth-century iwi engagement with the government. She is a parent of Kōhanga Reo and Kura Kaupapa Māori, and is currently involved with a native language revitalisation project with the Federal University of Rio de Janeiro and the Kaingang nation in Brazil. She visited the Kaingang nation in 2016.

Index

First published in 2017 by Massey University Press
Reprinted in 2018

Massey University Press, Private Bag 102904, North Shore Mail Centre
Auckland 0745, New Zealand
www.masseypress.ac.nz

A catalogue record for this book is available from the National Library
of New Zealand

Printed and bound in China by Everbest Ltd

ISBN: 978-0-9941363-7-4